Robert Browning, John Foster

Prose Life of Strafford

Robert Browning, John Foster

Prose Life of Strafford

ISBN/EAN: 9783744689144

Printed in Europe, USA, Canada, Australia, Japan

Cover: Foto ©Thomas Meinert / pixelio.de

More available books at **www.hansebooks.com**

PRO

LIFE OF ST

WITH AN

INTRODUC

By C. H. FIRTH, M.

AND

FOREWORD

By F. J. FURNIVALL, M.A,

———•••———

PUBLISHT FOR

The Browning Soc

By KEGAN PAUL, TRENCH, TR

LONDON. 1892.

THREE times during his life did Browning speak to me about his prose Life of Strafford. The first time he said only—in the course of chat—that very few people had any idea of how much he had helpt John Forster in it. The second time he told me at length that one day he went to see Forster and found him very ill, and anxious about the *Life of Strafford*, which he had promist to write at once, to complete a volume of *Lives of Eminent British Statesmen* for Lardner's *Cabinet Cyclopædia*. Forster had finisht the Life of Eliot—the first in the volume—and had just begun that of Strafford, for which he had made full collections and extracts; but illness had come on, he couldn't work, the book ought to be completed forthwith, as it was due in the serial issue of volumes; what *was* he to do? 'Oh,' said Browning, 'don't trouble about it. I'll take your papers and do it for you.' Forster thankt his young friend heartily, Browning put the Strafford papers under his arm, walkt off, workt hard, finisht the Life, and it came out to time in 1836, to Forster's great relief, and past under his name. A third time—in the spring of 1889, I think, almost the last time I saw Browning—he began to tell me how he had written almost all Forster's *Life of Strafford;* but I stopt him by saying that he'd told me before, and we went on to chat of something else.

At the first and second times, I had the *Eminent British Statesmen* on my shelves, and once thought of reading the Life of Strafford and asking the poet to point out his large share of it to me. But life in London is such a hurry that anything which gets into a busy man's head is driven out by another thing within the next half-hour. Later, my *Statesmen* volumes went to one of the Free Libraries that appeald to me for books, and I never lookt at the *Life of Strafford* till after Browning's death. Then Prof. S. R. Gardiner one day in the British Museum renewd our talk of some years before about this Life. I took it off the shelves, read the last paragraph (p. 278 below) and felt—as every other Browning student will feel—that I could swear it was Browning's. Let the reader judge :—

A great lesson is written in the life of this truly extraordinary person. In the career of Strafford is to be sought the justification of the world's "appeal from tyranny to God." In him Despotism had at length obtained an instrument with mind to comprehend, and resolution to act upon, her principles in their length and breadth,—and enough of her purposes were effected by him, to enable mankind to see " as from a tower the end of all." I cannot discern one false step in Strafford's public conduct, one glimpse of a recognition of an alien principle, one instance of a dereliction of the law of his being, which can come in to dispute the decisive result of the experiment, or explain away its failure. *The least vivid fancy will have no difficulty in taking up the interrupted design, and by wholly enfeebling, or materially emboldening, the insignificant nature of Charles; and by according some half-dozen years of immunity to the "fretted tenement" of Strafford's " fiery soul,"—contemplate then, for itself, the perfect realisation of the scheme of " making the prince the most absolute lord in Christendom." That done,—let it pursue the same course with respect to Eliot's noble imaginings, or to young Vane's dreamy aspirings, and apply in like manner a fit machinery to the working out the projects which made the dungeon of the one a holy place, and sustained the other in his self-imposed exile.*—The result is great and decisive ! It establishes, in renewed force, those principles of political conduct which have endured, and must continue to endure, "like truth from age to age."

Is it not clear that the passage in italics is a poet's conception, and not a historian's ? Is it not clear that Browning had thought of a character-study of Strafford, Eliot and Vane, a monodrama of each, which—like *Andrea del Sarto, Fra Lippo Lippi* and the like—would have been to us worth half-a-dozen of his drama of *Strafford?* Does not the fact of Browning's having written, or being engaged on, the Life of Strafford in 1836, explain why—when Macready, on May 26, 1836, askt Browning to write him a play,—the poet at once suggested Strafford: Strafford, a man intensely interesting to the analyser of character in verse,—a man knowing the better and choosing the worse,—but impossible for a dramatist who brings in the heroes of the Commonwealth, unless he alters the facts of history; just as impossible as Shakspere found King John, tho' he could keep his Bastard Falconbridge clear of annals.

When I first spoke to Prof. S. R. Gardiner about the Life of Strafford, I found that he knew Browning's authorship of almost all of it, and was convinst of the fact from his own knowledge of Forster's work and of history. 'It is not a historian's conception of the character, but a poet's. I am certain that it's not Forster's.' 'Yes, it makes mistakes in facts and dates, but, it has got the man—in the main.' Prof. Gardiner had also seen a letter of Browning's—now no longer extant, he believes—in which Browning claimd his part of the *Life of Strafford*, as he also did in talk with the Professor in like words to those he used to me. The fact of Browning's authorship is also known to his family and close friends. No doubt can exist on the point, though here and there in the *Life* an 'I' (as if John Forster's) occurs as a deliberate blind. The only question is, where Browning starts, and whether—as Mr. Firth suggests—he incorporated any of Forster's work in his text. Of the latter point I am not able to judge; but on the former, I recollect Browning's use of *waddle* in his goose-critic letter,

"19 *Warwick Crescent, W., February* 10*th*, 1887.

"Dear Sir,
"I am sure you mean very kindly, but I have had too long an experience of the inability of the human goose to do other than cackle when benevolent, and hiss when malicious; and no amount of goose criticism shall make me lift a heel against what *waddles* behind it.
"Believe me, dear sir, yours very sincerely,
"Robert Browning."

(*Browning Society's Papers*, Part IX, p. 187.)

and I claim as Browning's the passage on James I, p. 7 below :

"He wrote mystical definitions of the prerogative, and polite 'Counterblasts to Tobacco'; issued forth damnation to the deniers of witchcraft, and poured out the wrath of the Apocalypse upon popery; but whenever an obvious or judicious truth seemed likely to fall in his way, his pen infallibly *waddled* off from it."

On p. 6, I think this opinion of James I is also Browning's : "He was not an absolute fool, and little more can be said of him." Also, above it, "He came to this country in an ecstasy of infinite relief" strikes me as Browning's and not Forster's; and I suppose that Browning started with the second paragraph on p. 6. "James I had many reasons to be weary of his own kingdom," &c.

Other pieces that I think like Browning are the sentence (with quotations) 3 pages long on p. 69-71, from *In one and the same day*, to *laugh together;* that of nearly a page, 241-2, from "It was well and beautifully said" to "a different devotion;" pages 60-4 with the "divers ill-spelt [1] and solemn sillinesses from the king," the "prism of CIRCUMSTANCE" and the reference to the Ezzelin of *Sordello*, which Browning had set aside to write this Life and his play of *Strafford*—what had Forster to do with Ezzelin?—the discussion of Strafford's character, and his "fatal liking for the weak and unworthy king"; p. 124-6, with their "pick-thank chuckle of old good-humour," their

"Pleasure was a Silenus in the court of James. In that of Charles the Second, it was a vulgar satyr. Under

[1] Later printers' readers would have uniformd this into 'spelled,' as they've done 'burnt,' 'dipt,' into 'burned,' 'dipped,' &c. When will one, more consistent than his fellows, turn 'Jesus wept,' into *weeped?* 'Leapt' has past into 'leaped,' &c. The British public follow their blind guides into the ditch.

Charles the First, it was still of the breed, but it was a
god Pan, and the muses piped among his nymphs. . . .
As nine-tenths of common gallantry is pure vanity, so a
like proportion of the graver offence of deliberate seduction is owing to pure will and the love of power,—the
love of obtaining a strong and sovereign sense of an
existence not very sensitive, at any price to the existence
of another" (p. 125).

"It is a vulgar spirit only that can despise a woman
for making no remonstrances ; and a brutal one, that can
ill-treat her for it.   A heart with any nobleness left in it,
keeps its sacredest and dearest corner for a kindness so
angelical" (p. 126).

But I should weary the reader if I extracted bits in
which I see Browning's touch, on pages 21, 30, 49, 59,
84-5, 116, 143, 144, 149, 158, 162, 207, 228-9, 230, 236
and the whole close of the volume.   I however note that
Browning owed much to Donne, and that he mentions
Strafford's care for that poet too :

"The soul of the earl of Strafford was indeed lodged,
to use the expression of his favourite Donne, within a
'low and fatal room' (p. 228).   "But ever by the side
of the body's weakness we find a witness of the spirit's
triumph —a vindication of the mightiness of will !" (p.
229).   "Then, when every energy was to be taxed to the
uttermost, the question of his fiery spirit's supremacy was
indeed put to the issue, by a complication of ghastly
diseases ! " (p. 230).

There are also bits of analysis and philosophizing on
character which are surely Browning's ; and above all
there are the conception and working out of the per-
sonality and character of Strafford, "that he was consistent to himself throughout" (p. 60 at foot), that his one
object was to make Charles "the most absolute lord in

Christendom," and that this explains all apparent inconsistencies and vanities in his conduct. The *Life* also
seems to me written by a man who did not know the
period thoroughly, and did not work the details of contemporary history into it as a historian familiar with them
would have done. It is the work of a poet-analyser of
a statesman's character, rather than a historian's picturing
of him in his own time and surroundings.

The present reprint is due to Mr. Dana Estes, the Chairman of the Boston Browning Society. Both Messrs. Smith
& Elder, and Messrs. Longmans (whose firm publisht
the original edition of 1836 in Lardner's *Cabinet Cyclopædia*) declined to reprint the *Life of Strafford*. Mr.
Dana Estes is head of the firm of Estes and Lauriat in
Boston, U.S.A., and had seen a reproduction of my
letter in the *Pall Mall Gazette* of April 12, 1890, claiming the work for Browning. He wrote to me that his
firm would share the cost of the reprint with any other
publisher if I could find one. I accepted his offer on
behalf of the Browning Society, and agreed that none of
its copies should be sent for sale to the United States.
It was of course necessary to have the book up to date,
and to get the views of a modern historian on it and
Strafford. Prof. S. R. Gardiner and Mr. C. H. Firth of
Oxford are the acknowledged authorities on the period ;
and as Prof. Gardiner was too busy and also felt
somewhat bound by Browning's desire that he should not
make B.'s authorship public, Mr. Firth most kindly undertook to write the Introduction needed for the *Life*, and
compile us a table of the chief dates and events in

Strafford's career.   (The reader will notice how few dates Browning, poet-like, has given.)   Mr. Firth also suggested the addition of an Appendix II of the chief fresh Letters and documents of and about Strafford, which Prof. Gardiner and others have printed of late years.   Our London and Boston Browning Societies are greatly indebted to Mr. Firth for his valuable help, and all Browning students will thank him for his contribution to this book.   They will also feel grateful to our member Mr. Benjamin Sagar, for his famously full Index.

3 St. George's Sqr. London, N.W.
26 November, 1890.

INTRODUCTION

By C. H. FIRTH.

FORSTER in the life of Eliot, which he published in
1836, quotes a few lines from a poet, "whose genius,"
he says, "has just risen amongst us." In a footnote
he explains that the writer of the verses is "the author
of *Paracelsus*, Mr. Robert Browning. There would be
little danger in predicting that this writer will soon be
acknowledged as a first-rate poet. He has already proved
himself one."[1] Under what circumstances it was that
Browning undertook to write the life of Strafford for his
friend Forster, Dr. Furnivall explains in his 'Forewords.'
A biography written under such conditions naturally
shows occasional traces of haste and incompleteness.
Moreover, the evidence at the disposal of a biographer
in 1836 was in many respects defective ; and time has
brought to light so many new facts and new documents
that there is much to add to any life of Strafford written
so long ago, and something to correct in it.

On the other hand, even in 1836 a biographer of
Strafford had a larger amount of information at his disposal than in the case of any other statesman of the

---

[1] *British Statesmen*, vol. ii. p. 104.

seventeenth century. The article in *Biographia Britan-nica*, and the life in Macdiarmid's *British Statesmen*, supplied Browning with two tolerably full and careful accounts of Strafford's career. He had also Sir George Radcliffe's invaluable memoir of his friend, and the admirable selection from Strafford's letters published by Dr. Knowler in 1739. Of this last Browning observes: " The collection of documents known by the title of the Strafford papers, seems to me to contain within itself every material necessary to the illustration of the public and private character of this statesman, on an authority which very few will be disposed to contest, for the record is his own. . . . Hereafter I mean to restrict myself almost entirely to the authorities, illustrations, and suggestions of character, that are so abundantly furnished by that great work."

Evidently the subject which from the first attracted Browning was Strafford's character rather than his career. Unlike some biographers, he does not treat his hero merely as one of a series of statesmen, and confine himself to his public life, " as if the shop were all the house." He is interested in every aspect of Strafford's life, and every side of his character. He shows us what sort of a husband and father he was, and how faithful a friend. He describes his daily habits, his recreations, and his tastes. He brings out his fondness for fishing, hawking, and hunting, as well as his love of art and poetry.

Browning's conception of biography is further illustrated by the passage in which he discusses Strafford's desertion of the popular party. The supposition of a sudden and complete change in any man's character is dismissed with a touch of scorn. He seeks to discover, what Pope would have called "the ruling principle" of Strafford's character, or "the law of his being," as Browning prefers to term it—and finds in it the key to his political conduct. He demands from his hero fidelity to his own nature, not constancy to one party or one set of opinions. He requires, in a word, not political but dramatic consistency. "What it is desired to impress upon the reader before the delineation of Wentworth in his after years, is this—that he was consistent to himself throughout." [1] Unhappily, the execution of the design falls short of the conception. Phrases such as "the development of the aristocratic principle," and "the intensity of the aristocratic principle," hardly furnish the required explanation of Strafford's conduct. [2] His political career is not treated with the freedom from prejudice which seemed to be promised. Strafford is judged too much by the standards of 1832, and too little by the standards of 1632. To this result, the want of evidence about Strafford's earlier career, and an insufficient acquaintance with the conditions and ideas of his time, also contributed. Browning himself seems to have been scarcely satisfied with his own portrait of Strafford. It is curious to contrast the biography with the play written a year later. One might almost say that in the first Strafford was represented as he appeared to his opponents, and in the second as he appeared to himself;

[1] Pp. 60, 278.   [2] Pp. 2, 4, 59.

or that, having painted Strafford as he was, Browning painted him again as he wished to be. In the biography Strafford is exhibited as a man of rare gifts and noble qualities; yet in his political capacity, merely the conscious, the devoted tool of a tyrant. "In him Despotism at length obtained an instrument with mind to comprehend and resolution to act upon her principles in their length and breadth."[1]

In the tragedy, on the other hand, Strafford is the champion of the King's will against the people's, but yet looks forward to the ultimate reconciliation of Charles and his subjects, and strives for it after his own fashion. He loves the master he serves, and dies for him, but when the end comes he can proudly answer his accusers, "I have loved England too."

It seems as if the play were written to supplement and correct the biography. Each contains a part of the truth.

To judge Strafford fairly and to represent him truly, we have to take into account what he aimed at, as well as what he achieved, and to consider his political creed in close relation to the conditions of his time, and the ideas of his contemporaries.

From the outset of his career, Wentworth sought employment in the service of the State, or as he would have expressed it "the Commonwealth." It was not only the desire for credit and influence in his native country, which led him to seek office, nor was it simply his "abstract veneration for power."[2] It was also, as he says in his defence, the "chaste ambition . . . to have as much

1 P. 278.   2 P. 64.

power as may be, that there may be power to do the more good in the place where a man lives."[1] Eager to promote the public weal, he rejoiced in the labours it demanded. He describes himself truly, as "ever desiring the best things, never satisfied I had done enough, but did always desire to do better."[2] In the service of the State alone could such a man find full scope for his energies, and from the King's commission alone could he obtain the authority his aims required. He had grown up under the influence of the Elizabethan traditions, and looked to the monarchy, not to the people, as the source of authority; to the King, not to the Parliament, as the natural ally of a reformer.

Wentworth represented Yorkshire in the Parliament of 1614. In December 1615 he was made Custos Rotulorum for the West Riding of Yorkshire, and as such, first in the Commission of Peace for that district. On July 10th, 1619, he was appointed a member of the Council of the North. In 1620, at the desire of the Government he again stood for Yorkshire, and used his local influence to secure the return of Sir George Calvert, one of the Secretaries of State, as his colleague. He seemed marked out for the King's favour, and in 1621, the newsletters predicted his approaching elevation to the peerage, and even reported that he would take the title of Viscount Raby.[3]

At this moment, however, Wentworth's rise came to a stop. During the Parliament of 1621 he had

---

[1] Rushworth, *Trial of Strafford*, p. 146.   [2] *Trial*, p. 161.
[3] *Court and Times of James I.*, i. 169, 285.

wavered in his support of the Government. His attitude
was conciliatory throughout. He supported the King's
demand for a subsidy for the defence of the Palatinate.
In language which recalls his later utterances, he urged
the Commons not to seek " to capitulate with the
King," to "consider of the King and people together
and indivisibly," to avoid "leaving a kind of misunderstanding between the King and his people." But
anxious as he was to press on with practical legislation, and to prevent barren disputes about privileges,
he could not quietly submit to the King's denial of
freedom of speech to Parliament. "Sir Thomas Wentworth," says the reporter . . . "would have us stand on
it that our privileges are our right and our inheritance."
Vexed also by the sudden dissolution which followed the
protest of the Commons, he was yet far from any thought
of active opposition, and still aimed at office. The path
was more difficult, but " with patience, circumspection,
and principally silence," it might still be passed.[1]

Silence was Wentworth's resource throughout the
debates of the Parliament of 1624. The nation was
eager for war, and Buckingham seized the opportunity
to put himself at the head of the movement. Unmoved
himself by the popular feeling, Wentworth knew that it
was useless to struggle against it. His own views on
European politics were uninfluenced by religious considerations, and he cared little for the fate of the German
Protestants. He had no share in the Puritan antipathy
to Spain, and scoffed at the exultation with which "all

[1] *Letters*, i. 19.

the cobblers and bigots and zealous brethren" of London hailed the dismissal of the Spanish ambassador.[1] For dynastic reasons he desired the restoration of the Prince Palatine, but he would have sought it by diplomatic means only. The King of England, he held, was bound neither in justice nor honour to venture his people's prosperity for the recovery of the Palatinate. In 1637, King Charles thought of going to war with Spain for that purpose, and asked Wentworth's opinion on the question. There can be little doubt that the principles which dictated his answer then guided his conduct now. "The first consideration ariseth, whether this war tends in any sort to the wealth or safety of the crown of England, or not rather to the decay of trade, and losing the greatest entrance to the enlargement thereof that hath of many years been opened unto us, whilst those two great monarchs of France and Spain are now at odds, the commodities and commerce consequently of both, of necessity to pass through our merchants, to their mighty enriching, to the extreme improvement of the customs, and the great increase of shipping." Instead of rushing on "the bleeding evil of an instant and active war," let the King turn his attention homewards, and seek first the welfare of England.[2] The advice which Wentworth gave in 1637, he would have given in 1624 also. Consistently insular in his view of foreign politics, he was anxious to avoid interference in continental struggles, eager to amend laws, to redress grievances, and to "do the

---

[1] *Letters*, i. 21. [2] *Letters*, ii. 60, 62.

business of the Commonwealth." As a member of the Parliament of 1625, he neither attacked Buckingham personally, nor refused the subsidies the King demanded, but allowed his dissatisfaction with their policy to be clearly seen. As yet he was scarcely numbered with the opposition. The King still styled him "an honest gentleman," and if Buckingham by a trick excluded him from the Parliament of 1626, it was sedulously excused as an accident. Wentworth submitted quietly to his exclusion from Parliament. "It was better," he declared, "to be a spectator than an actor," and he announced his resolve not to contest with the King unless he were constrained thereto.

It is significant that at this very time he applied for the Presidency of the Council of the North.[1] Other motives no doubt besides ambition led him to desire it. Serving the King in the parts where he lived, he could keep out of the sterile constitutional struggles in Parliament, and avoid all responsibility for the foreign policy of which he disapproved. His application was made almost directly to Buckingham, was followed by explanations, and ended in a promise of friendship. Buckingham, however, would tolerate no neutrals amongst his friends, and required active support. There is little doubt that Wentworth's refusal to take part in the collection of the forced loan of 1626 was the cause of his dismissal from the dignity of Custos Rotulorum, and from his other official posts. His further refusal to subscribe to that loan himself was

[1] Appendix, p. 290.

followed by imprisonment in the Marshalsea and at Dartford. How reluctantly Wentworth exchanged the attitude of " cold, silent forbearance," for the " active heat " of opposition his conduct shows. His refusal to pay was courteous, his bearing at the Council-board firm but conciliatory.[1] It is evident from his letters to Weston that he regarded himself as personally attacked by Buckingham, and as the victim of a breach of faith on the part of the favourite. Immediately he was dismissed he sought to represent his fidelity to the King, complained that he had been maliciously misrepresented to his Majesty, and expressed the hope of presenting hereafter "more ripe and pleasing fruits of my labours in his service."

Thus personal and political motives alike combined to make Wentworth one of the leaders of the Opposition during the first session of the Parliament of 1628. Yet fiercely as he attacked the King's ministers, he was careful to exonerate the King. "This hath not been done by the King . . . but by projectors," is the conclusion of his catalogue of grievances. Vehement though his language was, it was evident that he sought to heal, not to widen, the breach between Charles and England. "Whether we shall look upon the King or his people, it did never more behove this great physician the parliament, to effect a true consent amongst the parties than now." Sovereign and subject alike had suffered by Buckingham's policy. "Both are injured; both to be cured. . . By one and the same thing hath the King

[1] Appendix, p. 291.

and people been hurt. . . I speak truly both for the interest of the King and people." The remedy he proposed was "no new thing," no transfer of power from King to Parliament, but simply the reinforcement of the ancient laws by a new law to provide security from arbitrary imprisonment, and freedom from arbitrary taxation. Instead of the Petition of Right with its recital of past illegalities he advocated a statute to decide what should be legal in the future, to fix the limits of the subject's liberty and the Crown's prerogative, and to lay the foundation of future union between King and people. That done he was willing to leave the King a discretionary power to use in cases of emergency. "Let us make what laws we can, there must—nay, there will be—a trust left in the Crown."

Between the refusal of the Commons to allow for exceptions, and the reluctance of the King to submit to rules, Wentworth's reconciling scheme fell to the ground. Other leaders seized the direction of the House, and sought to impose more rigid restrictions on the Crown. It was not without expressing some misgivings that Wentworth supported the Petition of Right. "I have discharged my conscience and delivered it. Do as you please. God, that knows my heart, knows that I have studied to preserve this Parliament, as I confess the resolutions of this House, in the opinion of wise men, stretch very far on the King's power, and if they be kept punctually will give a blow to Government." The struggle for the Petition of Right was long and bitter, and if its acceptance removed the grievances of which Wentworth had complained, it did not bring back the good understanding which his plan had aimed at restoring. He saw new subjects of dispute arise, and religious grievances with which he had no sympathy came to the front. With the failure of his leadership his part in the struggle was over, and there was nothing now to prevent him from seeking again, as he sought in 1626, to serve the King in the parts where he lived.

On July 22nd, 1628, he was raised to the peerage, and on Dec. 10th became President of the Council of the North. Buckingham's death (Aug. 23rd, 1628) opened the way to further promotion. On Nov. 10th, 1629, he entered the Privy Council, and became Lord Deputy of Ireland in January 1632.

As Browning observes, "much good wrath" has been thrown away on political apostacies.[1] What really requires explanation is not why Wentworth left the ranks of the Opposition, but how he ever came to act with it. He cannot be termed an apostate, for he renounced no article of faith; much less a convert, for he accepted no new creed. His aim remained the same. He still sought to spend his powers in the fruitful work of practical reform. He still hoped to reconcile King and people. If the Wentworth of 1640 differed from the Wentworth of 1628—and differed for the worse—it was because new duties had brought new conditions; but the change which their influence effected was gradual and unconscious. Neither can it fairly be said that Wentworth left the side of the people and adopted the side

[1] P. 61.

of the King.   Nothing misleads so much as the application of the ideas of modern politics to the times before party government was born or dreamt of. The first axiom of Wentworth's political creed was that there were not and could not be two sides; and he never saw that what had once been a truth was rapidly becoming a mere phrase. "Divide not," he warned the Irish Parliament, "between the interests of the King and his people, as if there were one being of the King, and another being of his people. This is the most mischievous principle that can be laid in reason of State. . . You might as well tell me an head might live without a body, or a body without a head, as that it is possible for a King to be rich and happy without his people be so likewise, or that a people can be rich and happy without their King be so also. Most certain it is, that their well-being is individually one and the same, their interests woven up together with so tender and close threads, as cannot be pulled asunder without a rent in the Commonwealth."[1]   When he entered on his government at York, he thus declared his object as a ruler. "To the joint individual well-being of sovereignty and subjection, I vow all my cares and diligence through the whole course of my ministry." "I thank God," he reiterated on his scaffold, "that in all my employment since I had the honour to serve his Majesty, I never had anything in my heart but what tended to the joint individual prosperity of King and people."[2]

In his view the liberties of the people and the prerogative of the Crown were perfectly compatible and harmo-

---

[1] *Letters*, i. 298.   [2] Appendix, p. 292 ; *Trial*, pp. 640, 759.

nious parts of the constitution. Each must be kept "within the modest bounds set and appointed for them by the sobriety and moderation of former times." Sometimes he represented them as two streams, running side by side, each to be restrained from growing at the cost of the other, "not rising one above another in any kind, but kept in their own wonted channels. For if they rise above these heights, the one or the other, they tear the banks, and overflow the fair meads equally on one side and the other." At other times he pictured the constitution as a musical instrument. "All the strings of this government and monarchy have been so perfectly tuned through the skill and attention of our forefathers, that if you wind any of them anything higher, or let them lower, you shall infallibly interrupt the sweet accord that ought to be entertained of King and people."[1]

According to Wentworth, it was the duty of the King's faithful servants to labour to defend this balance of the constitution, to protect the rights alike of King and people, and "to preserve each without diminishing or enlarging either."

The sin of Buckingham and his underlings was that they had "extended the prerogative of the Crown beyond its first symmetry which makes the sweet harmony of the whole."[2] The sin of Sir David Foulis and his fellow aristocrats was "that they had sought to impair the regal power; had with rough hands laid hold upon the flowers of it, and with unequal and swaggering paces trampled upon the rights of the Crown." In the

[1] *Trial*, pp. 182, 640.　　　　[2] *Ibid.* p. 795.

one case he wished to set such a stamp upon the laws "as no licentious spirit shall dare hereafter to enter upon them." In the other he urged such an exemplary punishment of the offender as should for the future "retain licentious spirits within the sober bounds of humility and fear."[1]   Throughout, as leader of the Opposition, as President of the Council of the North, and as Lord Deputy of Ireland, Wentworth regarded himself as defending the constitution against those who sought to assail it. "Stare super antiquas vias" is a maxim always in his mouth.

So long as King and people could contrive to agree, this theory of the constitution would work perfectly. Wentworth bent all his efforts to promote that agreement, and it was with the hope of promoting it that he entered the King's service in 1628. The letters to Weston in which he expressed his views have unhappily not survived, but Weston's reply enables us to conjecture their contents. "My heart," protested Weston, "hath ever been full of those ends you wish. If honesty did not lead me to it, yet wisdom would for my own profit and safety. By the good agreement between the King and his people, I may be happy; without it, impossible for me to be so."[2]   It was Wentworth's misfortune that he entered the King's service not merely at a time when King and people differed, but when the difference was too great to be healed; whichever prevailed, the harmonious balance of the constitution must be destroyed.   One of the two, either the liberty

<hr>

[1] Appendix, p. 292.   [2] *Letters*, p. 47.

of the people or the authority of the King, must increase at the expense of the other. So soon as Wentworth came to perceive this necessity, he preferred the second alternative. " He always thought," writes Radcliffe, " that regal power and popular privileges might well stand together. . . Yet it being most hard and difficult to keep the interests of King and People from encroaching one upon another, the longer he lived his experience taught him that it was far safer that the King should increase in power than that the people should gain advantages on the King: that may turn to the prejudice of some particular sufferers, this draws with it the ruin of the whole."[1] " The authority of the King," said Wentworth to the Council of the North, " is the keystone which closeth up the arch of order and government, which contains each part in due relation to the whole, and which once shaken, infirmed, all the frame falls together into a confused heap of foundation and battlement, of strength and beauty."[2] For that reason the preservation of the King's prerogative was more important than the preservation of the people's liberties. In the fundamental laws of the land the property of the subject was " the second table," but the prerogative of the King the first, and " hath a something more imprinted upon it. For if it hath a divinity imprinted upon it, it is God's anointed ; it is he that gives the powers. And Kings are as Gods on earth, higher prerogatives than can be said, or found to be spoken of the property or liberty of the subject."[3]

[1] *Letters*, ii. 434.　　　[2] P. 292.　　　[3] *Trial*, pp. 182, 646.

Wentworth held that this view of the Royal power was perfectly compatible with the existence, the usefulness, and the dignity of parliamentary institutions. In his dying speech he repudiated as a calumny the charge of hostility to parliaments. "I was so far from being against parliaments that I did always think the parliaments of England were the most happy constitutions that any kingdom or nation lived under, and the best means under God to make the King and people happy."[1] There was much truth in this protest. Wentworth did not share his master's dread and hatred of parliaments. He thought that a temporary intermission of such assemblies was necessary until the "peccant humour" was purged forth, "that once rightly corrected we may hope for a parliament of a sound constitution indeed." The success with which he had managed the Irish Parliament encouraged him (and encouraged others also) to think of the calling of a parliament again in England.[2] He it was who persuaded the King, in Dec. 1639, after so many years' intermission, again to make trial of a parliament.

Yet it was impossible to exalt the rights of kingship without at the same time diminishing the rights of parliaments. Strafford regarded them as useful machines for making good laws or amending bad ones, but he never considered them fit to guide the policy of a government or control its administration. They were useful also, according to his view, as the recognised constitutional form through which the king was to

[1] *Trial*, p. 759.   [2] *Letters*, i. 41, 420.

seek and obtain the co-operation of his subjects. He represented Charles to the Irish Parliament, as "ever best pleased to tread the ancient paths in public services to take his people along with him, to have you yourselves co-operate with him for the individual good of you both." It was their business to supply the king with money to carry out the policy on which his wisdom had determined, "a supply which in all wisdom, good nature, and conscience they are not to deny."[1]

"My master expects the honour of your trust," he told the Irish Parliament, explaining at the same time that it was the refusal to trust the king which had caused "the misfortunes these meetings have run of late years in England."[2] This trust, moreover, must be complete, there must be no attempt at "laying clogs or conditions on the king;" "conditions are not to be admitted with any subjects."[3] Should the Irish parliament refuse to trust the king their opposition would be futile, as well as undutiful. "The king desires this great work may be settled by Parliament, as the more beaten path he covets to walk in, yet not more legal than if done by his prerogative royal, where the ordinary way fails him. If the people then be so unwise as to cast off his gracious proposals, and their own safety, it must be done without them. . . . Could they fight against their own well-being; yet let them rest assured, his majesty, as Pater Patriae, would not suffer it, but save them even whether they would or no, do that by his own power, which he first

[1] *Trial*, pp. 614, 657; *Letters*, i. 183, 287.
[2] *Letters*, i. 289.   [3] *Letters*, i. 184, 237, 290.

expected to have accomplished with their concurring assents."[1] So too when the English Parliament in 1640 had refused to provide the king with money for the war against the Scots, Wentworth asserted that the king might raise supplies without the grant of Parliament. It was, he said, a " case of extreme and unavoidable necessity. And the king may in that case use, as the common parent of the country, what power God Almighty hath given him, for preserving himself and his people, for whom he is accomptable to Almighty God. In these cases he hath a power given him by God Almighty which cannot be taken from him by others; neither, under favour, is he able to take it from himself."[2] He might exercise that power even when the necessity was less visible and the danger more remote. " I conceive," writes Wentworth in his criticism on Hampden's trial, "that the power of levies of forces at sea and land for the very, not feigned, relief and safety of the public, is such a property of sovereignty as were the crown willing, yet can it not divest itself thereof : Salus Populi suprema Lex ; nay, in cases of extremity even above Acts of Parliament." The king therefore was justified in levying ship-money without a parliamentary grant. " I conceive it was out of humour opposed by Hampden beyond the modesty of a subject and that reverence wherein we ought to have so gracious a sovereign, it being ever to be understood, the prospects of kings into mysteries of state are so far exceeding those of ordinary common persons, as they be able to discern and prevent dangers to the

---

[1] *Letters,* i. 238. [2] *Trial,* p. 550.

public afar off, which others shall not so much as dream of till they feel the unavoidable stripes and smart of them upon their naked shoulders. . . . Therefore it is a safe rule for us all in the fear of God to remit these supreme watches to that regal power, whose peculiar indeed it is; submit ourselves in these high considerations to his ordinance, as being no other than the ordinance of God itself; and rather attend upon his will, with confidence in his justice, belief in his wisdom, assurance in his parental affections to his subjects and kingdom, than feed ourselves with the curious questions, with the vain flatteries of imaginary liberty, which, had we even our silly wishes and conceits, were we to frame a new common-wealth even to our own fancy, might yet in conclusion, leave ourselves less free, less happy, than now we are." [1]

To reconcile the nation to the loss of the control over the Government which it was unfit to exercise, Went-worth meant to give it the solid realities of even-handed justice and material prosperity. He too cherished the vision of an ideal commonwealth framed after his own fancy. "Once freed from the conditions and restraints of subjects," the king would be able to effect unhin-dered whatever the welfare of his subjects required. His "excellent wisdom," ever studying "the just and moderate government of his people," and ministering back to them in return for their subsidies "the plenties and comforts of life," would guide all classes to work together for the common weal. His justice, "search-ing and severe in punishing the oppressions and wrongs

[1] *Letters,* ii. 388.

of his subjects," would protect the poor against the rich, and the friendless against the powerful. The "love and protection" of the king would be repaid by the loyalty of the people. In the end the nation would be reconciled to the king's absolutism by the beneficence of his rule, parliaments would submit to become the king's helpers instead of striving to be his masters, and the people would cease to desire "imaginary liberty."

In England, at all events, such a scheme as Strafford's was foredoomed to failure. It had its source rather in the traditions of the past than the necessities of the present, and the conditions required for its success were lacking. To establish an intelligent despotism two things were needful: an intelligent despot, and a people willing to forego the right of thinking for itself. Charles I. neither sympathised with the desires of his people nor understood their needs, whilst his infirmity of purpose prevented him from following any systematic policy. Evils and abuses there might be in the social fabric; but no evil and no danger great enough to induce the English nation to surrender, even for a time, the claim to govern itself.

In Ireland, however, the conditions were very different. There parliamentary institutions were mere forms, and had never been anything more. Enough oppression and enough disorder existed to make the people desire "to fly from petty tyrants to the throne." Hence Wentworth's policy met with a marvellous temporary success. How swiftly he restored order, how greatly he increased the material prosperity of Ireland, Browning's pages well show.[1] What he fails to show is Wentworth's attempt to establish that reign of impartial justice which was equally important to Wentworth's mind, and an equally necessary part of his policy. The Lord Deputy's report to the king in 1636 shows the object which he had set before himself. "Justice," he told Charles, "was dispensed without acceptation of persons; the poor knew where to seek and to have his relief, without being afraid to appeal to his Majesty's catholic justice against the greatest subject; the great men contented with reason, because they knew not how to help themselves, or fill their greedy appetites, where otherwise they are as sharp set upon their own wills as any people in the world : that was a blessing the poorer sort, this a restraint the richer, had not formerly been acquainted with in that kingdom." [2]

Independent evidence shows how successful Strafford was in attaining this aim. My Lord Deputy, writes a correspondent to Lord Fairfax, " hath achieved high honours in respect of justice." "Dives hath no advantage of Lazarus," was the news which reached Sir John Bingley from his friends in Ireland. " Whilst I was in Ireland," says a third witness, "the poor cried, never so good a Lord Deputy."

One of the first things which struck him when he arrived in Ireland was the way in which the tax for the maintenance of the army had been levied. " Most unconscionably the landlords and moneyed men, to ease themselves, had laid it upon the poor and bare tenants."

[1] Pages 179, 184.　　　　　　　[2] *Letters*, ii. 18.

He arranged that henceforwards the burden of subsidies "should lie upon the wealthier sort, which, God knows, hath not been the fashion of Ireland." The relief of the tenants was also one of the objects of certain alterations made by Strafford in the system of land tenure —alterations which were likewise intended to break the influence of the great noblemen, and attach the smaller landholders more closely to the crown. Strafford's "masterpiece," according to Secretary Coke, was this "changing of the tenures of the lower sort of Irish from their oppressing lords to their gracious king."[1]

"The people in general," wrote Strafford in 1637, "are in great quietness, and if I be not much mistaken, well satisfied, if not delighted with his Majesty's gracious government and protection. It being most sure that the lower part of the Irish subject hath not in any age lived so preserved from the pressures and oppressions of the great ones, as now they do, for which I assure you they bless God and the king ; and begin to discern and taste the great and manifold benefits they gather under the shadow and from their immediate dependence upon the crown, in comparison of the scant and narrow coverings they formerly borrowed from their petty yet imperious lords."[2] In the spring of 1640, when Strafford left Ireland, it seemed as if his purpose had been attained. "This people," he writes, "is abundantly comforted and satisfied in your justice, set with exceeding alacrity to serve the crown the right way in these doubtful times, and much trusting and believing us your Majesty's

---

[1] *Letters*, i. 238, 334, 401.　　　[2] *Letters*, ii. 93.

poor ministers : all this in as high a measure as your own princely heart can wish."   " God be praised," were his words a few months earlier, " no king can be more absolute than your Majesty is amongst us." [1]

Yet all this appearance of success was delusive. Strafford's work failed to endure, and its failure was in part due to his own errors.   In his desire to realise his conception of good government as rapidly as possible he had regarded all means as legitimate.   His severity had alienated the nobles and officials who had hitherto formed the governing class in Ireland. Presbyterian and Puritan colonists had been driven into opposition by his determination to enforce conformity to the Anglican Church.   His plantations of Clare and Ormond, and his intended plantation of Connaught, had roused the fears of the native Irish for their lands. The meeting of the Long Parliament set free all these different resentments, and destroyed the strong government he had set up.   A year later the outbreak of the Irish rebellion, caused largely by Strafford's agrarian policy, swept away the material prosperity he had created. But even with twenty years of absolute power, he could hardly have effected what he sought to do in six or seven, for he relied upon force to effect social changes which force alone was insufficient to accomplish, and left out of count the necessity of obtaining the co-operation of the people he governed.

Whilst in Ireland Strafford gained only apparent and partial success, in England he had to struggle from the

[1] *Letters*, ii. 387, 402.

first with failure and defeat.   In July 1639 the king summoned him to his side to advise on the measures to be taken to suppress the rebellion in Scotland.

He had not been consulted when the disturbances in Scotland first began.   On July 3rd, 1638, the king had written to ask him what forces could be drawn from Ireland, but even then he was not consulted on the conduct of the war in general.   He had given some assistance during the first Scotch war, but not as much as he could have done had he been more fully trusted. "Where trusts and instructions come too late," he complained, "then the business is sure to be lost."   Now that the game was lost, when the first war had ended in an ignominious peace, he was at last called to restore the fortune of a sinking cause.   He arrived in London on Sept. 22nd, 1639. " From that time he became, what he had never been before, the trusted counsellor of Charles, so far at least as it was possible for Charles to trust any one.   During the fourteen months which followed he was the great minister, striving with all the force of his iron will to rescue his master from the net in which his feet were inextricably entangled." [1]

Browning treats this part of Wentworth's life very inadequately, no doubt because there are very few letters amongst the Strafford correspondence relating to it, though there was ample material in other collections of papers then published.[2]

---

[1] Gardiner, *History of England*, ix. 73.

[2] E. g. *The Hardwicke State Papers, The Clarendon State Papers*, and *Rushworth*.

The year 1640 was the culminating point in Wentworth's career. On Jan. 12th, 1640, he was created Earl of Strafford, and a week later he was raised from the rank of Lord Deputy of Ireland to the higher dignity of Lord Lieutenant. In the summer he was entrusted with the chief command of the King's English army (Aug. 18), and honoured with the Order of the Garter (Sept. 24). Charles said openly that he trusted him more than all his Council, and the Queen, so long hostile, told him that she esteemed him the most capable and faithful servant her husband had.[1] As the catastrophe drew nearer, the manifestations of their confidence redoubled. "The King," wrote Strafford on Nov. 5th, 1640, "hath given me great demonstrations of his affection, and strong assurances as can be expressed in words. The Queen is infinitely gracious to me, above all that you can imagine, and doth declare it in a very public and strange manner, so as nothing can hurt me, by God's help, but the iniquity and necessity of these times."

But trust had come too late, and power crumbled in Strafford's hands as he grasped it. The aim of his policy was to subdue the Scots and to rule Scotland directly from England. He would carry on the war, he had written in 1638, till the Scots had received the common Prayer-book used in our churches in England without any alteration, till the bishops were settled peaceably in their jurisdiction. "Nay, perchance till I had conformed that kingdom in all, as well for the temporal as eccle-

---

[1] Gardiner, *History of England*, ix. 110 ; Whitaker, *Life of Radcliffe*, p. 218.

siastical affairs, wholly to the government and laws of England; and Scotland governed by the King and Council of England, in a great part at least as we are here" [in Ireland]. All opposition was to be suppressed and chastised. The Scots were to be " cudgelled back into their right wits again"; the English Puritans to be " whipped home into their right wits "; English country gentlemen who murmured to be taught that " their part was obedience and not dispute." " He could not comprehend how honest men could look on the Scots' resistance from a point of view different to his own." He believed it possible to carry out this policy with the support of the English nation and by the aid of the English parliament. His first step was to counsel a new levy of ship-money; his next to persuade the King to call a parliament (Dec. 5, 1639). Caring little for the forms of the constitution himself, he never understood their importance to others, and was unprepared for the depth and strength of the feeling which the King's arbitrary rule had roused. He thought that the plea of necessity would be accepted, and these violations of the constitution condoned. He fancied that all would end in a reconciliation between the King and his subjects. To the assertion that the King might use extra-legal means to preserve the state, he added the promise " that when the present danger of the commonwealth was by the wisdom, courage, and power of the King prevented, and the public weal secured; in a time proper and fit, the King was obliged to vindicate the property and liberty of the subject from any ill prejudice that might fall from such a precedent."[1]   A new statute, such as he had proposed in 1628, defining the bounds of the King's prerogative and the subject's liberty, passed by parliament and assented to by the King, and the King and his people would again be happy and united.

In the spring of 1640 Wentworth hurried back from Ireland—though racked by gout and dysentery—to take his stand by the King's side in the coming struggle.   As he had prophetically written eight years earlier—" I have not so learned my master, nor am I so indulgent to my own ease, as to let his affairs suffer shipwreck whilst I myself rest secure in harbour.   No, let the tempest be never so great, I will much rather put forth to sea, work forth the storm, or at least be found dead with the rudder in my hands."[2]   The first blow to Strafford's policy was the rupture between the King and the parliament in May 1640.   Then came the failure of successive attempts to raise money, by a forced loan from the London merchants, assistance from the King of Spain, or the coinage of base money.   All hung now on the issue of the campaign.   Scarcely recovered from an illness which had brought him to death's door, Strafford was despatched to the north to take command of the army on the border.   On the 24th of August he left London, and the first day's travel brought back his sufferings.   " I am not very weary," he wrote to Radcliffe, "but much worse than I was this morning.   My pains are the same I had in my sickness, and the new grief which I have got again on my liver side gives me my former difficulty of

[1] Trial, pp. 566, 646, 669.   [2] P. 299.

breathing, and will no doubt force me to let blood. Yet hitherto I am able to endure travelling, I praise God, and so long as that holds I shall go on." He reached York on August 27th ; on the 28th Conway was routed at Newburn ; and on the 29th the Scots entered Newcastle. The sick General's first duty was to reorganise his beaten army. " Pity me," he wrote, " for never came any man to so lost a business. The army altogether unexercised and unprovided of all necessaries. That part which I bring now with me from Durham the worst I ever saw. Our horse all cowardly, the country from Berwick to York in the power of the Scot, an universal affright in all, a general disaffection to the King's service, none sensible of his dishonour. In one word, here alone to fight with all these evils without any one to help. God of His goodness deliver me out of this the greatest evil of my life." [1]

Still with desperate energy Strafford struggled to maintain the lost cause. To deprive the Scots of provisions he ordered the mills to be dismantled. Obliged to own the impossibility of expelling the Scots from Durham and Northumberland, he clung to the hope of holding Yorkshire against them. Remain on the defensive, and wear them out by time was his counsel to the King. In a piched battle the English army would infallibly be beaten, but in skirmishes they might hold their own against the Scots. The capture of a troop of Scotch plunderers who had penetrated into Yorkshire, and some trifling successes of the garrison of Berwick seemed to justify this view. Strafford bent all his efforts to restore discipline in his

[1] Whitaker, *Life of Radcliffe*, p. 203.

army,—"that mass of disorder and unsoldierliness" as Clarendon terms it. Want of money obliged him sometimes to persuade where he would have commanded; but when he had money he meant to take a shorter way, and in the camp at York he set up a gallows at the head of each regiment to show them the penalty of misconduct. At one moment he projected the expulsion of all the Scots from Ulster in order to render Ireland at least safe from Scottish invaders. At another time he proposed to bring over the Irish army—8000 foot and 2000 horse—to England, as all men whispered, not merely to fight the Scots, but to reduce the English to the King's will. Against those who refused to assist the King in his extremity he broke out with all his old vehemence. "You are bound," he told the Yorkshire gentlemen, " to attend his Majesty at your own costs and charges in case of invasion ; you are bound by the common law of England, by the law of reason, by the law of nature, and you are no better than beasts if you refuse in this case to attend the King, his Majesty offering in person to lead you on." Partly by threats, partly by concessions, he won them to pay their trained bands for two months, and to withdraw their petition for a parliament.

But the impossibility of raising money to maintain the army baffled all his efforts. Even on the personal guarantee of the peers London refused a loan. Even the King's Council in London dared not recommend taxation by prerogative. Everywhere the counties refused to pay their quota of coat-and-conduct money.[1]

[1] *Rushworth*, iii. 1235.

Unable longer to resist the universal cry for a parliament, Charles was obliged, on Sept. 24, to announce the issue of writs summoning one to meet for Nov. 3. To Strafford this meant ruin, but he hardly realized the greatness of the danger in which he stood. On Oct. 8, the Scotch Commissioners in a public paper denounced him as an incendiary, and declared that they meant to insist on his punishment.[1] "Whatsoever they have to say let them say it in a parliament, and all they can against me," answered Strafford.[2] Still in the great Council of the Peers he stubbornly resisted the demands of the Scots, and opposed every concession made to them. Almost alone in his opposition, he was obliged to submit to a truce on terms which he held dishonourable and unnecessary. On its conclusion the King left him in Yorkshire to command the army and keep the unpaid soldiers in order. With indomitable pride he refused to take any part in raising the contribution agreed on for the support of the Scots. He would not, he said, be an instrument for drawing new provinces under their yoke. He would rather bestow his whole estate on the King than one penny on them.

As soon as the parliament opened Charles discovered that it was necessary for his service to have Strafford again by his side, and summoned him to London. Browning represents him as begging the King to allow him to retire to his government of Ireland, or to some other place, where he might promote his Majesty's service, and not deliver himself into the hands of his enraged

[1] *Rushworth*, iii. 1293.　　　　　[2] *Hardwicke Papers*, ii. 265.

enemies.[1]   There is evidence that his friends urged him " to pass over to Ireland where the army rested at his devotion, or to transport himself to foreign kingdoms till fairer weather here should invite him home."   The Marquis of Hamilton advised him to fly, but as Hamilton told the King, the Earl was too great-hearted to fear.   Though conscious of the peril of obedience, he set out to London to stand by his master.

" I am to-morrow to London," wrote Strafford to Radcliffe, "with more dangers beset, I believe, than ever man went out of Yorkshire ; yet my heart is good, and I find nothing cold within me.   It is not to be believed how great the malice is, and how intent they are about it ; little less care there is taken to ruin me than to save their own souls.   Nay, for themselves I wish their attention to the latter were equal to that they lend me in the former ; and certainly they will rack heaven and hell, as they say, to do me mischief.   They expect great matters out of Ireland, therefore pray you lend an ear to what may stir there ; howbeit I know not anything yet."[2]

One desperate resource remained.   The intrigues of the parliamentary leaders with the Scots had come to Strafford's knowledge, and he had determined to impeach them of high treason.   He would prove that Pym

---

[1] Browning's statement (p. 239) of Strafford's intentions is founded on Whitelock, *Memorials*, p. 108, vol. i. ed. 1853. L'Estrange's *Reign of King Charles*, ed. 1656, p. 201 ; Sanderson, *Reign of King Charles*, 1658, p. 337 ; and Heylyn, *Life of Laud*, p. 461, agree in stating that Strafford refused to fly.   See also Clarendon, *Rebellion*, ii. 104.

[2] Whitaker's *Radcliffe*, p. 218.

and his friends had secretly communicated with the rebels, and invited them to bring a Scottish army into England. "At one blow he hoped to strike down the traitors, and regain for the crown the popularity it had lost."[1] Strafford arrived in London on Monday, Nov. 9, 1640, and spent the Tuesday in resting after his journey. On the morning of Wednesday the 11th he took his seat in the House of Lords, but did not strike the blow.

" The moment when his accusation should have been brought, if it was to be brought at all, was allowed to slip by. It is no explanation to say that the Lords were engaged in other business. In such a case as this business could be interrupted, and at all events there would be time to speak when it was concluded. The only reasonable supposition is that, when the moment for execution came, Charles drew back as he had so often drawn back before. After a short visit Strafford left the House without uttering a word."

Meanwhile some traitor about the court had revealed the secret of Strafford's intentions to his opponents. Already on Nov. 7 committees had been appointed to investigate the complaints of Ireland against Strafford,

---

[1] See Gardiner, *History of England*, ix. p. 232. The statement that Strafford intended to accuse his opponents is made in Laud's *History of the Troubles* (Works, iii. 295); by Rushworth (*Trial of Strafford*, p. 2); by Sanderson, *The Reign of King Charles*, p. 337; and in the *Memoirs of the Earl of Manchester*. Clarendon mentions it as a rumour (*Rebellion*, iii. 10). It is curious that Browning, who sees the importance of this fact, and makes good use of it in his play (Act III. scene ii.), says so little of it in this biography. Probably he only knew of it from Clarendon, who gives it with a doubt.

and the general grievances of England also. No man doubted that the result would be the accusation of Strafford, and this new discovery merely precipitated the attack. Seven articles of impeachment were hastily drawn up on the morning of Nov. 11th, and the same afternoon Pym presented them to the House of Lords. Strafford, committed at first to the custody of the Black Rod, was sent to the Tower on Nov. 25.

The "fiery trial" he had often anticipated had come at last. "I have much reason," he had written eight years earlier, "to carry my eyes along with me wherever I go, and to expect my actions, from the highest to the lowest, shall all be cast into the balance and tried whether heavy or light. Content in the name of God! let them take me up and cast me down. If I do not fall square, and—to use a word of art—paragon, in every point of duty to my master; nay, if I do not fully comply with that public and common protection which good kings afford their good people, let me perish, and let no man pity me." [1]

As Browning observes, Strafford was not unprepared to meet his changed fortunes. He faced them with magnanimous cheerfulness and courage. He relied on his own innocence of the charge brought against him, and was convinced that he could prove it. "As to myself," he wrote on Dec. 13, "albeit all will be done against me that art and malice can devise, with all the rigour possible, yet I am in great inward quietness and a strong belief God will deliver me out of all these troubles."

[1] P. 298.

"Some meaner minds," he wrote two days later, " may perchance think this my night, but indeed I am and have myself in a better opinion, never having done anything I need to be ashamed of; and am able in much tranquillity of mind to look through this foul weather. To suffer, so it be not for our ill doing, is the condition of our frail humanity, and to a constant mind it must not sure be very hard to undergo." "Here," he told Ormonde, " is my only danger, that I may not have time given sufficient for my clearing."[1]

In Browning's account of Strafford's trial the importance of the change of procedure from impeachment to attainder is inadequately appreciated,[2] nor are the facts correctly told. Strafford's confidence arose largely from the fact that he had not technically been guilty of high treason. After he had heard the detailed articles of impeachment (Jan. 30, 1641), he wrote to his wife, to Ormonde, and to Sir Adam Loftus, telling each of them that there was nothing capital in the charge against him.[3] During the first part of the trial his confidence increased. "To the best of my judgment," he wrote to Radcliffe, "we gain much rather than lose. I trust God will preserve us ; and, as [of] all other passions, I

---

[1] Letter to his Wife, p. 243 ; Letter to Loftus, 15 Dec. ; *Strafford Letters*, ii. 414 ; Letter to Ormonde, 3 Feb. 1641 ; Carte's *Ormonde*, ed. 1851, v. 246.

[2] In the play the significance of the change is very well brought out in the speeches attributed to Vane and Pym, Act IV. scene ii. lines 125—137, 170—183.

[3] Letter to his Wife, Feb. 4, p. 245 ; to Loftus, Feb. 4 ; *Stafford Letters*, ii. 415 ; to Ormonde, Feb. 3 ; *Carte*, v. 246.

am free of fear, the articles that are coming I apprehend not. The Irish business is passed, and better than I expected, their proofs being very scant. God's hand is with us, for what is not we might expect to have been sworn from thence? All will be well, and every hour gives more hope than other."[1]

On April 10, a serious quarrel broke out between the two Houses on the question of the admissibility of some fresh evidence. A riotous scene took place in Westminster Hall, and there seemed likely to be a permanent breach. " The Commons on both sides of the House," says Baillie, " raise in a fury, with a shout of Withdraw ! Withdraw ! Withdraw ! get all their feet, on with their hats, cocked their beavers in the King's sight. We all did fear it should go to a present tumult." " The King laughed," says another eye-witness, "and the Earl of Strafford was so well pleased therewith that he would not hide his joy."

The same afternoon the Commons decided to bring in a Bill of Attainder. " The secret of their taking this way is conceived to be to prevent the hearing of the Earl's lawyers, who give out that there is no law yet in force whereby he can be condemned to die for aught yet objected against him, and therefore their intent is by this Bill to supply the defect of the laws therein."[2] A member

---

[1] This letter is printed by Dr. Whitaker, p. 222, as a postscript to Strafford's letter of Nov. 5, 1640, but is really a separate letter of fourteen lines, and should be dated April 4, 1641. The internal evidence is conclusive.

[2] Baillie, i. 346 ; *Cal. State Papers Domestic,* 1640-1, p. 540. See Gardiner, ix. pp. 327, 330.

of the Commons adds, "If the House of Commons proceed to demand judgment of the Lords, without doubt they will acquit him, there being no law extant whereupon to condemn him of treason. Wherefore the Commons are determined to desert the Lords' judicature, and to proceed against him by Bill of Attainder, whereby he shall be adjudged to death upon a treason now to be declared."[1]

Under these circumstances "the rigid, strong, and inflexible party" in the Commons broke away from the control of their ordinary leaders, and adopted the Bill of Attainder brought in by Sir Arthur Hesilrige. It appears from the diary of Sir Symond D'Ewes that Pym was opposed to proceeding by Bill of Attainder, and wished to carry the impeachment to its close, in which desire he seems to have been also backed by Hampden. The Bill passed its first reading on April 10, the second on April 14, and the third on April 21.

One result of this change of procedure was that it entirely altered the King's attitude towards Strafford's trial. If the Lords passed the Bill the King's confirmation would be required. "Unhappy men," says Baillie, "putts the King daily in harder straits. Had the Commons gone on in the former way of pursuit, the King might have been a patient, and only beheld the striking off of Strafford's head; but now they have put them on a Bill which will force the King either to be our agent and formal voicer to his death, or else do the world

---

[1] *Twelfth Report of the Historical Manuscripts Commission,* Coke MSS. ii. 278.

knows not what."[1] Strafford's chief hope was in the Lords. They might decline to pass the Bill, or they might suggest some compromise which the Commons would be obliged to accept. Strafford himself, now less confident, suggested such a middle course. " It is told me," he wrote to Hamilton on April 24, " that the Lords are inclinable to preserve my life and family, for which their generous compassions the great God of mercy will reward them ; and surely should I die upon this evidence, I had much rather be the sufferer than the judge.

" All that I shall desire from your lordship is, that divested of all public employment, I may be permitted to go home to my own private fortune, there to attend my own domestic affairs, and education of my children, with as little asperity of words or marks of infamy as possibly the nobleness and justice of my friends can procure for me, with a liberty to follow my own occasions as I shall find best for myself. This is no unreasonable thing I trust to desire, all considered that may be said in my case (for I vow my fault that should justly draw any heavy sentence on me, I yet do not see :) yet this much obtained will abundantly satisfy a mind hasting first to quiet, and a body broken with afflictions and infirmities." [2]

A party in the House of Lords, headed by Lords Bristol, Clare, and Savile, endeavoured to forward an arrangement of the kind here suggested. The day before this letter to Hamilton was written, the King himself had promised Strafford in words quoted by Browning on

[1] Baillie, *Letters*, ed. Laing, p. 350.
[2] Burnet, *Lives of the Hamiltons*, pp. 232, 507, ed. 1852.

d

p. 252—that he should not suffer in "life, honour, or fortune." Charles now came forward himself and appealed to the Lords to consent to this compromise. His speech [1] was made on May 1st, and the Attainder Bill had passed its second reading in the Lords on April 27th. A week before the speech might have had some effect: it could have no effect now. [2]

More fatal even than the King's hesitation was his incapacity to confine himself to constitutional action, or to adhere persistently to the policy of relying on the Lords.

Schemes to bribe the Governor of the Tower to let Strafford escape, or to introduce into that fortress a body of troops devoted to the King, were connected with a wider plot to bring up the army from the north to overawe the Parliament. The King was directly involved in these designs, and their disclosure by Pym on May 5 ruined Strafford's last hope. The suspicions and the fears which their discovery excited put an end to the possibility of a compromise which should save Strafford's life. It was the revelation of the Army Plot rather than the dread of mob violence which induced the Lords to pass the Attainder Bill. On the morning of May 8, [3] the Bill passed the House of Lords by 26 to 19 votes, and it was presented to the King for his assent on the same afternoon. Four days earlier Strafford had written to the King to release him from his promise. [4]

---

[1] P. 264.   [2] Gardiner, *History of England*, ix. 347.

[3] Gardiner, ix. 355.

[4] May 4.   See the letter itself on p. 266.   Browning mistakenly places it after the passing of the Bill by the Lords.   See Gardiner, ix. 362.

Of the struggle which the King made before he yielded, Browning gives no account. His Privy Council with one accord advised him to yield. The judges when consulted replied that they held Strafford to have been guilty of treason. Out of five bishops summoned to discuss the moral question, only Juxon and Usher advised him to satisfy his conscience by refusing his assent. A shouting mob crowded the street and threatened an attack on Whitehall. Late on the evening of May 9 Charles gave way. At last the King protested at the council table that if his person only were in danger, he would gladly venture it to save Lord Strafford's life, but seeing his wife, children, and all his kingdom were concerned in it, he was forced to give way unto it; "which he did not express without tears."[1]

Of that consent Charles repented all his life. In one of his letters to the Queen he speaks of "that base, sinful concession concerning the Earl of Strafford." In another he writes, "Nothing can be more evident than that Strafford's innocent blood hath been one of the great causes of God's just judgments upon this nation by a furious civil war; both sides hitherto being almost equally punished as being in a manner equally guilty." When he was negotiating with the army in 1647, Berkeley describes him as specially opposing the suggested provisions against his adherents, " saying that he would have no man to suffer for his sake, and that he repented of nothing so much as the Bill against my Lord Strafford."

---

[1] Forster, *British Statesmen*, vi. 71. Letter of the Elector Palatine.

A well-known story quoted by Browning represents Strafford as receiving the news that the King had signed the Bill with the words—" Put not your trust in princes, nor in the sons of men, for in them there is no salvation." [1] The anecdote is generally quoted from White-locke's *Memorials*, published in 1682 ; but it first appeared in 1658 in Sanderson's *Life and Reign of Charles I.* A more authentic record of his feelings is contained in a letter written probably as soon as the Attainder Bill had passed the Lords. " God have mercy on our souls, for our bodies are theirs," cried Simon de Montfort, at Evesham, when he saw the advancing standards of Prince Edward's host on every side of his little army. Strafford uses almost the same words. " I am lost," he wrote to Guilford Slingsby. " My body is theirs, but my soul is God's. There is little trust in man ; God may yet, if it please Him, deliver me." Over the letter by which Strafford released the King from his promises there hangs a certain amount of obscurity. Its genuineness has been impugned, but without reason. [2] One authority dates it May 4, another May 7, a third May 9. [3] Mr. Gardiner thinks May 4 the most probable date ; Browning seems to adopt May 9. [4] The letter illustrates not only Strafford's generosity, but the unity of aim which inspired his political life. He begins by saying that his greatest grief is to be thought to be taken as a person that should endeavour to set things amiss between the King

---

[1] P. 272. [2] Rushworth, *Trial of Strafford*, p. 774.
[3] Rushworth, *Trial*, p. 744 ; *Strafford Letters*, ii. 432 ; *Brief and Perfect Relation*, p. 103. [4] P. 266.

and his people, and protests that his aim always had been to create a right understanding between them. " Yet the truth finds little credit, and I am myself reputed the cause of this great separation betwixt you and your people. . . . Here are before me the ruin of my children and family. . . . Here are before me the many evils which may befall your sacred person and the whole kingdom, should yourself and the parliament be less satisfied the one with the other than is necessary for the King and people. Here are before me the things most valued, most feared, by mortal men—life and death." His choice is made, though not without a conflict. " Out of much sadness I am come to a resolution of that which I take to be best becoming me, that is, to look upon that which is principally to be considered in itself, and that is doubtless the prosperity of your sacred person and the commonwealth.

" So now, to set your Majesty's conscience at liberty, I do most humbly beseech you, for the preventing of such mischiefs as may happen by your refusal, to pass the Bill ; by this means to remove . . . this unfortunate thing forth of the way towards that blessed agreement, which God, I trust, shall for ever establish betwixt you and your subjects."

It is this self-sacrifice which proves the sincerity of Strafford's political faith, and the unselfishness of the purpose with which he entered the King's service. He had professed then his desire to bring about a good agreement between the King and his people ; and now when he was put to the touch—when he found himself the

great obstruction to that agreement—he offered his own
life to restore it, and offered it not merely for the King's
sake, but for the sake of the commonwealth also. In
Browning's play, when Pym speaks of his labours and his
sacrifices for England, Strafford answers, " I have loved
England too." The poet was nearer to the truth than
the biographer, but to Englishmen in general Strafford
was simply the perfect instrument of tyranny drawn in
Browning's biography. No contemporary narrative shows
the hatred which the people felt for Strafford so well as
Hollar's picture of his execution. In the background
is the Tower, and further in the distance are the masts
of the ships in the river. In the foreground stands the
scaffold, Strafford kneels before the block, Usher and a
little group of friends are beside him, the executioner
raises his axe to strike. On the roofs and turrets of the
Tower and in all the open space before it presses an
innumerable throng of spectators. Right up to the
edge of the scaffold are wooden stands crowded with
gazers. The Puritanical citizens in their long cloaks and
steeple hats have brought their wives and sweethearts
to see the spectacle. One stand has broken down beneath the weight of the mass upon it. The keepers of a
second are fighting with a gang of young men who are
trying to climb on to it without paying. But the eyes of
all the rest of that great multitude are turned towards the
kneeling figure, waiting for the axe to fall.

" And to show how mad this whole people were,
especially in and about London, in the evening of the day
wherein he was executed, the greatest demonstrations of

joy that possibly could be expressed ran through the whole town and country hereabout; and many that came up to town on purpose to see the execution, rode in triumph back, waving their hats, and with all expressions of joy, through every town they went, crying, 'His head is off! his head is off!' and breaking the windows of those persons who would not solemnize this festival with a bonfire. So ignorant and brutish is a multitude."[1]

If Browning, like Strafford's contemporaries, judges the statesman with too great harshness, he treats the personal characteristics and the private life of Wentworth with great fairness. There are however occasional errors and omissions in his sketch, and on more than one point new evidence corrects and completes it. There is amongst the *Domestic State Papers* a letter from Sir Thomas Roe to the Queen of Bohemia, written in 1634, which helps us to realize the impression made by Wentworth on an unbiassed observer.[2]

"The Lord Deputy of Ireland doth great wonders, and governs like a king, and hath taught that kingdom to show us an example of envy, by having parliaments, and knowing wisely how to use them; for they have given the king six subsidies, which will arise to £240,000, and they are like to have the liberty we contended for, and grace from his Majesty worth their gift double; and which is worth much more, the honour of good intelligence and love between the king and his people, which I would to God our great wits had had eyes to see.

[1] *Memoirs of Sir Philip Warwick,* p. 163.
[2] *Calendar of Domestic State Papers,* 1634-5, pref. xxxviii.

This is a great service, and to give your Majesty a character of the man,—he is severe abroad and in business, and sweet in private conversation; retired in his friendships, but very firm; a terrible judge and a strong enemy; a servant violently zealous in his master's ends, and not negligent of his own; one that will have what he will, and though of great reason, he can make his will greater when it may serve him; affecting glory by a seeming contempt; one that cannot stay long in the middle region of fortune, being entreprenant; but will either be the greatest man in England, or much less than he is; lastly, one that may (and his nature lies fit for it, for he is ambitious to do what others will not) do your Majesty very great service, if you can make him."

Another contemporary, Sir Philip Warwick, whose position as Secretary to the Lord Treasurer must have brought him into contact with Wentworth, gives this brief description of his appearance. "In his person he was of a tall stature, but stooped much in the neck. His countenance was cloudy whilst he moved or sat thinking, but when he spake, either seriously or face-tiously, he had a lightsome and a very pleasant air; and indeed whatever he then did he performed very grace-fully." One part of this description recalls "the proud, glooming countenance" Baillie speaks of, and "the bent, ill-favoured brow" Wentworth himself refers to.[1] It suggests also Macaulay's description of Wentworth's "harsh dark features, and that fixed look, full of severity, of mournful anxiety, of deep thought, of dauntless reso-

[1] pp. 128, 189, 240.

lution, which seems at once to forebode and to defy a terrible fate, as it lowers on us from the living canvas of Vandyke."[1]

Warwick goes on to tell a strange tale of a vision which half revealed to Wentworth's father the fortunes of his son. "The greatness of the envy that attended him, made many in their prognostics to bode him an ill end; and there went current a story of the dream of his father, who being both by his wife, nighest friends, and physicians, thought to be at the point of his death, fell suddenly into so profound a sleep, and lay quietly so long, that his wife, uncertain of his condition, drew nigh his bed, to observe whether she could hear him breathe, and gently touching him he awaked with great disturbance, and told her the reason was, she had interrupted him in a dream, which most passionately he desired to have known the end of. For, said he, I dreamed one appeared to me, assuring me that I should have a son (for until then he had none) who should be a very great and eminent man: but—and in this instant thou didst awake me, whereby I am bereaved of the knowledge of the farther fortune of the child. This I heard when this Lord was but in the ascent of his greatness, and long before his fall: and afterwards conferring with some of his nighest relations I found the tradition was not disowned. Sure I am, that his station was like those turfs of earth or sea-banks which, by the storm swept away, left all the inland to be drowned by popular tumult."[2]

[1] *Essay on Hampden.*　　[2] *Memoirs of Sir P. Warwick*, p. 112.

According to Warwick, Wentworth's greatest fault was " a sour and haughty temper . . . . a roughness in his nature, which a man no more obliged by him than I was would have called an injustice; though many of his confidants who were my good friends (when I, like a worm, being trod on, would turn and laugh, and under that disguise say as piquant words as my little wit would help me with) were wont to swear to me, that he endeavoured to be just to all, but was resolved to be gracious to none, but to those whom he thought inwardly affected him. . . . It was a great infirmity in him that he seemed to overlook so many as he did; since everywhere, much more in Court, the numerous or lesser sort of attendants can obstruct, create jealousies, spread ill reports, and do harm; for as 'tis impossible that any power or deportment should satisfy all persons, so there a little friendliness and openness of carriage begets hope and lessens envy."

Whilst Wentworth took no trouble to conciliate his inferiors, he was careless how many of his equals he offended in the pursuit of his master's service. Browning relates at some length his quarrels with Lord Fauconberg and Lord Mountnorris, and quotes Wentworth's defence of his own severity. It was "the necessity of his Majesty's service," says Wentworth, which obliged him to use "seeming strictness," instead of "gracious smiles and gentle looks." One of the most serious of the feuds in which this conception of his duty engaged him was that with the Earl of Cork.[1]

[1] pp. 116, 192, 195, 201, 208.

Hitherto we have only had Strafford's account of the dispute, but lately the Earl of Cork's story has been published.[1] In his diary Cork describes the landing of the new Lord Deputy at Dublin (July 23rd, 1633), and the civilities which passed at their first meeting. " A most cursed man to all Ireland, and to me in particular," is the note on the Lord Deputy's character which he added later. The first quarrel arose over a tomb which Cork had erected in the chancel of St. Patrick's Cathedral, and which Strafford at Laud's instigation obliged him to remove.[2] A much more serious struggle took place concerning certain church lands which Cork had succeeded in securing. He was charged with having fraudulently obtained possession of the revenues of the College of Youghal, prosecuted in the Castle Chamber, sentenced to lose the greater part of the property in question, and to pay the King a fine of £15,000. Cork describes in detail his interviews with Strafford concerning this suit.[3] The Lord Deputy had urged him many times not to stand to his justification, but to compromise the matter and submit to a fine. The Lord Chancellor and the Primate gave similar advice. At last after many struggles he yielded to the Lord Deputy's

---

[1] *The Lismore Papers*, Diaries and Letters of Richard Boyle, first Earl of Cork, from MSS. belonging to the Duke of Devonshire, preserved at Lismore Castle, 10 volumes, edited by Rev. A. B. Grosart, D.D. (for private circulation), 1886—1888.

[2] pp. 165, 171.

[3] See *Lismore Papers*, Series I. vol. iv. p. 184 ; Series II. vol. iii. pp. 247—259. On the question of the tomb erected by the Earl of Cork, see *Lismore Papers*, I. iii. pp. 171, 175 ; iv. pp. 12, 39, 133.

menaces. On May 2, 1636, when the final hearing of the case was to have taken place, Cork was called into the Lord Deputy's Chamber. " As soon as I came in," writes Cork, " the Lord Deputy asked me whether I would have war or peace. I told him I did pursue peace, but it flew from me." Then he replied, " I have offered you peace, and sent many messengers in to you, but you will not embrace it ; and therefore I now must needs enter into the lists against you, and I do vow that I will censure you to pay the King thirty thousand pounds, take away the office of Treasurer from you, and send you prisoner to the Castle of Dublin before I come back hither again. And therefore it will behove you now to make such an offer as is fitt for me in his Majesty's name to accept of." I told him the offer I had made by my son was rejected, and therefore I had made a vow never to make an offer again. " Then let the Master of the Wards make an offer for you, for he knows my mind." Seeing no other remedy Cork allowed the Master of the Court of Wards to offer in his name a composition of £15,000 and the surrender of a portion of the property in question. " I am to pay his Majesty for my redemption out of the Court of Castle Chamber, though my innocency and integrity be clear as the sun at high noon, and that my own conscience neither doth nor can accuse me of any wilful crime or abuse worth any censure, yet to prevent censure I have yielded to pay the King £5,000 in hand, £5,000 more on Midsummer Day 1637, and another £5,000, to make my last payment, on Midsummer Day 1638, in all fifteen thousand pounds sterling, for which fine, or rather high ransom thus undeservedly imposed upon me, God forgive the Lord Deputy and his great Councillor, Sir George Radcliffe; yet as God shall enable me, I will by his grace pay it freely and willingly, for that it is to come to my good and gracious king and master, for whose service I would most willingly sacrifice life and estate. And my soul assures me so fully of his Majesty's religiousness and justice, that if he were rightly informed how undeservedly this mighty fine is thus drawn from me, he would not take one penny thereof."

Three days later Cork had another altercation with Wentworth. "I prayed him to consider well, whether in justice he could impose so great a fine upon me." Whereunto he replied, "God's wounds, Sir, when the last Parliament in England brake up, you lent the King fifteen thousand pounds. And afterwards in a very uncivil, unmannerly manner you pressed his Majesty to repay it you. Whereupon I resolved before I came out of England to fetch it back again from you by one means or other. And now I have gotten what I desired, you and I will be friends hereafter."

It was too late, however, to be friends with the man whom he had so humbled. The Lord Deputy gave stately entertainments to the Earl of Cork, dropped in to dinner with him in a gracious and friendly way; played cards with him and lost a few pounds over the game of maw, stood god-father to his grandchildren, and was solemnly reconciled with him by Laud. All this was useless. The injury he had done to Cork was too

great to be forgotten.   Cork's treatment was one of the
charges against Strafford at his trial.   "Old Richard,"
writes Strafford, "has sworn against me gallantly."   With
vengeful joy Cork jots down in his diary the circumstances
of Strafford's impeachment before the Lords.   " His
Lordship was called into the House as a delinquent, and
brought to the bar upon his knees (I sitting in my place
covered), where the charge of high treason being objected
against him, he being not permitted then to speak in his
defence, was presently committed to Mr. James Maxwell.
And this his dejection shows the uncertainty whereunto
the greatest men are subject unto."   With equal satisfaction he notes the termination of the trial.   " This
day after many long debates, and several hearings, the
oppressing Earl of Strafford, Lord Lieutenant of Ireland,
was by parliament attainted of high treason, where I sat
present, but eleven voices of all the Lords declaring not
content; and the 12th of this month he was beheaded
on the Tower Hill of London, as he well deserved." [1]

In discussing Strafford's friendships and enmities, the
question of his personal relations with Pym naturally
demands consideration.   The tradition of their early
friendship supplies one of the leading motives of Browning's play, and is also referred to in this biography.[2]
In the year 1700, Dr. James Welwood, one of the
physicians of William III., published a volume entitled
Memoirs of the most material transactions in England

---

[1] *Lismore Papers*, Series I. iv. pp. 142, 147, 150, 166; v. pp.
164, 176.
[2] pp. 143, 240.

for the last hundred years preceding the Revolution of
1688.   It consists of historical anecdotes and traditions,
but does contain a certain amount of fact and a few
documents.   Speaking of Strafford, Welwood tells the
following story.[1]   " There had been a long and intimate
friendship betwixt Mr. Pym and him, and they had gone
hand in hand in everything in the House of Commons.
But when Sir Thomas Wentworth was upon making his
peace with the Court, he sent to Pym to meet him alone
at Greenwich ; where he began in a set speech to sound
Mr. Pym about the dangers they were like to run by the
courses they were in ; and what advantages they might
have if they would but listen to some offers which would
probably be made them from the Court.   Pym understanding his speech stopped him short with this expression : " You need not use all this art to tell me you
have a mind to leave us ; but remember what I tell you,
you are going to be undone.   But remember, that though
you leave us now I will never leave you while your head
is upon your shoulders."   The incident is not very
probable, and though Welwood might have heard the
story from some good source he does not mention his
authority.   He certainly exaggerates their political agreement and perhaps their personal intimacy also.   The
papers of Pym and Wentworth, so far as they have
survived, give no support to the story of their friendship.
On the other hand there can be little doubt that the two
men were well acquainted with each other, though one
was a Devonshire man and the other a Yorkshire man.

[1] p. 47.

Pym entered the Middle Temple in 1607, and seems to
have lived generally in London.   Wentworth entered
the Inner Temple in 1607, and studied law much more
seriously than most gentlemen of his wealth and rank.
More than one of his despatches and the whole of his
defence bear witness to the extent and thoroughness of
his legal knowledge.   According to Radcliffe " he was
excellently well studied in that part of the English law
that concerns the office of a justice of peace; insomuch
that one of the judges of assize, a great lawyer, was well
pleased to learn his opinion in a matter about the poor
and the statutes made concerning them.   By constant
attention at the Star Chamber for seven years together,
he learned the course of that Court. . . . He spent
eight years' time, besides his pains and money, in soliciting the businesses and suits of his nephews, going every
term to London about that only, without missing one
term in thirty, as I verily believe."[1]   It was probably
while Wentworth attended the Law Courts and pursued
his legal studies, between 1614 and 1624, that his
intimacy with Pym began, and it was doubtless cemented
by their association in the parliaments of 1621 and
1624.   There can be little doubt that Welwood is right
in representing it as coming to a sudden end in 1628,
when Wentworth became one of the King's ministers.
In his letters, when Strafford had occasion to mention
Pym, he speaks of him with a certain scorn; "your
Prynnes and Pyms, a generation of odd names and odd
natures."[2]   He says nothing of any past intimacy.   Pym

---

[1] Strafford, *Letters*, ii. pp. 434, 436.   [2] Strafford, *Letters*.

on the other hand, on Nov. 24th, 1640, when he reported to the House of Commons the charges against Strafford, began his speech by saying that he had "long known the person charged by acts of friendship." [1]

When the trial opened, Pym attacked Strafford with extraordinary bitterness, to which Strafford replied that "he hoped shortly to clear himself of all those foul aspersions which his malicious enemies had cast upon him." Pym accused him at once of insulting the House of Commons by calling them his malicious enemies. "Whereupon the Lieutenant falling down upon his knees humbly besought them that they would not mistake him, and withall gave a large panaegyrique of their most just and moderate proceedings, protesting that if he himself had been one of the House of Commons, (as he had the honour once to be), he would not have advised them to have done otherwise against his dearest friend ; but withall told them that he might justly say he had his owne un-friends, which hee hoped in time to make known ; nor did he all this time speake one bitter word against Master Pym, though justly incensed, which hath infinitely advanced his reputation."

The next day, in answer to a speech from Glyn, Strafford said "That it did strike him to the heart to be attacked of such a wicked crime by such honourable persons, yea that it wounded him deeper in regard that such persons who were the companions of his youth, and

---

[1] *Note-Book of Sir John Northcote,* ed. by A. II. A. Hamilton, 1877, p. 1.

with whom he had spent the best of his days, should now rise up in judgment against him." [1]

The last of these passages may no doubt refer to the managers of the impeachment in general, and not to Pym in particular. The earlier one seems to me directly aimed at Pym. It contains just the brief sarcastic reference to their old friendship which a proud man might make to an old friend who had unjustly accused him.

Browning draws a dramatic picture of Pym suddenly meeting Strafford's gaze, and losing his self-possession "when he met the fixed and wasted features of his early associate." But there is no evidence for this striking incident. All that the authorities say is, that during Pym's answer to Strafford's defence his memory for a moment failed him. [2]

Strafford's friendship with Laud, which Browning also discusses, [3] has been further illustrated since he wrote, by the publication of fifty letters from the Archbishop to the Lord-Deputy. [4] The intimacy and the confidence between the two men rose naturally from their characters and position. Each had an unselfish devotion to the Monarch he served, and to the ideas which he hoped to realize through the Monarchy. Each needed a friend and ally. "I am alone," wrote Laud to Wentworth, "in those things which draw not private profit after them."

---

[1] *A Briefe and Perfect Relation of the Answers and Replies of Thomas, Earle of Strafford*, 4⁰., 1647, pp. 7, 8.

[2] P. 263. *Baillie's Letters*, i. 348; *Briefe and Perfect Relation*, p. 67.   [3] P. 163.

[4] *Laud's Works*, vol. vii. Library of Anglo-Catholic Theology, 1860.

Wentworth describes the Irish officials as "a company of men the most intent upon their own ends which ever I met with," and himself as "charged with many cares, and like to bear out the heat of the day alone.   Without Radcliffe and Wandesford sure I were the most solitary man that ever served a king in such a place."   To succeed in Ireland he needed assistance against court intrigues in England, and therefore besought Laud for his "continued hand of support and help."   What was at first a political alliance became in the end a close and uninterrupted friendship.[1]

In the same way Strafford's famous friendship with Lady Carlisle grew out of his need of an ally near the Queen.   "I judge her ladyship very considerable," he wrote to Laud in 1637; "she is often in place, and extremely well skilled how to speak with advantage and spirit for those friends she professeth unto, which will not be many.   There is this further in her disposition, she will not seem to be the person she is not, an ingenuity I have always observed and honoured her for."[2]

The story which represents Lady Carlisle as Strafford's mistress seems based on a misunderstanding both of her character and of Strafford's.   Her beauty brought her adorers of all ranks, courtiers, and poets, and statesmen ; but she remained untouched by their worship.   "Yet will she freely discourse of love," writes Toby Mathews,[3]

---

[1] *Strafford's Letters,* i. 96, 194, 300.

[2] *Ibid.* ii. 120.

[3] A collection of letters made by Sir Tobie Mathews, Kt., with a character of the most excellent Lady, Lucy, Countess of Carlisle, 1660.

"and hear both the fancies and powers of it; but if you will needs bring it within knowledge, and boldly direct it to herself, she is likely to divert the discourse, or, at least, seem not to understand it. By which you may know her humour, and her justice; for since she cannot love in earnest, she would have nothing from Love. So contenting herself to play with love, as with a child." She filled her mind, he continues, "with gallant fancies, and high and elevated thoughts," and "her wit being most eminent among the rest of her great abilities," affected the conversation of those who were most famed for it. Later still she chose her friends amongst those "of the most eminent condition, both for power and employments," sought to influence the men who guided events, and found her pleasure in political intrigues.

A contemporary compares her to Sempronia, "the great stateswoman," of Jonson's Catiline. This love of power was what attracted her to Strafford, and their intimacy needs no other explanation. "A nobler nor a more intelligent friendship," writes Strafford, "did I never meet with in my life."[1]

Browning describes Strafford as "a man of intrigue," and mentions, besides Lady Carlisle, Lady Carnarvon and Lady Loftus as his mistresses.[2] But these statements are based on very insufficient evidence. In the case of Lady Carnarvon the suggestion is entirely based on a confusion of names. Lord Conway in a letter to the Lord-Deputy tells a certain story of Lord Wentworth and Lady Carnarvon, which is quoted in full by Browning

---

[1] Whitaker, *Life of Sir G. Radcliffe*, p. 221.   [2] P. 129.

on p. 130.　But the Lord Wentworth there referred to is not the Lord-Deputy himself, but his young kinsman Thomas Wentworth, son of Thomas Wentworth, Earl of Cleveland and Baron Wentworth of Nettlested.　Up to 1640 the younger Thomas Wentworth was styled by courtesy Lord Wentworth, and in that year he was summoned to the House of Lords as Lord Wentworth of Nettlested.　He is mentioned in a song on the gallants of the time, and in the answer to it, amongst "the wags wantonly-minded and merry conceited," "jovial boys as ever tavern bred," whose special qualifications were drinking and courting ladies.[1]　In the Civil Wars he served under Prince Rupert, was a well-known cavalry leader, and died in 1664.[2]

The Lady Loftus mentioned by Browning was Eleanor, daughter of Sir Francis Ruish, who married in 1621 Sir Robert Loftus, son of that Irish Lord Chancellor with whom Strafford had such a violent quarrel.　The statement that she was Strafford's mistress is based on a passage in Clarendon, who speaks of letters from Strafford to that lady, "found in her cabinet after her death," and made public during Strafford's impeachment.[3]　There is no trace of any such letters, or of any imputation based on them, in the voluminous records of Strafford's trial. Such a charge, however, was made by some of the libellous pamphlets of the period, and was probably carelessly taken from them by Clarendon.[4]　The rumour

---

[1] *Wit Restored*, ed. Hotten, pp. 134, 136.
[2] *Collins' Peerage*, ed. Brydges, vi. 208.
[3] Pp. 132, 214.　　　　[4] *Somers Tracts*, ed. Scott, iv. 286.

is mentioned by Sir Philip Warwick, but evidence of any other kind ·is entirely lacking. The intimacy between Strafford and Lady Loftus is sufficiently accounted for by the fact that his brother Sir George Wentworth had married her younger sister, Frances Ruish.[1] "Strafford's own language in speaking of the lady is inconsistent with the charge, whilst the respectful admiration which it reveals would account for the rise of scandalous rumours."[2] He writes to Conway on Aug. 13, 1639, saying, " we have sadly buried my Lady Loftus, one of the noblest persons I ever had the happiness to be acquainted with; and as I had received greater obligations from her ladyship than from all Ireland beside, so with her are gone the greatest part of my affections to the country; and all that is left of them shall be thankfully and religiously paid to her excellent memory and lasting goodness."[3]

The chief subject of disagreement between the Lord Deputy and Chancellor Loftus was the refusal of the latter to make the settlement on his daughter-in-law which had been promised when the marriage took place. Wentworth and the Irish Council made a decree enforcing this settlement (Feb. 1, 1638), which was reversed by the Long Parliament (May 3, 1642), and the whole question was again tried by the House of Lords during

---

[1] *The Fairfax Correspondence*, vol. i. pp. lxi—lxvii, contains half a dozen letters from Wentworth, relative to the marriage of his brother; two are addressed to Lady Jephson, mother of Lady Loftus, and two to Frances Ruish herself.

[2] Gardiner, *History of England*, ix. 71.

[3] *Strafford Letters*, ii. 381.

the reign of Charles II. Had there been any truth in this particular charge, it would assuredly have been brought forward in the course of these proceedings ; but the very numerous petitions and papers relating to the case contain no trace of any such accusation.[1]

Browning justly refuses to credit Baillie's scandalous story of the death of Strafford's second wife, Arabella Holles, and it has since been effectually refuted by a letter published amongst the Fairfax papers.[2] On the other hand he is hardly fair in his criticisms of Strafford's behaviour to his third wife, seeing how little is really known about the circumstances of the marriage. Browning prints at length five letters from Strafford to this lady.[3] These five letters were given in 1686 to Ralph Thoresby, preserved in his Museum at Leeds, and first printed in the article on Strafford in *Biographia Britannica* (1766). The author of the article also gave extracts from eight other letters which, since the dispersion of Thoresby's Museum, have entirely disappeared. Fortunately part of the correspondence had remained in the possession of the Rhodes family, descended to Lord Houghton, and was printed by him in the miscellany of the Philobiblion Society. These letters, eleven in all, are reprinted by Miss Elizabeth Cooper in her *Life of Strafford.*

A few words in conclusion, on the sources of informa-

---

[1] See Mr. Gilbert's report on the papers of the Marquis of Drogheda, *Ninth Report Historical MSS. Commission*, Pt. ii. pp. 293—328.   [2] Pp. 94, 260 ; *Fairfax Correspondence*, i. 237.

[3] Pp. 120, 242, 245.

Charitie to repryve untill Saterday." The errors and
corrections of the letter testify to the perturbation of the
unhappy King.[1]

———————

A TABLE

OF THE PRINCIPAL DATES AND EVENTS IN THE

LIFE OF THOMAS WENTWORTH, EARL OF STRAFFORD.

Born, April 13, 1593 ;

knighted by James I., December 6, 1611 ;

travelled in France and Italy, December 1612—February
1614 ;

succeeded his father as second baronet, September 1614 ;

appointed Custos Rotulorum for the West Riding of
Yorkshire, Dec. 1615 ;

appointed a member of the Council of the North, July
10, 1619 ;

High Sheriff of Yorkshire, November 13, 1626 ;

committed to the Marshalsea for refusing the loan, May
1627 ;

created Baron Wentworth of Wentworth Woodhouse, July
22, 1628 ;

created Viscount Wentworth, December 13, 1628, and
appointed president of the Council of the North ;

made a privy-councillor, November 10, 1629 ;

appointed Lord-Deputy of Ireland, January 6, 1632 ;

landed in Ireland, July 23, 1633 ;

created Earl of Strafford, January 12, 1640 ;

———

[1] *Report of the Royal Commission on Historical Manuscripts*,
I. 10 ; *ibid.* III. 3.

appointed Lord Lieutenant of Ireland, January 13, 1640;
leaves Ireland for the last time, April 13, 1640;
captain-general of the Irish army, August 3, 1640;
lieutenant-general of the army in England, August 18, 1640;
Knight of the Garter, September 12, 1640;
sent to the Tower, November 11, 1640;
beheaded, May 12, 1641.

THOMAS WENTWORTH married—

(1) Oct. 22, 1611, Lady Margaret Clifford, eldest daughter
    of Francis fourth Earl of Cumberland; she died
    Aug. 1622.

(2) Feb. 24, 1625, Lady Arabella Holles, second daughter
    of John first Earl of Clare; she died Oct. 1631.

(3) Oct. 1632, Elizabeth, daughter of Sir Godfrey Rhodes.

Strafford left three daughters and one son. The
youngest daughter, Margaret, died unmarried; the
second, Arabella, left no issue; the eldest, Anne,
married in 1654 Edward Watson, second Lord Rockingham. Their son, William, second Earl of Strafford,
died in 1695, leaving no children. "With him ended,"
says Hunter, "the regular male succession of the
Wentworths of Wentworth Woodhouse, which had continued from the time of Henry III."[1] The honours of
the family became extinct, except the barony of Raby,
which descended to Thomas Wentworth, grandson of
Sir William Wentworth the great earl's younger brother.
This Thomas Wentworth distinguished himself as a
soldier and diplomatist, was one of the negotiators of

[1] *South Yorkshire*, ii. 89.

the Treaty of Utrecht, and was created Earl of Strafford by Queen Anne in 1711. The second line of Earls of Strafford which he founded became extinct in 1799. But the title of Earl of Strafford was revived in 1847 in favour of John Byng, great grandson of the negotiator of the Treaty of Utrecht, whose grandson is the present Earl of Strafford.

Woodhouse and the other estates of the great Earl of Strafford passed to Thomas Watson, the third son of his daughter Anne and Lord Rockingham, who assumed the name of Wentworth. His son, successively created Lord Malton (1728), Earl of Malton (1734), and Marquis of Rockingham (1746), published the collection of Strafford's letters, and was the father of Charles Watson Wentworth, Marquis of Rockingham, twice Prime Minister of George III. On Rockingham's death in 1782 the Wentworth estates passed to the Fitzwilliam family, his sister Anne having married William, Earl Fitzwilliam. Her son, the popular Earl Fitzwilliam who was Lord Lieutenant of Ireland in 1795, took the arms of Wentworth, and prefixed in 1807 the name of Wentworth to that of Fitzwilliam; so that the present Wentworth-Fitzwilliam family are the direct descendants of Strafford through his daughter Anne.

BROWNING'S
LIFE OF STRAFFORD.

1593—1641.

THOMAS WENTWORTH was born on the 13th of April, 1593, in Chancery-lane, at the house of his mother's father, Mr. Robert Atkinson, a bencher of Lincoln's Inn.[1] He was the eldest of twelve children, and the heir of "an estate, which descended to him through a long train of ancestors, who had matched with many heiresses of the best families in the North, worth at that time 6000*l.* a year."[2] His father, sir William Wentworth, continued to hold a manor which his ancestors had held from the time of the Conquest downwards.[3]

The youth of Wentworth was passed, and his mind received its earliest and strongest impressions, in the midst of the aristocratic influences. And he was by no means taught to disregard them. He must have considered the various ramifications of the family pedigree

---

[1] Radcliffe's "Essay towards the Life of my Lord Strafforde," published as an appendix to "The EARL OF STRAFFORDE'S LETTERS AND DISPATCHES," 2 vols. folio. Dublin edit. 1740. vol. ii. p. 429. Biographia Britannica, vol. vii. p. 4172.

[2] Knowler's Dedication to the Letters.

[3] An account of the Wentworths will be found in Collins; and see Thoresby's Ducatus Leodiensis.

B

with a very early pride and zeal, to have been so well prepared, on his sudden elevation to the peerage, with the formidable list of progenitors that were cited in his patent. It was there set forth, among other grand and notable things, that he was lineally descended from John of Gaunt, and from the ancient barons of Newmark, Oversley, and so forth; and that his ancestors, either by father or mother, had matched with divers houses of honour; as with Maud countess of Cambridge, daughter to the lord Clifford of Westmoreland; with Margaret, daughter and heir to the lord Philip de Spencer; the lords D'Arcy of the North; Latimer, Talboys, Ogle; Ferrers earl of Digby; Quincy earl of Winchester; Beaumont earl of Leicester; Grantmesnil baron of Hincley and lord high steward of England; Peveril earl of Nottingham; Leofric earl of Mercia; and Margaret duchess of Somerset, grandmother of Henry VII.[1] It was from the high conventional ground of such proud recollections, that Thomas Wentworth looked forward to the future.

Little account of his early education has been preserved, but he afterwards proved that no accomplishment suited to rank and lofty expectations had been omitted, and it is characteristic of the encouragement given by his father to his aristocratic tendencies, that the college selected for the completion of his studies should have been that which was founded by the illustrious grandmother of Henry VII., whom he claimed as one of his ancestors. He was sent to St. John's college, Cambridge.[2] Here he soon gave evidence of the powers of a fine intellect, and of that not ungenerous warmth of disposi-

---

[1] Collins' Peerage of England, vol. ii. pp. 20, 21.
[2] Radcliffe's Essay.

tion which is lavish of gratitude and favour in return for personal service. He met with a tutor, Mr. Greenwood, whose useful attentions to him at this time were secured for the future by a prompt appreciation of their value; he availed himself of them through his after life, and never at any time failed, faithfully, and even affectionately, to remember and reward them.[1] I may add, in further proof of this characteristic quality, that we find him shortly after profiting by the active service of a person named Radcliffe,[2] connected with his family by some claims of clanship, and that, from this time, Radcliffe never left his side. He had been found useful.

Wentworth left his college while yet very young; he cannot have been more than eighteen. But he had received benefits from his residence there, and he did not fail to exhibit his recollection of these also, when the power and opportunity arose.[3] Not that it required, in this particular case, the circumstance of service rendered, to elicit Wentworth's return. The memory of his proudly recollected ancestress was abundantly sufficient to have

---

[1] I shall have other occasions to allude to this. It may be worth while to add, that Greenwood was himself a man of ancient family, and not likely, on that account, to prove less suitable to Wentworth. See Biog. Brit. vol. vii. p. 4173. note C.

[2] Strafford Papers, vol. i. p. 9.

[3] Strafford Papers, vol. i. pp. 125. 189.; ii. p. 390. I may allude to this again. On his promotion to the earldom, two years before his death, he acknowledged, in warm phrase, the congratulations of the provost and fellows of his old college:—"After my very hearty commendations, so mindful I am of the ancient favours I received in that society of St. John's, whilst I was a student there, and so sensible of your present civility towards me, as I may not upon this invitation pass by either of them unacknowledged. And therefore do hereby very heartily thank you for renewing to me the sense of the one, and affording me the favour of the other. And in both these regards shall be very apprehensive of any occasions, wherein I may do any good offices either towards that house or yourselves, the provost and fellows thereof."

called it forth; "being," as he himself, shortly after this, writes to one of his country neighbours, "I must confess, in my own nature, a great lover and conserver of hereditary good wills, such as have been amongst our nearest friends."[1]   When a hereditary good will happened to be associated with one of his greatest ancestral glories, it ran little chance of being lessened or lost.

The next circumstance I trace in the scanty memorials of this portion of his history, is his acquisition of the honour of knighthood.[2]   This title was then to be purchased at a reasonable rate of money; doubtless Wentworth so purchased it; and the fact may be taken, along with the evidences I have already named, in further corroboration of the development of the aristocratic principle.   Though still extremely young, this remarkable person had been left to all his independence of mature manhood; was treated with deference by his father; and even now, having not yet passed his eighteenth year, aspired to the hand of Margaret, eldest daughter of the earl of Cumberland, whom he married before the close of 1611.[3]   If it has seemed strange to the reader, that the immediate successor to an ancient baronetcy should have sought to feed his love of rank by the purchase of a

---

[1] Strafford Papers, vol. i. p. 25.

[2] The writer in the Biog. Brit., and Mr. Mac-Diarmid, assign a later period to this, but without authority.   Radcliffe distinctly, in his Essay, names the year 1611; and there is extant a letter of sir Peter Frecheville's to Wentworth's father, sir William Wentworth, dated in this year, which commences thus:—"I do unfeignedly congratulate the honourable fortunes of my cousin, your eldest son;"—in reference, as must be supposed, to the youth's new title. While on this subject I may add, that Mr. Mac-Diarmid has also fallen into error in attributing certain praises (vol. i. p. 1. of the Strafford Papers) to Thomas Wentworth:—they distinctly relate to his brother William, then educating for the bar.

[3] Radcliffe's Essay.

paltry knighthood, here is the probable reason that influenced him. A title of any sort matched him more fittingly with a lady of title. Immediately after his marriage, in November, 1611, he went into France. Mr. Greenwood, his former tutor, joined him there, and remained with him.[1]

Strange events at that moment shook the kingdom of France. Henry IV. assassinated, the parliament invaded and beset, Marie de' Medicis regent, Sully disgraced, Concini in favour! These things sunk deep into the mind of Wentworth. "Il put faire dès lors," exclaims the comte de Lally-Tolendal, "de profondes réflexions sur les horreurs du fanatisme, sur les abus du pouvoir, sur le malheur d'un pays dépourvû de ces loix fixés, qui, dans l'impossibilité d'annéantir les passions humaines, les balancent du moins l'une par l'autre, et les forcent par leur propre intérêt à servir, même en dépit d'elles, l'intérêt général."[2] Without adopting M. de Lally-Tolendal's exact construction, it is certain that the events I have named, occurring as it were in the immediate presence of Wentworth,[3] were not calculated to weaken his

---

[1] Radcliffe's Essay.

[2] This is the only remark with any pretension to originality I have been able to find through the course of a long "Essai sur la Vie de T. Wentworth, Comte de Strafford," which the comte de Lally-Tolendal (penetrated with profound disgust at the patriotic party in England, and with the striking resemblance between Strafford's fate and that of his own unfortunate father) undertook to write for the instruction of his countrymen. He perpetrated a very ridiculous tragedy on the same subject.

[3] He does not appear to have visited France only, at this period, as has been supposed. He went on to Venice, where he formed a friendship with sir Henry Wotton. We find him afterwards, in his correspondence, contrasting to his friend the ambassador, "these cold and sluggish climates," with "the more sublimated air of Italy."—*Papers*, vol. i. p. 5. Wotton continued his ardent friend and admirer.

impressions in favour of strict establishment, and in scorn of popular regards. The image of a Ravillac, indeed, haunted his after life ![1]

Meanwhile events, in themselves not so startling and painful as these, but not the less ominous of a stormy future, were occurring in England. In the biography of Eliot I confined myself strictly to an explanation of the circumstances of general history under which he entered his first parliament: I must now retrace my steps.

James I. had many reasons to be weary of his own kingdom, when the death of Elizabeth seated him on the English throne. He came to this country in an ecstasy of infinite relief. Visions of levelling clergy and factious nobles had vanished from his aching sight. In hopeful conceit he turned to his Scotch followers, and remarked, they had at last arrived in the land of promise.

His first interviews with his English counsellors were no less satisfactory. " Do I mak the judges? do I mak the bishops?" he exclaimed, as they pointed out to his delighted attention the powers of his new dominion— "then, Godis wauns! I mak what likes me law and Gospel." There is enough of shrewdness in this remark to express James's character in that respect. He was not an absolute fool, and little more can be said of him. It is a pity he was not, since he was deficient in much wisdom. It is the little redeeming leaven which proves troublesome and mischievous; the very wise or the very foolish do little harm. His "learning," such as it was— though not open to the serious censure which is provoked by his preposterous vanity in the matter of "kingcraft," his disgraceful love of personal ease, and his indecent and shameless fondness for personal favourites—never

[1] His letters afford very frequent evidence of this.

furnished him with one useful thought, or a suggestion of practical benefit.[1]   He wrote mystical definitions of the prerogative, and polite " Counterblasts to Tobacco ;" issued forth damnation to the deniers of witchcraft[2], and poured out the wraths of the Apocalypse upon popery; but whenever an obvious or judicious truth seemed likely to fall in his way, his pen infallibly waddled off from it. He expounded the Latin of the fathers at Hampton Court[3], but avoided the very plain and intelligible Latin of Fortescue.

[1] Bacon's opinion has been urged against this, as evidence of genuine praise or of the basest sycophancy.   He dedicated his greatest work, the " Advancement of Learning," to James.   It is worth while, however, to quote the exact words of this dedication. They are very curious.   If they were meant seriously, never was so much flattery ingeniously mixed up with so much truth.   They savour much more of irony.   " I am well assured," writes Bacon, " that this which I shall say is no amplification at all, but a positive and measured truth ; which is, that there hath not been, since Christ's time, any king or temporal monarch, which hath been so learned in all literature and erudition, divine and human.   For let a man seriously and diligently revolve and peruse the succession of the emperors of Rome, of which Cæsar the dictator, who lived some years before Christ, and Marcus Antoninus, were the best learned ; and so descend to the emperors of Græcia, or of the West, and then to the lines of France, Spain, England, Scotland, and the rest ; and he shall find his judgment is truly made.   *For it seemeth much in a king, if by the compendious extractions of other men's wits and labour, he can take hold of any superficial ornaments and shows of learning, or if he countenance and prefer learning and learned men : but to drink indeed of the true fountain of learning, nay, to have such a fountain of learning in himself, in a king, and in a king born, is almost a miracle.*"   This makes out too formidable an exception to be quite complimentary, and perhaps James's irreverent joke about the book itself was not unconnected with its dedication.   " It is like the peace of God," he said, " it passeth all understanding !"   It was a fair retort upon the sycophancy of James's more profligate flatterers, when Henry IV. of France admitted that he might be " Solomon—*the son of David.*"

[2] See the preface of his " Dæmonologie."

[3] An extraordinary account of the indecent conduct of James at this conference is given by Harrington, an eye-witness (Nugæ Antiquæ, vol. i. p. 181.) and is worth referring to. Barlow, a partial

Not so the great men, his opponents, who were now preparing for a constitutional struggle, of which Europe had as yet given no example.   At the close of Elizabeth's reign they had risen to a formidable party, they had wrung concessions even from her splendid despotism, and won for themselves the courteous title of "mutineers."[1] They soon found that they had little to fear from her successor.   He had no personal claims on their respect[2],

---

observer of the king and bishops, gives a long account of the discussion in his Phœnix Britannicus, p. 140. *et seq.* edit. 1707.   See also Winwood's Memorials, p. 13.   James and his eighteen abject bishops boasted that they had thoroughly beaten their four puritan adversaries ; and beat them, it must be confessed, they did, with the rudest and most atrocious insults ; certainly not with learning.   In the latter respect, Dr. Reynolds, the puritan leader, had the advantage of perhaps any other man in England.   See Hallam's Const. Hist. vol. i. p. 405.

[1] Sloane MSS. 4166.   Letter of Sir E. Hoby to Sir T. Edmonds, dated Feb. 12, 1605.   See also Hallam's Constitutional Hist. vol. i. p. 401.   A curious tract in the Sloane MSS. 827. confirms the loss of Elizabeth's popularity, and states its cause, in a short history of the queen's death, and the new king's accession.   See, too, the proceedings in the case of Peter Wentworth (a Cornish Wentworth), Parl. Hist. vol. iv. p. 186. *et seq.*   The name of Wentworth fills up more than one illustrious era of the English history.

[2] The news of the progress of his journey from Scotland had travelled before him !   "By the time he reached London," says Carte, a friend of the Stuarts, "the admiration of the intelligent world was turned into contempt."   The reader will find good reason for this in Harrington's Nugæ Antiquæ, vol. i. p. 180. ; Wilson, in Kennet, vol. ii. p. 667. ; Neal, p. 408. quarto edit. ; Fuller, part ii. p. 22. ; Hallam, vol. i. pp. 402, 403.   Nor is it likely that this contempt should have been diminished by his personal aspect, which Weldon (quoting Balfour) has described, and Saunderson (in his Aulicus Coquinariæ—an answer to Weldon's book) has not dared to contradict.   "He was of a middle stature," says Balfour, "more corpulent throghe his clothes then in his body, zet fatt enouch ; his clothes euer being made large and easie, the doubletts quilted for steletto proofe ; his breeches in grate pleits and full stuffed : he was naturally of a timorous dispositione, which was the gratest reasone of his quilted doubletts : his eye large, euer roulling after aney stranger cam in his presence ; insomuch as maney for shame have left the roome, as being out of countenance ; his beard was werey thin ; his toung too large for his mouthe, vich euer made him speake

no dignity to fence in royalty. They buckled on the armour of their privileges, and awaited his ludicrous attacks without respect and without fear.[1]

James soon commenced them, and with a hand doubly defenceless. He had impoverished his crown, by conferring its estates on his needy followers; he had deprived it of the sympathy and support of the wealthier barons, in disgusting them with his indiscriminate peerage creations.[2] From this feeble hand, and a head stuffed with notions of his royal "divinity," he issued the first of his proclamations for the assembling of parliament. It contained a deadly attack on the privileges of the house of commons, in an attempt to regulate the parliamentary elections. This was resented, and defeated, and so the fight began.[3]

full in the mouthe, and made him drinke werey uncomelie, as if eatting his drinke, wich cam out into the cupe in eache syde of his mouthe ; his skin vas as softe as tafta sarsnet : wich felt so becausse he neuer washt his hands, onlie rubbed his fingers' ends slightly vith the vett end of a napkin. His legs wer verey weake ; having had, as was thought, some foule play in his youthe ; or rather, befor he was borne ; that he was not able to stand at seuin zeires of age ; that weaknes made him euer leaning on other men's shoulders."— " His walk," subjoins Wilson, "was ever circular." The satirical Francis Osborne has certainly completed this picture :—"I shall leave him dressed for posterity," says that writer, "in the color I saw him in, the next progress after his inauguration ; which was as green as the grass he trod on ; with a feather in his cap, and a horn, instead of a sword, by his side. How suitable to his age, calling, or person, I leave others to judge from his pictures."—*Trad. Mem.* c. xvii.

[1] An ominous hint of relative advantage may be quoted from the Journals, vol. i. p. 156. "That a people may be without a king, a king cannot be without a people."

[2] See Bolingbroke on the History of England, pp. 237, 238. Harris's Life of James, pp. 69. 71. "A pasquil," says Wilson, "was pasted up at St. Paul's, wherein was pretended an art to help weak memories to a competent knowledge of the names of the nobility."—p. 7.

[3] See Commons' Journals, p. 147. *et seq.* 166. ; Carte, vol. iii. p. 730. ; Winwood's Memorials, vol. ii. p. 18. ; Bolingbroke's

The popular party proclaimed their intentions at once, with boldness, and in explicit language. They warned the king of his imprudence; they spoke of the dissolute and abandoned character of his court expenses. They did not refuse to assist his wants, but they maintained that every offer of money on their part should be met with corresponding offers of concession on the part of the crown. They brought forward a catalogue of grievances in the practice of the ecclesiastical courts, in the administration of civil justice, and in the conduct of the various departments of the government. For these they demanded redress.[1] Artifice and intrigue were the first answers they received, and a prorogation the last.

James had now sufficient warning, but, nevertheless, plunged blusteringly forward. With no clear hereditary right to the crown[2], he flouted his only safe pretension—the consent and authority of the people. With no personal qualities to command respect, he proclaimed himself a "lieutenant and vicegerent of God," and, as such,

---

Remarks, p. 250. Hume observes that "the facility with which he departed from this pretension is a proof that his meaning was innocent." (vol. v. p. 12.) Fear, his saving characteristic, is the more obvious solution.

[1] They tried to get the upper house to join them in these complaints, but vainly. Their lordships refused. See Somers Tracts, vol. ii. p. 14.; Commons' Journals, pp. 199. 235. 238. For the principal grievances, see Journals, pp. 190. 215. 251. &c.; Hallam's Court Hist. vol. i. pp. 412. 415.; and Lingard's History, vol. vi. pp. 23. 27. 88—93. quarto edit.

[2] Mr. Hallam has admirably and fully discussed this point, Const. Hist. pp. 392—400. I have no doubt the king was able to feel his want of clear pretensions acutely; but his blundering shrewdness taught him no better mode of concealing it, than by magnifying the inherent rights of primogenitary succession, as something indefeasible by the legislature. We find him frequently, with much testiness, reminding the commons—"you all know, I came from the loins of your ancient kings"—a sure proof that he feared they did *not* know it. See Parl. Hist. vol. v. p. 192.

adorned and furnished with "sparkles of divinity." In total ignorance of the nature and powers of government, nothing could shake his vain conceit of the awe to be inspired by his regal wisdom. The commons, however, left no point of their claims unasserted or uncertain ; they reserved no "arcana imperii," after the king's fashion. They drew up in committee a "Satisfaction" of their proceedings, for the perusal of James, who makes an evident allusion to it in a letter of the time.[1] It is vain to say, after reading such documents as this, that liberty, a discrimination of the powers and objects of government, was then only struggling to the light, or had achieved no distinct form and pretension. It was already deep in the hearts and in the understandings of men. "What cause," they eloquently said, "we your poor commons have, to watch over their privileges, is evident in itself to all men. The prerogatives of princes may easily, and do daily, grow. The privileges of the subject are, for the most part, at an everlasting stand. They may be, by good providence and care, preserved ; but being once lost, are not recovered but with much disquiet."

[1] This remarkable paper will be found at length in Petyt's Jus Parliament. ch. x. p. 227. ; and is extracted into Mr. Hatsell's first vol. of Precedents, Appendix. No. 1. Hatsell states, that it was not entered on the Journals. This is partly a mistake, for at p. 243. the first paragraph will be found. Rapin alludes to it ; and Mr. Hallam has made very spirited use of it (vol. i. p. 418.), though he seems to labour under misapprehension in stating that Hume was ignorant of its existence. Hume, on the contrary, makes special allusion to it (vol. v. p. 15.) ; quotes a passage from it ; speaks of it as drawn up "with great force of reasoning, and spirit of liberty ; " attributes it to Bacon and Sandys ; and inclines to think that it had not been presented to the monarch by the house. The last supposition is certainly incorrect ; and Mr. Hallam produces a letter which appears to indicate the feelings with which the king regarded it (vol. i. p. 419.). About this time, it may be added, mention is made in the Journals, that fresh seats were required for the extraordinary attendance of members.—p. 141.

Another session succeeded, and the same scenes were again enacted, with the same results. In vain were monopolies cried down, and the merchants lifted their voices unavailingly against the inglorious peace with Spain. After this prorogation, James's obstinacy held out for upwards of two years, when want of money overcame it.

The session of 1610 was a most distinguished one, and called the unjust prerogative to a rigorous reckoning. James had most illegally, in the face of two great charters, and twelve other parliamentary enactments, imposed certain duties on imports and exports. Bates, a Turkey merchant, refused payment of one on currants, and carried his case into the exchequer.[1] The judges there refused him justice, in terms more disgraceful and sub-versive of liberty, than even the iniquitous decision. Against this, and in no measured terms, the commons now protested. Lawyers, more learned than the judges, exposed, in masterly reasoning, the ignorance and cor-ruption of barons Fleming and Clark. Sir Francis Bacon appealed with all his eloquence to the reverence of past ages, and the possession of the present; but Hakewill proved[2], in an argument of memorable clear-

[1] A very learned preface to the report of the case of Bates in the State Trials, comprising the entire argument on the question, has been written by Mr. Hargrave. Coke, in his 2d Inst. p. 57., proves the illegality of the decision ; though, in his Reports (p. 12.), he had inclined to its favour, on other grounds than those stated by the judges. See also Birch's Negotiations, and an eloquent and very learned note on the subject of impositions, in Mr. Amos's Fortescue, pp. 28—31. 142, 143. I cannot leave the latter work without adding, that various and extensive as is the learning displayed in it, it is for those only to appreciate Mr. Amos's profound acquaintance with constitutional law and history, who, like myself, have to acknowledge, with the deepest gratitude, information personally communicated.

[2] See his speech, State Trials, vol. ii. p. 407. Mr. Hallam's statement of the discussion is interesting, vol. i. p. 433—438.

ness and vast knowledge, that the only instances adduced
were on forbidden articles, and therefore false as precedents ; and Bacon appealed in vain.   Still more vain was
the rage of the monarch, who hastened to the house to
lay his arrogant commands upon them.   He told them,
after a comparison savouring of blasphemy, that it "was
seditious in subjects to dispute what a king may do in
the height of his power." [1]   They answered in a remonstrance of great strength and spirit, and of much learning. [2]
After producing a host of precedents, they passed a bill
against impositions ; but, to use Hume's phrase, "the
house of lords, as is usual, defended the barriers of the
throne," and threw out the bill. [3]

I may allude a little further to the proceedings of this
distinguished session, since they illustrate forcibly the
exact relative positions of the crown and parliament at
the period of Wentworth's return.

Unwearied in exertion, the house of commons now
fastened on a work that had been published by Dr.
Cowell, one of the party of civilians encouraged against
the common lawyers, and which contained most monstrous doctrines on the subject of kingly power. [4]   They

[1] It is worth referring to this speech, as given in King James's
Works, pp. 529. 531.   The discontent it provoked will be found by
referring to Winwood's Memorials, vol. iii. p. 175. ; Commons'
Journals, p. 430. ; and Miss Aikin's James, vol. i. p. 350.
[2] It will be found at length at Somers' Tracts, vol. ii. p. 159.
[3] Hume, referring to this measure, observes :—"A spirit of liberty
had now taken possession of the house.   The leading members,
being men of independent genius and large views, began to regulate
their opinions more by the future consequences which they foresaw,
than by former precedents which were laid before them ; and they
less aspired at maintaining the ancient constitution, than at establishing a new one, and a freer, and a better." (vol. v. p. 34.)   However
true this may be in reference to future proceedings, it is certainly
incorrect as applied to the present.
[4] See Roger Coke's Detection, vol. i. p. 50. edit. 1694.   These

compelled James to suppress the book.   The wily Cecil
had striven to effect a compromise with them, by the proposition of a large yearly revenue to the crown, in return
for which he promised that the liberality of the sovereign
in the matter of grievances should be commensurate.
He had entreated, however, without success, that the
subsidies should have priority: the commons were
resolute in enforcing the condition before yielding the
grant.   The fate of their impositions' bill had instructed
them.   Cecil now pressed again for the subsidies; they
persisted in the further entertainment of grievances.
They complained of the ecclesiastical high commission
court, and its disregard of the common law; they protested against the recent system of substituting proclamations for laws; they sought redress for the delays of
the courts in granting writs of prohibition and habeas
corpus; they questioned the right of the council of
Wales to exclude from the privileges of· the common law
four ancient English counties; they remonstrated against
patents of monopolies, and a late most unjust tax upon
victuallers; but, above all, they strove to exonerate the
country from the feudal burthens.[1]   They did not dispute
that these in right belonged to the crown; but they
negotiated for their abolition; for they never then insisted
on a right, except with proofs and precedents in their
hands for claiming it as such.   In that particular stage of
the contest, the necessity and justice of such caution
is apparent, and forms an important feature of their
struggles.

---

passages have since been suppressed, and it is now considered a
useful book.   See Hume's admirable note, vol. v. p. 37.

[1] See the Parl. Hist. vol. v. pp. 225—245.   Also, the Commons'
Journals for 1610.   Winwood, vol. iii. p. 119.

The negotiation now commenced. James did not care to abolish purveyance[1], which was sought for; but with that was coupled a demand for the exchange of every other kind of tenure into that of free and common socage.[2] "What!" said James, "reduce all my subjects, noble and base, rich and poor, to hold their lands in the same ignoble manner?" The indignant "father of his people" would not listen to it; and, after some delay, a compromise was struck. The tenure by knight service was retained; but its most lucrative and oppressive incidents, such as relief, premier seisin, and wardship, were surrendered, along with purveyance. Still the commons delayed; for Cecil's demands were exorbitant. They resolved to pause some short time longer, that they might ascertain the best mode of levying so large a sum with the least distress to the nation. The session had already been protracted far into summer; a subsidy was granted for immediate wants; and a prorogation took place.

The loss of the Journals of the ensuing session renders it difficult to follow their proceedings. It is certain, however, from other sources, that the events of the interim had resolved the leaders of the house on aban_ doning the terms proposed. They saw no signs of greater justice at the outports, or in the proclamations, or in the ecclesiastical courts. The most important of their petitions on particular grievances had been refused, and now, when they sent one up to the throne for the allowing prisoners on a capital charge to bring witnesses in their own defence, the king protested to them, that in

---

[1] An admirable note on purveyance will be found in Amos's Fortescue, pp. 134, 135.

[2] Parl. Hist. vol. v. p. 229. *et seq.*

his conscience he could not grant such an indulgence. "It would encourage and multiply forgery," he said: " men were already accustomed to forswear themselves, even in civil actions; what less could be expected when the life of a friend was at stake?"[1]   Such was the exquisite philosophy of James.   A coolness ensued; threats followed; a prorogation was again the intermediate argument, with a dissolution within nine weeks as the final one.   Those nine weeks were employed in vain in the purpose of weakening the popular party; and, on the day threatened, seven years from their first assembling, the dissolution took place.[2]

The interval which ensued was one of profusion, debauchery, and riot in the court[3], and of attempted oppression and wrong against the people.   Fortunately, the spirit of liberty had strengthened to resistance. " The privy seals are going forth," says a contemporary writer[4], " but from a trembling hand, lest that sacred seal should be refused by the desperate hardness of the prejudiced people."   It was refused; and the shameful expedient was abundantly resorted to by the court, of selling the honours of the peerage, and of creating a number of hereditary knights, who should pay tribute for their

---

[1] Commons' Journals, p. 451.   Lords' Journals, p. 658.   Winwood, vol. iii. p. 193.

[2] A curious letter of the king, illustrative of the angry feelings that prevailed at the dissolution, exists in Marden's State Papers, p. 813. See Hallam, vol. i. p. 451.

[3] Observe the account in Fulke lord Brooke's Five Years of King James; Mrs. Hutchinson's Memoirs; Weldon, p. 166.; Coke's Detection, vol. i. pp. 42—49.   The court presented, at this moment, a disgusting scene of profligacy.   It requires a strong stomach even to get through a perusal of the details.   Ladies rendered themselves especially notable, not merely for laxity of virtue, but for the grossest drunkenness.   See Nugæ Antiquæ, vol. i. p. 348.

[4] In Winwood's Memorials, vol. iii.

dignity.[1] All would not serve, however; and Bacon, reckoning somewhat unduly on his own skill[2], prevailed upon the king to summon another parliament.

At this eventful moment Wentworth came back to England, and was immediately returned knight of the shire for Yorkshire.[3] It is now my duty to follow him through the commencing passages of his public life, and I hope to do this faithfully. I have felt very strongly that the truth lies (as it generally does in such cases) somewhere between the extreme statements that have been urged on either side, by the friends and the foes of Wentworth.

One of his latest biographers[4], who brought to his task a very amiable feeling and desire—which wasted itself at last, however, in an excess of sweetness and candour—sets out with a just remark. "The factions which agitated his contemporaries," Mr. Mac-Diarmid observes, "far from ceasing with the existing generation, divided

[1] An account of this proceeding will be found in Lingard's History, vol. vi. quarto edit. from Somers' Tracts. See also Hallam, vol. i. p. 461. ; Aikin, vol. i. p. 389. The project appears to have been the suggestion of Salisbury. See Baker's Chronicle, p. 416. edit. 1679. ; Guthrie, vol. iii. p. 704. ; and Macaulay's History, vol. i. p. 75.

[2] MS. in the possession of Mr. Hallam, Const. Hist. vol. i. pp. 461, 462.

[3] The writer in the Biographia Britannica, and Mr. Mac-Diarmid, reject sir George Radcliffe's dates without the slightest scruple, but without the smallest excuse. They are all of them extremely accurate, and it is quite certain that Wentworth sat in the parliament of 1614. The writers in the Biog. Brit. plead in apology that Radcliffe's own statement—"my memory is (of late especially) very bad and decayed"—quite warrants their freedom with his dates ; but they seem to have overlooked the fact, that Radcliffe distinctly restricts the decay of his memory to facts he has *altogether* forgotten. "Seeing my unfaithful memory," he subsequently says, "hath lost part of the occurrences which concerned my lord, I am loth to let slip that, *which yet remains.*"

[4] Mr. Mac-Diarmid, Lives of British Statesmen, 2 vols.

posterity into his immoderate censurers, or unqualified admirers; and writers, whether hostile or friendly, have confounded his merits and defects with those of the transactions in which he was engaged. Even in the present day, an undisguised exposure of his virtues and vices might be misconstrued by many into a prejudiced panegyric, or an invidious censure of man, as well as of the cause." Now, from this I shall certainly, in some measure, secure myself by the course I propose to adopt. The collection of documents known by the title of the " Strafford Papers," seems to me to contain within itself every material necessary to the illustration of the public and private character of this statesman, on an authority which few will be disposed to contest, for the record is his own. The general historical statement I have already given, was necessary to bring Wentworth more intelligibly upon the political scene; but hereafter I mean to restrict myself, almost entirely, to the authorities, illustrations, and suggestions of character, that are so abundantly furnished by that great work. The letters it contains, extending over a period of more than twenty years, comprise the notices of the country gentleman, the anxieties of the parliament-man, the growing ambition of the president of the North, the unflagging energy of the lord deputy, the intense purpose and reckless daring of the lieutenant-general, and the cares, magnanimously borne, of the ruined and forsaken aspirant, about to render the forfeit of that life, which three kingdoms had pronounced incompatible with their well-being. Their evidence is the more unexceptionable, that they are no hasty ebullitions, the offspring of the moment, a sudden expression of sentiments to be disavowed in succeeding intervals of calm. With a view, as it would seem, to guard against the inconveniences of a naturally fiery and uncontrollable temperament, Strafford wrote with singular deliberation; and his perspicuous and straightforward despatches[1] deliver the results of a thorough conviction. "He never did any thing of any moment," remarks sir George Radcliffe, "concerning either political or domestical business, without taking advice; not so much as a letter written by him to any great man, of any business, but he showed it to his confidents if they were near him. The former part of his life, Charles Greenwood and myself were consulted with; and the latter part, Chr. Wandesford came in Charles Greenwood's room, Charles Greenwood desiring not to be taken away from his cure; they met almost daily, and debated all businesses and designs, *pro et contra:* by this means his own judgment was very much improved, and all the circumstances and probable consequences of the things consulted were discovered and considered."[2] From the high praise which is given by sir George to this practice, it is to be inferred, moreover, that it was no cheap expedient to obtain an obsequious and all-approving set of counsellors; for he complacently subjoins, that such a course "is very efficacious to make a wise man, even though he advise with much weaker men than himself: for there is no man of ordinary capacity, that will not often suggest some things which might else have been let slip without being observed; and in the debatings of things, a man may give another hints and occasions to observe and find out

---

[1] It is much to be regretted that Mr. Brodie, whose work contains several valuable suggestions towards the life of Strafford, should suffer himself to depreciate so strongly the merit of his letters and despatches, and his intellectual attainments generally. I shall have ample occasion to refute this.

[2] Essay.

that, which he that speaks to it, perhaps, never thinks on; as a whetstone," &c.; concluding with that very original simile. It may also be remarked here, that, of his more important despatches to the king, Wentworth was accustomed to transmit duplicates to the leading members of the council. Thus, in a letter to secretary Cooke, he writes: " Having such confidence in your judgment and good affection both towards his majesty's service and myself, I hold it fit to give you a clear and particular understanding of all my proceedings in these affairs; to which end I have sent you the duplicates of all my despatches to his majesty and others, as you will find in the pacquet this bearer shall bring unto you; only I desire you will be pleased not to take notice thereof, unless it be brought unto you by some other hand. These businesses have cost me a mighty labour, having been at first written over by my own hand. And I have been as circumspect and considerate therein as possibly I could. And now, I beseech you, help me with your judgment, in any thing you shall find amiss; and let me clearly and speedily be led into the right path, in case I have erroneously, in any thing, swerved from that which is best and honourablest for our master; for it would grieve me more than any other thing, if my weakness should lead him into the least inconvenience: and this you ever find in me,—that no man living shall more promptly depart from an error than myself, that have, in good faith, no confidence in my own judgment, how direct and intent soever my affections may be." What these letters want, therefore, in those sudden and familiar outbreaks which are to be looked for in a less guarded correspondence, is amply made up in the increased authority of the matter thus carefully elaborated, and

cautiously put forth.   Nor are instances altogether wanting, in which the curb is set aside, and the whole nature
of the writer has its resistless way.

I have remarked on the aristocratic influences which
surrounded Wentworth's youth.   Every thing had tended
to foster that principle within him.   His ancient lineage,
extending, at no very distant period, to the blood royal
—the degree of attention which must have early attached
itself to the eldest of twelve children—his inheritance of
an estate of 6000*l.* a year, an enormous fortune in those
days—his education—all the various circumstances which
have been touched upon—contributed to produce a
character ill fitted to comprehend or sympathise with
"your Prynnes, Pyms, Bens, and the rest of that generation of odd names and natures,[1]" who recognised, in
the struggling and oppressed Many, those splendid
dawnings of authority, which others were disposed to
seek only in the One.   From the first we observe in
Wentworth a deep sense of his exact social position and
its advantages.   This is explained in a passage of a
remarkable letter, written at a later period to his early
tutor, Mr. Greenwood, but which I shall extract here, since
it has reference to the present time.   " My sister Elizabeth writes me a letter concerning my brother Mathew's
estate, which I know not how to answer till I see the
will; nor do I know what it is she claims—whether
money alone, or his rent-charge forth of my lands, or
both.   Therefore I desire the copy of the will may be
sent me, and her demand, and then she shall have my
answer.   This brother, that she saith was so dear unto

---

[1] Strafford Papers, vol. i. p. 344. Such was Wentworth's ill-
judged classification.   " Ben " may be presumed to have meant sir
Benjamin Rudyard.

her, had well tutored her, or she him, being the couple of all the children of my father that I conceived loved me least; it may be they loved one another the better for that too.   However it prove, I know not; but this I am most assured,—that in case any of the three brothers died without issue, *my father ever intended their rent-charge should revert to me, and not lie still as a clog upon my estate; or that any daughter of his, whom he had otherwise provided for forth of the estate, should thus intercept his intentions towards his heir.   But how often hath he been pleased to excuse unto me the liberal provisions taken forth of my estate for my brothers and sisters?   And as often hath been assured by me, I thought nothing too much that he had done for them; and yet I can make it confidently appear, that he left not my estate better to me than my grandfather left it to him, by 200l. a year; nay, some that understand it very well have, upon speech had with me about it, been very confident he left it me rather worse than better than he received it.*   But I shall and can, I praise God, and have heretofore, patiently looked upon their peevishness and frowardness towards me, and all their wise and prudent councils and synods they have held against me, as if they had been to have dealt with some cheater or cozener, not with a brother, who had ever carried himself justly and lovingly towards them; nor do I, or will I, deny them the duties I owe unto them, as recommended unto my care by my father. Nay, as wise as they did, or do, take themselves to have been, I will say, *it had not been the worse for them, as I think, if they had taken less of their own foolish empty fancies, and followed more of my advice,* who, I must needs say, take myself to have been full as able to have directed their course, as they themselves could be at that age."[1] Here the remark cannot but occur, of the very early age at which these extraordinary "excuses " from a father to a son must have been proffered and accepted! Sir William Wentworth died in 1614[2], shortly after his son, who had scarcely accomplished his twenty-first year, was returned to parliament from Yorkshire. This patriarchal authority, then, this strong sense of his hereditary rights of property, was of no late assumption; and in after life it was Wentworth's proud satisfaction that he came not to Ireland "to piece up a broken fortune."[3]—"For," says he elsewhere, "as I am a Christian, I spend much more than all my entertainments come unto; yet I do not complain; my estate in England may well spare me something to spend." At his so early maturity, being called to the family inheritance by the death of his father, a new charge devolved to him in the guardianship of his elder sister's children, the issue of sir George Savile, which trust he faithfully discharged. His own account of his family regards, generally, given in the passage quoted, appears to me to be perfectly just. His disposition was kind, but exacting. Those of his relations who paid him proper deference, received from him attentions and care. And it is remarkable to observe, in those brothers, for instance, who continued attached to him through all his fortunes—one an intimate counsellor, another a " humble poster in his affairs "—the complete deference they at all times cheerfully paid to him.

Such was the new member for Yorkshire, who took his seat in the parliament of 1614. I have described the condition of affairs. They had arrived at such a point, that not to declare in favour of the popular party, was to

[1] Strafford Papers, vol. i. p. 484.   [2] Radcliffe's Essay.
[3] Strafford Papers, vol. i. p. 138. and see vol. i. p. 79.

exert an influence against them. The liberal strength had not declined in the present assembly. The confederacy of "undertakers[1]," banded for the purpose of influencing the elections, had pursued their vile avocations without effect. The new members were staunch; resumed complaints against monopolies and other unjust grants; called the bishop of Lincoln to account for disrespectful words; and received the tribute to their honesty of a dissolution after two months' sitting[2], and of imprisonment, in many cases, afterwards.[3] During these two months, Wentworth had continued silent;— not unobserved, but silent. I have examined the Journals, and find no trace of his advocacy of either side in the great struggle.[4]

[1] For the origin of these "strange ugly kind of beasts," as the king, in his subsequent confession of their existence, oddly called them, see Wilson, in Kennet, vol. ii. p. 696. For James's present false denial of their having been employed, see Carte, vol. iv. pp. 19, 20. ; Bacon's Works, vol. i. p. 695. ; Commons' Journals, p. 462.

[2] "This house of commons," says Hume, "showed rather a stronger spirit of liberty than the foregoing, so little skill had the courtiers for managing elections." (vol. v. p. 49.) It subsequently received from the politer courtiers the title of the "addle" parliament, from the circumstance of its not having been allowed to pass a single bill. Aikin, vol. i. p. 439. See a curious fact mentioned in D'Israeli's Character of James, p. 158., and the king's assertion, in his remarkable commission for the dissolution.

[3] The compilers of the Parliamentary History have denied this; but see debate on it in Journals of Feb. 5. 12. and 15. 1621 ; and Hatsell's proof, vol. i. p. 133, 134. edit. 1796. Hume admits the statement, vol. v. p. 50.

[4] In some of the less precisely accurate histories,—in Echard's, Oldmixon's, and Mrs. Macaulay's—Wentworth had been erroneously ranked as one of the "factious" members of this session, who had earned imprisonment after the dissolution by a violent personal attack on the king. Mr. Brodie set the mistake completely at rest, by showing its origin. A *Mr.* Thomas Wentworth, a very popular member, represented Oxford in all the parliaments of James, and in the two first parliaments of Charles. It was he who spoke violently, and was imprisoned. It was he also who took the active part against Buckingham in the second parliament, which had been

At the close of the session he returned to Yorkshire, and a year passed over him at his country residence, engaged, to all appearance, in no pursuits less innocent than his favourite sport of hawking. Let the reader judge, however, if his personal ambitions had been forgotten. Sir John Savile, the father of the afterwards lord Savile—and not, as has been invariably stated by modern writers, the lord Savile himself[1]—at this time held an office of great esteem in the county,—that of custos rotulorum, or keeper of the archives, for the West Riding. So strong an influence, however, had for some time been moving against Savile in the county, that the lord chancellor Ellesmere was induced to interfere. It is

---

ascribed to sir Thomas Wentworth (who did not sit in that parliament at all), even by Rushworth. In expressing great surprise at this mistake on the collector's part, however, Mr. Brodie overlooks the circumstance of its having arisen from a mere error of the press. Had it been otherwise, it would have been difficult (considering that Rushworth attended the house himself, and was necessarily acquainted with the persons of the different members) to have received even Mr. Brodie's authority and that of Wentworth's own letters, against the indefatigable collector. But the context of Rushworth shows the error to have been merely one of the press. He is stating the argument of the *lawyers* of the house on the difference between "common fame" and "rumour;" and observes, "It was declared by sir Tho. Wentworth, Mr. Noy, and *other* lawyers in the debate," &c.—Now *Mr.* Wentworth was a lawyer, and an eminent one, the author of a legal treatise of great merit on Executors, and recorder of Oxford; but sir Thomas Wentworth was none of these things. The mistake does not occur again. See Rushworth, vol. i. p. 217. The author of the History continued from Mackintosh has fallen into Rushworth's error, vol. v. p. 33.

[1] It is singular that this mistake should have occurred; for occasionally, in the Papers, he is called "the old knight," "old sir John," &c. (vol. i. p. 38. &c.); and in his own letter to the lord chancellor Ellesmere, on which the whole of the present business turns, he expressly alludes to "service of forty years under the late queen of gracious memory."—*Strafford Papers*, vol. i. p. 2. But so incorrectly are circumstances looked at, which do not seem to bear immediately on the matter in hand, yet are to illustrate it afterwards not unimportantly.

instructive to observe that sir Thomas Fairfax, a near kinsman of Wentworth's, was the most active against Savile. I quote a passage of a letter from Sheffield, the lord president of the north, to Ellesmere:—"I desired much to have waited upon you myself, to present an information lately made unto me, of the evil carriage of one sir John Savile, a gentleman of Yorkshire, one of the principal in commission, that maketh use of his authority to satisfy his own ends, if sundry complaints be true, which of late have been made unto me, touching one particular, which in my opinion is a matter of foul condition, and which I am bold to intreat your lordship to give me leave to make known unto you by the relation of sir Thomas Fairfax, a gentleman of good worth, to whom the particulars of that matter is well known." The result was, that in 1615 Savile was removed, and sir Thomas Wentworth appointed to the office. The court had not forgotten the good services of his silence, and Wentworth was not ungrateful. "Calling to mind," he afterwards writes to Weston, "the faithful service I had the honour to do his majesty, now with God, how graciously he vouchsafed to accept and express it openly and sundry times, I enjoy within myself much comfort and contentment. . . . You can best witness the opinion, nay, I might say the esteem, his late majesty held of me."[1]

But a new actor now appears upon the scene, in whose hands James had become a puppet, and to whose shameless influence he had surrendered all his esteems and regards. Having discharged the duties of his new office for nearly two years, Wentworth received (near the close of 1617) a startling notice from no less a person than his grace the duke of Buckingham. Old Savile had been

---

[1] Letter, dated 1626, Strafford Papers, vol. i. p. 35, 36.

busy with him. "These are to let you understand, that, whereas his majesty is informed that sir John Savile yielded up his place of custos rotulorum voluntarily unto you, whom now his majesty hath received into favour again, and purposeth to employ in his service, his majesty will take it well at your hands, that you resign it up again unto him with the same willingness, and will be mindful of you to give you as good preferment upon any other occasion."[1] Buckingham, however, had committed a mistake here. Wentworth replied to this notice in a letter which has unfortunately been lost,[2] but whose import may be gathered from some passages in Buckingham's reply :—"The reasons set down in your letter are so substantial to prove that sir John Savile made no voluntary resignation of the place to you, but yielded it up rather out of a necessity to avoid that which otherwise would have fallen upon him, that I see it was a misinformation given to his majesty and to me, which occasioned the writing of my letter unto you." Other grounds of apology are added, and Buckingham proceeds :—"Upon these grounds I thought it could neither be any wrong nor disgrace to move you in that business; but I pray you believe, that I am so far from doing the least indignity to any gentleman of your worth, that I would be ready upon any occasion to do you the best service I could. Therefore I desire you not to trouble yourself either with any doubt of further proceeding in this matter, which went so far only upon misunderstanding, *or with so long a journey to give me satisfaction, seeing I have fully received it by your letter, and have acquainted his majesty* with the true state of the business, as you have set it down." Buckingham subscribes himself his " very

[1] Strafford Papers, i. p. 4.   [2] No. See it in App. II below.

assured friend," and then, in a very curious and significant postscript, betrays good reason for his sudden change of style, and sufficiently explains the shrewd and determined course that had been adopted by Wentworth : " I beseech you to excuse me to my lord of Cumberland and my lord Clifford, that I write not to them now, as I purpose to do at more leisure ; for now I made haste to signify that which I have to you, that I might spare you so troublesome a journey." So Wentworth continued in his place, and old Savile, eaten up with mortified spleen, waited his first opportunity of retaliation.

Wentworth foiled him at that game too, by striking the first blow ! A new parliament was spoken of, and a strong opposition from the Savile party against Wentworth significantly indicated. He went instantly up to London; spoke carelessly, it may be supposed, to his friends at court, of his indifference about standing any contest ; and so won from the ministerial party an *intreaty* that he would stand, and endeavour to bring in one of the secretaries of state along with him.[1] Wentworth then consented, returned to Wentworth Woodhouse, and commenced his election exertions. In these his character had full play ; and here, in the first great effort of his public life, were amply vindicated his achievements of a later period. The energy and activity he exhibited, amounted almost to a marvel ! Every difficulty sank before him. Doubts were satisfied, jealousies put to shame, indifference moved to action, enmity even to friendship, dishonesty foiled in its own way, friends stimulated, the opposition of those who still continued enemies diverted. I mean to quote these letters at some

---

[1] "I was at London *much intreated, and indeed at last enjoined,* to stand with Mr. Secretary Calvert."—*Strafford Papers,* vol. i. p. 10.

length hereafter, in immediate illustration of the character of the lord president and lord deputy, to the right understanding of which they appear to me to offer a remarkable assistance. Wentworth of course triumphed, for nothing could withstand his vigour and resources. He went to the poll, after all, on the day of his election, with Calvert, in no vain reliance on friendly professions, but with positive lists, furnished him by the petty officers of the several hundreds, of the names of those voters who had distinctly engaged to support his interests.[1]

It may be supposed into what a deadly feud the hatred of the Saviles had now been provoked. From this time we hear little more of the father : the son, sir John Savile the younger, supplies his place. He was a person of mean intellect ; but he had a restless ambition, and was active in intrigue. He had " suck'd in with his milk," as Clarendon says, a particular malice to Wentworth ; and through his life he had many opportunities of showing how steadily he remembered that "Strafford had shrewdly overborne his father."[2]

Disgraceful occurrences had filled up the interval between the last parliament and this parliament of 1621. The exaction of benevolences[3]; the usurpations of the

[1] Strafford Papers, vol. i. p. 13.

[2] Clarendon's History of the Rebellion, vol. ii. p. 155. folio edit.

[3] " The benevolence goes on. A merchant of London, who had been a cheesemonger, but now rich, was sent for by the council, and required to give the king 200*l*., or to go into the Palatinate and serve the army with cheese, being a man of eighty years of age. He yielded rather than pay, though he might better have given nine subsidies according as he stands valued. This was told to me by one that heard it from his owne mouth. They talk also of privy seals. His majestie at Theobald's, discoursing publicly how he meant to governe, was heard to say he would governe according to the good of the common-weale, but not according to the common will." Such is an extract from a MS. letter of that day. Harl. MSS. 389. It is partly quoted in Ellis's Original Letters, 2d series, vol. iii. p. 241. It is very characteristic.

star-chamber; the deaths of the unfortunate Arabella Stuart, of the promising youth prince Henry[1], and of the accomplished Overbury; the rapid rise of Villiers; the pardon, and dark allusions of Somerset[2]; the disgrace of Coke;—these are some of the events which had blotted the history of the nation. And these were of home growth. Abroad, mischief had been equally busy; for the small remnant of foreign policy in the government disappeared with Cecil. The weak and unassisted Frederick, son-in-law of the English king, had been ignominiously driven from his new dominions by Spinola; Prague had furnished its disasters; and the protestant interest—the faith, of which, as he had abundantly assured Vorstius, James conceited himself the defender—was trampled down every where.

Proportioned to the disgust and indignation with which these things had been contemplated by the popular party, were the feelings with which they now assembled

---

[1] For some account of the strange circumstances attending the death of this prince, see Osborne, p. 531.; Burnet, vol. i. p. 10.; Winwood, vol. iii. p. 410.; Harris's Life of James, p. 301, 302. Fox, in his letter to lord Lauderdale, stated his conviction that Henry had been poisoned. The report of the physicians, however, is unanimous on this point, and unfavourable to the supposition. See Cornwall's Memoir, in the 2d vol. of Somers' Tracts; and the admirable remark of Hume, vol. v. p. 48.

[2] See Osborne, p. 534.; Weldon, pp. 95. 168. 125.; and Harris, pp. 82—86.; for *certain remarkable points* in the character of James. With respect to the allusions of Somerset, see Weldon, p. 118.; the king's letters to Bacon, in the Cabala; Birch's edition of Bacon, vol. iii.; and Von Raumer's 63d letter, in his Illustrations of History. Sir Walter Scott has a curious note, in his edition of Somers' Tracts (vol. ii. p. 488.), on this mysterious affair. See also Somers' Tracts, vol. ii. pp. 335, 336.; and Brodie's History, pp. 15—19. I have no inclination to venture an opinion on so extremely unpleasant a subject; but if suspicions reasonably prevailed before, the publication of Von Raumer's work on the history of the sixteenth and seventeenth centuries is not likely to lessen them. Dr. Lingard has put forward objections, which see in his History, vol. vi. p. 116. quarto edit.

in this parliament of 1621. The early sittings were distinguished by active and resolute steps in behalf of privilege. It is not necessary to allude to them at any length here. Some great state criminals were subsequently struck down; and after a few months, the parliament was dissolved by proclamation, and the king committed himself in many acts of foolish violence.[1]

Wentworth had taken little or no part in these proceedings. He avoided the risk of endangering a certain show of country independence, by active opposition to what was called the country party, and held the most moderate of courses between the court and the people. The service he had already rendered to the former in the matter of Calvert's return, he had been enabled to render palatable to his county by the circumstances of the Savile feud; and it now left him to a convenient kind of neutrality in other respects, which might be felt, in secret quarters, as no less serviceably intended to the court. I find him acting on committees in this parliament, but never putting himself forward as a speaker. Shortly after, he explained his policy in this respect, in a letter to his brother-in-law lord Clifford. Alluding to parliaments, he says,—"For my opinion of these meetings your lordship knows sufficiently, and the services done there coldly requited on all sides, and, which is worse, many times misconstrued. I judge further, the path we are like to walk in is now more narrow and slippery than formerly, *yet not so difficult but may be passed with circumspection, patience,* AND PRINCIPALLY SILENCE."[2] The present dissolution Wentworth regretted; but he made silence chiefly serve to assist him in this also. "As for

---

[1] See Rushworth, vol. i. pp. 52—55.
[2] Strafford Papers, vol. i. p. 19.

the disaster," he writes to lord D'Arcy, "fallen upon this so hopeful a parliament, albeit I should take pleasure to relate it, yet the enclosed proclamation for dissolution might well save me the labour; much more then, when I cannot think a thought of it but with grief, will it well become me to be silent." [1]

He had moved his family up from Wentworth Wood-house before the session; and they resided, during its continuance, in Austin Friars.   Here his body first began to show its extreme frailty.   He had "a great fever," says sir George Radcliffe; one of those pestilential fevers, it is to be presumed, which so often ravaged the close and crowded streets of London; and which at the same time (1622) struck his wife more fatally.   He removed from London, but too late to save the lady Margaret. She died shortly after, leaving no issue, but a memory which he held in respectful regard.

In his intercourse with his court friends at London Wentworth had zealously interested himself in behalf of two or three of his brothers.[2]   The anxiety with which he sought to get them fairly "settled" somehow, was extremely characteristic.   The first thing we now find him engaged in at Wentworth Woodhouse after his domestic loss, is the following-out of these exertions for the youths of his family.   He writes to sir Edward Conway, one of the king's principal secretaries of state, to remind him of his promises in behalf of "the bearer, my fifth brother, who, intending to try his fortune in the wars, desires more than in any place to serve as a gentle-man of the company under my cousin your son."   He apologises for not having seen the secretary before leaving

---

[1] Strafford Papers, vol. i. p. 15.
[2] See Strafford Papers, vol. i. pp. 14. 16. 18.

London, on the score of the sudden necessity of his illness. "If you would vouchsafe him," he continues, " so much of your favour, as to recommend him by your letters in such sort, that my cousin may be pleased to afford him his good direction and counsel, and cast his eye upon him as a kinsman (if his carriage may be such as may deserve it), I should judge myself much bound unto you for this, as for other your many noble curtesies bestowed upon me. And this I will be answerable for, —that he shall approve himself, by God's grace, religious, honest, well governed, and daring enough. I conceive, likewise, (if it might stand with your good pleasure) that a letter of recommendation to sir Horace Vere might stand him in good stead, which I humbly submit to your wisdom, and myself to your honourable censure for this my boldness." This is the same thought, the reader will perceive, as that which suggested itself to Eliot when writing to Hampden of his younger son. Sir Edward Conway at once granted the request, and Michael Wentworth was sent off to the wars. Not without a letter from his brother, however, of excellent purpose and advice. Among many sound suggestions for his professional advancement, he observes,—" Methinks it were good to keep a journal-book of all that passeth during your being in the army; as of your removes, your skirmishes, your incampings, the order of your marches, of your approaches, of your retreats, of your fortifications, of your batteries, and such like; in the well and sound disposal whereof, as I conceive, consists the chief skill and judgment of a soldier." The letter concludes admirably :—" Only let me add this one counsel,—that if you come in person to be brought on in any service, I conceive you shall do well to go on with the sober and

stayed courage of an understanding man, rather than
with the rash and ill-tempered heat of an unadvised youth.
In which course too, I conceive, you may sufficiently
vindicate yourself from the opinion of fear and baseness,
and gain a good esteem among the wiser sort.   And,
indeed, a man that ventures himself desperately beyond
reason (besides that thereby he too much undervalues
himself) shall by men of sure and sad brains be deemed,
without doubt, unfit for government and command, that
exerciseth none of it first over his own unruly and mis-
leading passions."   This conduct, so deprecated here by
Wentworth, is a description of that very conduct which
it is the general custom to ascribe to the earl of Strafford ;
but incorrectly, as I trust I shall be able to show.

His health had now strengthened, and with it a flow
of good spirits came.   Sir George Calvert, the king's
secretary of state, was selected for the first advantage of
these.   " Mr. Tailor telling me," Wentworth writes, "he
would see you before the end of this week, I might not
omit to present my service unto you in these few lines.
Matter worthy your trouble these parts afford none, where
our objects and thoughts are limited in looking upon a
tulip, hearing a bird sing, a rivulet murmuring, or some
such petty, yet innocent pastime, which for my part I
begin to feed myself in, having, I praise God, recovered
more in a day by an open country air, than in a fortnight's time in that smothering one of London.   By my
troth I wish you, divested of the importunity of business,
here for half a dozen hours, you should taste how free
and fresh we breathe, and how *procul metu fruimur
modestis opibus*,—awanting sometimes to persons of
greater eminency in the administration of commonwealths.
But seeing this is denied to you in your course, and to

me as part of my misfortune, I shall pray you may ever receive as full contentment in those more weighty as we do in these lighter, entertainments." [1]

This "innocent pastime," nevertheless, did not withhold him from the parliament, which was now summoned. Its proceedings have been described in the life of Eliot. Wentworth played his usual cautious part, and returned to Wentworth Woodhouse, at its adjournment, a better friend than ever, more playful and more confidential, to his majesty's "principal secretary of state." Calvert himself had gone to his country seat at Thistleworth, and is congratulated by his correspondent with many classical similitudes and quotations, on having "retired to the delights of his Tusculanie, *ereptus specioso ejus damno.*" An amusing anecdote of James, then hunting with his court at Rufford, concludes the letter. "The loss of a stag, and the hounds hunting foxes instead of a deer, put the king, your master, into a marvellous chaff, accompanied with those ordinary symptoms better known to you courtiers, I conceive, that *to us rural swains;* in the height whereof, comes a clown galloping in, and staring full in his face: *His blood!* (quoth he) *am I come forty miles to see a fellow?* and presently in a great rage turns about his horse, and away he goes faster than he came; the oddness whereof caused his majesty and all the company to burst out into a vehement laughter; and so the fume for that time was happily dispersed."

Seven days after this, the "rural swain" of Woodhouse writes again to his selected confidant. He begins by a laughing mention of having written some politics recently to his "cousin Wandesford, *as being a statist,*" a politician, a meddler in state affairs; "but here with you," he adds,

[1] Strafford Papers, vol. i. p. 16.

" I have matters of other guess stuff to relate,—that our harvest is all in, a most fine season to make fish-ponds, our plums all gone and past, peaches, quinces, and grapes almost fully ripe, which will, I trow, hold better relish with a Thistleworth palate, and approve me how to have the skill to serve every man in his right cue. These only we countrymen muse of, hoping in such harmless retirements for a just defence from the higher powers, and, possessing ourselves in contentment, pray with Dryope in the poet,—

> ' Et siqua est pietas, ab acutæ vulnere falcis
> Et pecoris morsu, frondes defendite nostras.'

—Thus, you see, Ovid serves us at every turn. How bold we are with you since you entred our list; and how we take time, while time serves ! For, Michaelmas once come, and your secretary's cloak on your shoulders, I trust, you shall find us better manner'd than to interrupt your serious hours with our toys." On the arrival of Michaelmas, however, the parliament was again adjourned, for the purpose, as it afterwards appeared, of a final dissolution. Our rural swain, in consequence, despatches with an airy sauciness to his state friend, in a tone between jest and earnest, some slight shades of significant advice, dashed with a sort of reminder that the writer—though given to looking at tulips, and hearing birds sing, and rivulets murmuring, and keeping sheep from biting his hedges, and such like innocent pastime—might yet be called upon, as an effect of want of employment, to play the part of an " unruly fellow in parliament." The words of this letter are eminently happy and well chosen. " Now," says Wentworth, " that you have given us a put-off till February, we are at good ease and leisure to pry (the true effects of want of employment) saucily out of our own calling into the mysteries of state; to cast about for a reason of this sudden change. In a word, we conclude, that the French treaty must first be consummate before such unruly fellows meet in parliament, lest they might appear as agile against this, as that other Spanish match. For my part I like it well, and conceive the bargain wholsom on our side, that we save three other subsidies and fifteenths. Less could not have been demanded for the dissolving of this treaty, and still the king your master have pretended to suffer loss (no doubt for our satisfaction only), which certainly we should have believed, and reputed ourselves great gainers, and that rightly too. *For is it a small matter, trow you, for poor swains to unwind so dextrously your courtly true-love knots? You think we see nothing; but believe it, you shall find us legislators, no fools; albeit, you of the court (for by this time I am sure you have, by a fair retreat from Thistleworth, quit your part of a country life for this year) think to blear our eyes with your sweet balls, and leave us in the suds, when you have done. Thus much for the common-weal.* For your own self, I am right glad for your ague recovered; hoping it will cleanse away all bad-disposed humours, and give entrance consequently unto a settled continuing health, wherein no man alive shall be more pleased. In the alacrity of which faith, and out of an earnest desire to be made an eye-witness thereof, you shall have (God willing) within these few weeks to attend you, your honour's ever most humbly, most readily to be command, THOMAS WENTWORTH."

It is just possible that these hints might have been taken at last by the court party, but that Wentworth's

proposed journey was retarded by a sudden return of
illness.   In the spring, Radcliffe observes, "as I take it,
he had a double tertian ; and after his recovery, a relapse
into a single tertian ; and, a while after, a burning
fever."   On his recovery from these afflicting disorders,
he came instantly up to London.   Charles now sat upon
the English throne, and Buckingham's influence reigned
over the royal councils more absolutely than even in
James's time.   This, it is probable (for he had had good
reason to suspect a personal dislike on Buckingham's
part), induced Wentworth to venture more openly among
the popular party, and by that means convey to the king,
inaccessible through his minister, the importance of his
talents and services.   I shall show very soon how
extremely anxious he was to exhibit himself, as it were,
personally to the king.   We find him now, accordingly,
in frequent communication with Denzil Hollis, and others
of the popular men.   He had, from the first, provided a
convenient organ of communication with them, in the
person of his kinsman Wandesford, who subsequently
proved so accommodating a patriot.   Soon after this
(one of the results of his visits to the house of Hollis's
father, the earl of Clare), he married the lady Arabella
Hollis, "younger daughter of the earl, a lady exceeding
comely and beautiful, and yet much more lovely in the
endowments of her mind." [1]

Wentworth now began to be talked of as an accession
to the liberal party, and the court grew somewhat alarmed.
On the meeting of parliament, his election for Yorkshire
came into dispute, and, as I have shown in the memoir
of Eliot, the ministerial men supported his claims.   No
doubt this arose from a desire, by some little sacrifice in

----

[1] Radcliffe's Essay.

a matter of no essential concern, to nip slightly the budding patriot. Eliot's opposition threw him out. What has been already suggested on this subject [1], is corroborated by some occasional allusions in the Strafford papers. Wentworth's friend, sir Richard Beaumont, for instance, writes in answer to his earnest request :—"My occasions are, and have been such, as with no convenience I can come up to London ; for which I am very sorry, that I shall not enjoy your good company this summer, and give what assistance I could to make good our York election, which I hold as clear as the noon sun, for if it be tolerated that men shall come six, seven, nay, ten apprentices out of a house, this is more like a rebellion than an election. The gentry are wronged, the freeholders are wronged." [2] Sir Richard Beaumont goes on to allude to the borough of Pontefract, observes that he is much beholden for the honour of having been elected there, but hints a private reason which will prevent his accepting, and suggests the name of another friend to be returned on a new writ. "I should have been willing to have kept your place for you, or for any friend of yours, and served in it, and yielded it up of an hour's warning to have done you service ; but as it is," &c. It would appear from this, that Wentworth had already, against the chance of defeat, secured a seat to fall back upon, in the borough of Pontefract. [3]

When the parliament commenced proceedings, Wentworth partly showed gratitude to the court, and partly redeemed his new alliance. He spoke with extreme moderation, and advised a grant of subsidies, while at the

[1] Memoir of Eliot, pp. 31, 32.
[2] Strafford Papers, vol. i. p. 27.
[3] See Letter to the Mayor of Pontefract, vol. i. p. 26.

same time he intimated opposition to Buckingham. The adjournment to Oxford then took place; but, on their re-assembling, while Eliot and others were dooming the minister to impeachment, *Wentworth continued silent.* The cause of this will very soon appear.

He returned to Yorkshire. Necessity, in a few months, called together another parliament. He set to work instantly to prepare for his election; but, in the midst of his arrangements, to the infinite surprise of himself no less than of his friends, an announcement reached him that his name was among those of the men disabled from serving, by Buckingham's notable scheme of pricking them sheriffs of their respective counties. Wentworth was now sheriff of Yorkshire. Sir Arthur Ingram, a cautious friend, writing to him at this moment, gave him one consolation :—"*It was told me by two counsellors, that in the naming of you, the king said, you were an honest gentleman, but not a tittle to any of the rest. This much advantage have you that way.*" He had previously said that every exertion to prevent the step had been used, but added, " I think, if all the council that was at court had joined together in request for you, it would not have prevailed: for it was set and resolved what should be done before the great duke's going over, and from that the king would not change a tittle." [1] Buckingham had gone by this time into Holland; and it would thus appear that Charles, though inclined favourably to Wentworth, did not dare to contravene the order of his minion.

Be that as it might, here was a great occasion. It was soon announced to Wentworth that the pricked men were resolved to make a struggle, to defeat the unusual

[1] Strafford Papers, vol. i. p. 29.

tyranny that had sought to disable them from parliament.
" I met with sir Francis Seymour here, at Reading," writes
the cautious Ingram; "I find by him that he is very
desirous to be of the house, notwithstanding he is chosen
sheriff; he hath taken, as he telleth me, very good advice
in it; and he hath been resolved, that he may be
returned, and serve for any town or city that is out of
his own county. He would gladly that you would favour
him so much as to get him chosen for some place in the
north, and he will, if it stand with your good liking, have
you chosen in the west. This he did desire me to write
to you of, and that you would send him or me an answer
so soon as you can. This, his desire, I have by these
few lines made known unto you, leaving it to your own
wisdom to do therein what you shall think good. *For
my own poor opinion, it is a thing that no doubt will displease the king exceeding much, and, therefore, to be well
considered of. On the other side, I think the house would be
exceeding glad of it, and would hold you in, in spite of any.*
That which induceth sir Francis the rather in this is,
that he knoweth that sir Edward Coke, and sir Robert
Philips will be both returned. But, good sir, out of
the love I bear to you, I dare not give you any
encouragement in it."[1] Wentworth's conduct upon this
was decisive of the character I am endeavouring to
represent. With the ready and resolved purpose of a
man who is already decided on the *main* course to be
pursued, yet is not unwilling that it should receive corroboration or modification from his friends, he instantly
consulted several of them. Observe how characteristically this is conveyed, in a letter from his father-in-law,
lord Clare : " *You resolve, in my opinion of this particular*

[1] Strafford Papers, vol. i. p. 30.

rightly; for we live under a prerogative government, where book-law submits unto *lex loquens;* then be these extraordinaries, that rely rather upon inference or interpretation than the letter, too weak staves for such subjects to lean upon.   This is a novelty and a stranger, that a sheriff, who, according to the received rule of our forefathers, is tied to his county as a snail to his shell, may cause himself to be chosen a burgess, or servant for a borough, and so in a sort quit the greater and the king's service for a subject's and a less: *therefore, as a novelty, it is rather to be followed than to begin it,* and as a stranger to be admitted as a probationer, and to be embraced upon further acquaintance.   For my part, I shall be glad if sir Edward Coke and sir Robert Philips can make their undertaking good; and I could wish sir Francis Seymour were a burgess, *so you were not seen in it: and if any of them, without your knowledge and consent, shall confer any such place upon you, you are no way in fault thereby;* and yet Cæsar's wife must be free from suspicion; so as I may conclude, it is not good to stand within the distance of absolute power.   But I see the issue: the question will fall between the king and the parliament; the house will demand her member, and the king denies his officer, and the king's election was prior, so as in conclusion some drops of displeasure may fall upon the borough, *whose charter is always in the king's reach.*   But this is my chimera, and the lion may be less terrible than the picture.   Howsoever this well succeeding would put the courtier out of his trick, secure the parliament better, and the subject in general, and make great ones more cautious in wrestling with that high court.   *Yet as you write, son, this business is of such a nature, as it is much better to be a spectator than an actor, and in this I give you no opinion; I only confirm yours.*"[1] His resolution now perfectly assured, Wentworth writes in playful confidence to his kinsman, Wandesford, whose services he relied on to keep him as well as possible with the popular members. He begins by a pleasant piece of humour: "*Returna brevium* is the office of a sheriff indeed,—but in this, that in this high calling (and now sworn too,) I answer your long letter, is more than in justice, scarcely in favour, you could expect from me; and little less than incivility in you thus to abuse a simple gentleman in his place, and put me beyond the length of my tether, it being my part this year, *laconicum agere,* as becomes best, to say truth, a man of affairs,—attendant upon justices, escheators, juries, bankrupts, thieves, and such kind of cattle. Well then, still to pursue, as a good officer should do, the duties of my vocation, I will tell you, my purpose is to carry myself in such a temper, that for my expense it shall participate of moderation and sobriety, without the least tincture of wantonness or petulancy, which will both better express the sense wherewith I take it from above, and be more suiting with that just regard I owe the gentry of this country, to whom I have been so much beholden; of whom I should be too much forgetful, and of my own modesty too, if I did any ways intend (at least as far as my indiscretion could go,) to bring the former licentious custom in again so much to their prejudice. Therefore, in a word, come king, come judge, I will keep myself within the articles made when sir Guy Palmes was sheriff; and run dog, run cat, drink a red ryal by the place at least, by God's leave." He goes through many topics very amusingly, and then observes.

[1] Strafford Papers, vol. i. p. 31.

" *You will partly see by the enclosed, how the pulse beats above,*"—which I take to be an allusion to the letter (he afterwards desires it to be enclosed back to him,) of his friend Ingram, in which the king's feeling had been so favourably expressed. "*For my own part,*" he continues, "*I will commit others to their active heat, myself, according to the season of the year, fold myself up in a cold silent forbearance, apply myself cheerfully to the duties of my place, and heartily pray to God to bless sir Francis Seymour.* For, my rule, which I will not transgress, is, ' *Never to contend with the prerogative out of a parliament ; nor yet to contest with a king but when I am constrained thereunto.*' " [1]

Wentworth faithfully adhered to these intentions ; and while "the great, warm, and ruffling parliament" in London was infusing, by the boldness of its acts and words, new spirit and strength into the country, he remained quiet in Yorkshire, discharging his duty, as his humourous classification had described it, among "justices, escheators, juries, bankrupts, thieves, *and such like cattle.*" It is true he had found time to attend in London for certain purposes that are speedily to be explained, but he did not meddle with parliament matters there, returning to Yorkshire again as quiet as before, and, indeed, a little more contented.[2]

Soon afterwards, before the proceedings of the parliament had closed, and while attending a county meeting in his office of high sheriff, a paper was handed to Wentworth. It was the king's warrant dismissing him from the office he had so ardently desired to hold of custos rotulorum ! Giving way to momentary astonishment and indignation, he publicly told the meeting in

<hr>

[1] Strafford Papers, vol. i. pp. 32—34.   [2] Ibid. p. 35.

what manner he had just been discharged, and that his successor was to be old sir John Savile. "Yet I could wish," he added, "they who succeed me, had forborne this time this service, a place in sooth ill chosen, a stage ill prepared, for venting such poor, vain, insulting humour. I leave it," he concluded, "not conscious of any fault in myself, nor yet guilty of the virtue in my successor, that should occasion this removal."[1]

This was admirable for a *public* display. As soon as he had arrived at Wentworth Wood House, however, he dispatched the following letters, one almost immediately after the other, to "the right honourable sir Richard Weston, knt., chancellor of his majesty's exchequer!" They fully explain, it will be seen, the whole course of Wentworth's recent conduct. "I have been beholden unto you," he begins, "for many courtesies, which in your own particular I will undoubtedly ever thankfully acknowledge. Give me leave then to put you in remembrance of some things wherewith you formerly have been acquainted; as also to give you an account of some things which have happened since. *At the dissolved parliament in Oxford, you are privy how I was moved from and in behalf of the duke of Buckingham, with promise of his good esteem and favour; you are privy that my answer was, I did honour the duke's person, that I would be ready to serve him in the quality of an honest man and a gentleman; you are privy, that the duke took this in good part, sent me thanks; as for respects done him, you are privy, how during that sitting I performed what I had professed. The consequence of all this was the making me sheriff the winter after. It is true, the duke, a little before Whitsuntide last, at Whitehall, in*

<hr>

[1] Strafford Papers, vol. i. p. 36.

*your presence, said, it was done without his grace's know-
ledge, that he was then in Holland.   At Whitehall, Easter
term last, you brought me to the duke, his grace did, before
you, contract (as he pleased to term it) a friendship with
me, all former mistakes laid asleep, forgotten.   After, I
went, at my coming out of town, to receive his commands,
to kiss his grace's hands, where I had all the good words
and good usage which could be expected, which bred in
me a great deal of content, a full security.   Now the consequence here again is, that even yesterday I received his
majesty's writ for the discharging me of the poor place of
custos rotulorum which I held here,* whose good pleasure
shall be cheerfully obeyed ; yet I cannot but observe as
ill luck of it, that the reward of my long, painful, and
loyal service to his majesty in that place, is to be thus
cast off without any fault laid to my charge that I hear
of, and that his grace too was now in England.   I have
therefore troubled you with this unartificial relation to
show you the singleness of my heart, resting in all
assurance justly confident, you shall never find that I
have for my own part in a tittle transgressed from what
had passed betwixt us.   All which I confess, indeed, to
this bare intent and purpose and no other, that I might
preserve myself in your opinion a man of plainness and
truth.   Which obtained I have fully my end, and so I
rest in the constant condition of your truly affectionate
friend to dispose of, THOMAS WENTWORTH."   The courteous conclusions of Wentworth's letters have a signi-
ficancy at times.   The next letter to Weston, following
up the purpose of the last, runs thus : " *Calling to mind
the faithful service I had the honour to do his majesty
now with God, how graciously he vouchsafed to accept and
express it openly and sundry times, I enjoy within myself*

much comfort and contentment. On the other side, albeit therein still strongly dwell entire intentions (and by God's goodness shall, with me to my grave) towards his sacred majesty that now is, yet I may well apprehend the weight of his indignation, being put out of all commissions, wherein formerly I had served and been trusted. This makes me sensible of my misfortune, though not conscious of any inward guilt, which might occasion it; resting infinitely ambitious, not of new employment, *but much rather to live under the smile than the frown of my sovereign.* In this strait, therefore, give me leave to recommend to you the protection of my innocence; *and to beseech you, at some good opportunity, to represent unto his majesty my tender and unfeigned grief for his disfavour, my fears also that I stand before his justice and goodness clad in the malevolent interpretations, and prejudiced by the subtle insinuations, of my adversaries;* and lastly, my only and humble suit, that his majesty will princely deign, that either my insufficiency or fault may be shown me; to this only end, that if insufficiency, I may know where and how to improve myself, and be better enabled to present hereafter more ripe and pleasing fruits of my labours in his service; if a fault, that I may either confess my error and beg his pardon, or else, which I am most confident I shall do, approve myself throughout an honest well-affected loyal subject, with full plain and upright satisfaction to all that can, by the greatest malice or disguised untruth, be objected against me. The contentment of others in my actions is but subordinate, and consequently neither my principal study nor care. Thus have I presumed upon you, further than any particular interest of mine can warrant, out of a general belief in your wisdom and nobleness, *the rather too because I conceive you can best witness the opinion, nay I might say the esteem, his late majesty held of me.* All which, nevertheless, as in good manners and discretion I ought, I submit wholly to your best pleasure, *without importunately pressing further herein than may stand with your conveniency,* your other respects, and, however, retain with me the lasting truth of your honour's most humbly, most readily to be commanded, THOMAS WENTWORTH." [1]

It did not suit with Weston's convenience to answer these letters at the time, but it is probable that no word of them was withheld from the king. Buckingham was still too powerful to be in any thing gainsayed, and it was clear that he had formed a violent dislike to Wentworth. He sought now to mortify him as much as possible through the means of Savile. The son of the " old knight," or the " old cavalier," as one of Wentworth's correspondents [2] calls him, was promoted to a barony and an office in the household. It is not difficult, on mature consideration, to assign an intelligible reason for these proceedings by Buckingham, though at first they appear startlingly gratuitous. He had, in truth, an equal motive to be jealous of Wentworth, in the way of favour, as in that of opposition. While it is possible that he did not very clearly understand the policy that had been shown by Wentworth in either case, it is more than probable that he feared to be undone by him in both. In

---

[1] Strafford Papers, vol. i. pp. 34, 35.

[2] Lord Mansfield, who appears to have remonstrated with the duke of Buckingham himself, while Wentworth thus remonstrated, as it were, with the king, respecting the late proceedings. " I writ my mind," says Mansfield to Wentworth, " at full to my lord duke ; and, I protest to God, no more sparing the old cavalier or his nature than I would speak of him to you, nor mincing my desires or my nature, which is not to do curtesies for injuries." It is most probable that this was done at Wentworth's desire. See Papers, vol. i. p. 43.

favour, he might already have received occasion to suppose Wentworth likely to prove a formidable rival, (not dreaming that a large capacity could never so impose upon Charles as a mean one) ; and in opposition, he may still have thought him too likely to be dangerous, for a perfect trust. Nor was he without reason for suspicion, at least, on the latter score. Wandesford, the most intimate friend and kinsman of the quiet sheriff, had been one of the most active managers of the impeachment in the last session. And there were other causes of dread. Wentworth had had some communication with the intriguing archbishop Williams, and worse than all, was known to have frequently visited the person whom the duke more deeply feared, the archbishop Abbot. I quote from Abbot's narrative " concerning his disgrace at court," a passage elucidatory on this point. In describing the three of his acquaintances to whom exception had been taken by Buckingham, ("I know from the court, by a friend," he interposes, "that my house for a good space of time hath been watched, and I marvel that they have not rather named sixty than three,") the archbishop observes, "the third was sir Thomas Wentworth, who had good occasion to send unto me, and sometimes to see me, because we were joint executors to sir George Savile [1], who married his sister, and was my pupil at Oxford; to whose son also sir Thomas Wentworth and I were guardians, as may appear in the court of wards, and many things passed between us in that behalf; yet, to my rememberance, I saw not this gentleman but once in these three quarters of a year last past ; at which time he came to seek his brother-in-law,

---

[1] Sir George, it may be remarked, was not a "Yorkshire Savile."

E

the lord Clifford, who was then with me at dinner at Lambeth.[1]

The second parliament dissolved, privy seals were now issuing. Savile, still hot against his old opponent, prevailed with the court to send Wentworth a privy seal. The latter received it while his recent overtures to Weston remained yet unaccepted. It had the appearance of a cold rejection of them.[2] Still he hesitated as to his course. "I have been here now some two or three months," writes lord Baltimore to him, "a spectator upon this great scene of state, where I have no part to play; but you have; for which your friends are sorry. It is your enemies that bring you on the stage, where they have a hope to see you act your own notable harm; and therefore keep yourself off, I beseech you, *et redimas te quam queas minimo.*"[3] A letter from lord Haughton followed. "It was supposed," he informs Wentworth, "this humour of committing had been spent, till that your antagonist did revive it; who, I hear, brags he hath you in a toil or dilemma; *if you refuse, you shall run the fortune of the other delinquents; if you come in at the last hour into the vineyard, he hopes it will lessen you in the country.*"[4] Such was indeed the dilemma, the toil, in which Wentworth found himself; — but he hesitated still! His friends now became extremely anxious, and letter upon letter was dispatched to him. Their general cry was one of dissuasion, but in all events of immediate decision.[5] Lord Clifford wrote several times in anxious

---

[1] Rushworth, vol. i. p. 451. Written about the year 1628-9.

[2] In the Life of Eliot, I have sufficiently explained the court practices at this time. Privy seals were generally addressed to the "disaffected" only.

[3] Strafford Papers, vol. i. p. 37.   [4] Ibid.

[5] See the Papers, vol. i. pp. 37—40.

solicitude. "Your friends here do think, you take the best course in writing to the commissioners and coming up instantly, *if you are not yet resolved to lend:* but that being the point we all wish you would grant us; for, without that, we can have no hope of your safety for your health or person. *Then, the deferring of the answer will so lessen the gift, as the acceptance of it would be but faint and cold.* Whereas, if you would now assent to slip the money into some commissioner's hand, you might wave the trouble to appear, either in the country or here. I must tell you, that I have met here with many that are persuaded that you struck a tally here yourself when you were at London, and my answer to such was ignorance. Another sort there are, who inquire much after your coming up, and these I conceive not out of any good affection, because some of them have relation to old sir John." Lord Baltimore wrote more earnestly still. "If you resolve betimes to take this course, which I would to God you would, it may be yet interpreted obedience to your sovereign, and zeal to his service; *and whatsoever slackness hath been in it hitherto may be excused by your friends here, either by indisposition of health, or some other reason,* which your own judgment can better dictate unto you than my advice. I should say much more to you were you here, which is not fit for paper; but never put off the matter to your appearance here, for God's sake; but send your money in to the collectors in the country without more ado. *Your friends are much perplexed and in fear of you, and none more than I.*" Wentworth, thus driven, made up his mind, at last, to refuse to lend. He could no longer conceal from himself that a crisis had arrived, and he was not ignorant of a means (though he might have hitherto wished to avoid some incidents attached to it,) that would possibly force from it a perfect triumph.   He refused the loan, and was summoned to the council table at London.   He did not omit an opportunity to his main purpose that seemed to offer itself here.   Wandesford describes it in a letter written to him after his committal to the Marshalsea. "Now that you are reckoned with the afflicted, a man may pray safely for your deliverance ; and, seeing it would be no better, I am glad you come in so fair, and so-handsomely upon the point itself. *Sir Arthur tells me, the president reports well of your carriage at the table.* I shall be glad to hear of you in your present confinement, lest that prison and this season give you a nightcap in earnest."[1]

He only remained six weeks in the Marshalsea.   He was then removed to Dartford in Kent, where, Radcliffe observes, he "was not to go above two miles from that town."   This was an easy imprisonment, and, easy as it was, was still more alleviated by the presence of the lady Arabella.   She had already presented him with a boy, and, during his present restriction, gave birth to a girl.   The letters of her brother, Denzil Hollis, written at this period to Wentworth, are very delightful in many respects[2], and, in the disastrous news of the court schemes which they supplied, may have served to strengthen his present patriotic purposes.   "I am most glad," he writes, "to hear my sister is in so fair a way of recovering strength, since she last made you the second time a father : I wish she may many times do it to both your comforts, and every time still with more comfort than the former ; that yet in our private respects we may have

_____

[1] Strafford Papers, vol. i. p. 39.
[2] See Strafford Papers, vol. i. pp. 40—42.

some cause of joy, since the public affords us so little for you see how that goes on *de mal en pis*, as the French say." He then gives a vivid account of the melancholy Isle of Rhée expedition, and describing the numbers that had been lost, pleasantly concludes thus :—" In the mean time we have lost many good men, yet let us make the best of it, and, I hope, it will make our wives, instead of bearing wenches, which of late you say they have been much given to, fall to bringing of boys, young soldiers for the reincrew of our army : and I know no reason but mine should begin ; and she had as good do it at first, for if she do not, at her peril, I hope to make her go again for it ; and when my sister Arabella shall see how mine is served, I hope she will take fair warning, and do as she should do ; but I fear not her so much, for she has begun pretty well already. And now I will close my letter as you do yours (with thanks by the way for it, as also for the whole letter), heartily praying she may so continue, to make you a glad father of many goodly and godly boys,—and some wenches among, lest the seventh work miracles, as old wives will tell us,—and herself to be a joyful and good mother, as I know she is a good and loving wife, and long may she so be to your comfort and her own."

Wentworth and the other recusants released, they met, under the circumstances of extreme excitement which have been already described, in the famous third parliament. It is scarcely necessary to remark here, that the under current of intrigue which had been set in motion by Wentworth, was only known to his convenient friend Wandesford. It is not likely, from the tone of Hollis's letters, that he had ever been made acquainted with it. For the rest of the patriots, with the exception of the keen-sighted Eliot, they all held well with Wentworth, as a great and valuable supporter of the popular cause. He had long been known for his talents; their outburst in behalf of liberal principles had long, by a certain section of the leaders, been anxiously watched for; and now, disappointing none, even of those who had known them longest, and looked for them most impatiently, they burst forth amidst the delighted cheers of the house, and with a startling effect upon the court.

On the discussion of the general question of grievances, Wentworth rose. " May this day's resolution," he solemnly began, "be as happy, as I conceive the proposition which now moves 'me to rise, to be seasonable and necessary! For whether we shall look upon the king or his people, it did never more behove this great physician, the parliament, to effect a true consent amongst the parties than now. This debate carries with it a double aspect; towards the sovereign, and towards the subject; though both be innocent, yet both are injured; both to be cured. In the representation of injuries I shall crave your attention; in the cure, I shall beseech your equal cares, and better judgments. In the greatest humility I speak it, these illegal ways are punishments and marks of indignation. The raising of money by loans; strengthened by commission, with unheard-of instructions; the billeting of soldiers by the lieutenants; —have been as if they could have persuaded Christian princes, nay worlds, that the right of empire was to take away goods by strong hand; and they have endeavoured, as far as was possible for them, to do it. This hath not been done by the king (under the pleasing shade of whose crown, I hope we shall ever gather the fruits of justice), but by projectors; these have extended the prerogative of the king beyond its just limits, so as to mar the sweet harmony of the whole."

Wentworth then burst suddenly, and with great dramatic effect, (he studied this at all times) into the following rapid and passionate invective. "They have rent from us the light of our eyes! enforced companies of guests worse than the ordinances of France! vitiated our wives and daughters before our faces! brought the crown to greater want than ever it was, by anticipating the revenue; —and can the shepherd be thus smitten, and the flock not be scattered? They have introduced a privy council, ravishing, at once, the spheres of all ancient government! imprisoning us without bail or bond! They have taken from us—what shall I say? *Indeed what have they left us?* They have taken from us all means of supplying the king, and ingratiating ourselves with him, by tearing up the roots of all property; which, if they be not seasonably set again into the ground by his majesty's hand, we shall have, instead of beauty, baldness!"

For this, in the noblest language, the orator proposed his remedy. "By one and the same thing hath the king and people been hurt, and by the same must they be cured:—to vindicate—what? New things? No! our ancient, lawful, and vital liberties! by reinforcing of the ancient laws made by our ancestors; by setting such a stamp upon them, as no licentious spirit shall dare hereafter to enter upon them. And shall we think this a way to break a parliament? No; our desires are modest and just. I speak truly, both for the interest of the king and people. If we enjoy not these, it will be impossible to relieve him: therefore let us never fear but they will be accepted by his goodness. Wherefore I shall descend to my motion, which consists of four parts: two of which have relation to the persons, and two to the property of our goods. 1st. For our persons, the freedom of them from imprisonment, and from employments abroad, against our own consents, contrary to the ancient customs of this kingdom. 2d. For our goods, that no levies may be made, but by parliament; and no billeting of soldiers. It is most necessary that these be resolved, and that the subjects may be secured in both. Then, for the manner, it will be fit to determine it by a grand committee."[1]

Wentworth sustained, through the short but important proceedings of the session, the reputation he had achieved by this speech in the house and the country. He spoke on all the great questions and emergencies that occurred. Only two of his speeches, however, remain in any completeness. The second was delivered on one of secretary Cooke's pressing applications for the subsidies. "I cannot help lamenting," he said, "the unlawful courses and slights, for which the only excuse is necessity. We are required to give; but before we can resolve to give, it must be determined what we have to give. What heavy fogs have of late darkened our hemisphere, and yet hang over us, portending our ruin, none is so weak as to be ignorant of! What unsteady courses to dispel these mists, have been pursued, and thereby raised near us great storms, I take no pleasure to remember,—yet, in all bodies diseased, the knowledge precedes the cure. I will shortly tell the principals; next their remedies. I must reduce them into two heads: 1. whereby our persons have been injured; 2. whereby our estates have suffered."

"Our persons have been injured," continued Wentworth

---

[1] From a MS. in the Harleian Library. See Parl. Hist. vol. vii. pp. 369—371.

more earnestly, "both by imprisonment without law—nay, against law, boundless and without bank!—and by being designed to some office, charge, and employment, foreign or domestic, as a brand of infamy and mark of disgrace. Oh! Mr. Speaker, when it may not be safe to deny payments upon unjust exactions, but we must go to prison for it,—nor in this place, to speak our consciences, but we must be stamped to unwilling and unfitting employments! Our estates have been racked two ways; one in the loan, wherein five subsidies were exacted; and that by commission of men of quality, and instructions to prosecute the same, with an asperity which no times can parallel! And hence the other consideration, of the projectors and executioners of it. Nay, this was not all, but ministers, in their pulpits, have preached it as gospel, and damned the refusers of it—so then we are already doomed to damnation!

"Let no man," he said, in conclusion, after proposing a committee for grievances, "judge this way a break-neck of parliaments: but a way of honour to the king, nay of profit; for besides the supply which we shall readily give him, suitable to his occasions, we give him our hearts. *Our hearts, Mr. Speaker, a gift that God calls for, and fit for a king!*"[1]

There may have been more passion than logic in these speeches, but they had their effect. The court now saw more thoroughly the man they had discarded, and Weston hastened to answer his last letter! He reasoned here not unjustly—that it could scarcely be too late at any time to answer a letter, which in its terms so clearly proved the non-existence of any *lasting* obstacle, such as a firm point of principle. The present conduct of Wentworth,

---

[1] Parl. Hist., vol. vii. p. 442.

to Weston at least, could appear no other than a temporary resource.   Even Buckingham's continued objections
were therefore set aside, and, before the conclusion of
the session, a negotiation with Wentworth had opened;
—nay, almost before the burning words which have just
been transcribed, had cooled from off the lips of the
speaker, a transfer of his services to the court was decided
on!   We have indisputable evidence, that, on the 28th of
May, Finch was acting as a go-between.[1]   On the 26th
of June the parliament was prorogued.   On the 14th of
July sir Thomas Wentworth was created Baron Wentworth, and called to the privy council.   It is clear,
however, that *at the same time* he had stipulated to be
made a viscount, and lord president of the North [2], but
this apparently could not be done, till the death of
Buckingham had removed a still lingering obstacle.[3]

I have thus endeavoured to trace at greater length,
and with greater exactness than has been attempted
hitherto, the opening passages in the political history

---

[1] Strafford Papers, vol. i. p. 46.

[2] See Papers, vol. ii. p. 390.

[3] A passage in Rushworth (vol. viii. p. 768.) is corroborative of
the view which I have presented of Wentworth's public conduct.
The collector professes to give all those parliamentary speeches "in
which my lord of Strafford so discovered his wit and temper, that
the court took particular notice of him," and gives only the speeches
that were delivered in this third parliament.   It is clear that he had
not rendered himself at all formidable before.   Rushworth, indeed,
subsequently sets this at rest, by adding,—"*Now* he began to be
more generally taken notice of by all men, and his fame to spread
abroad, where public affairs, and the criticisms of the times, were
discoursed by the most refined judgments; those who were infected
with popularity flattering themselves that he was inclined to support
their inclination, and would prove a champion on that account; but
such discourse, as it endeared him to his country, so it begot to him
an interest in the bosom of his prince, who (having a discerning
judgment of men) quickly made his observation of Wentworth's, that
he was a person framed for great affairs, and fit to be near his royal
person and councils."

of this extraordinary man. The common and vulgar account given by Heylin [1] has been, it is believed, exploded, along with that of the no less vulgar Hacket. [2] All Wentworth's movements in the path which has been followed, appear to me to be perfectly natural and intelligible, if his true character is kept in view. From the very intensity of the aristocratic principle within him, arose his hesitation in espousing at once the interests of the court. This, justly and carefully considered, will be found the solution of his reluctant advances, and still more reluctant retreats. The intervention of a favourite was hardly supportable by one whose ambition, as he felt obliged to confess to himself even then, would be satisfied with nothing short of the dignity of becoming "the king's mistress, to be cherished and courted by none but himself." He was to be understood, and then invited,—rather than forced to an explicit declaration, and then only accepted. The purpose of the alternating attraction and repulsion of his proceedings, such as I have described them, submissive and refractory, might have been obvious, indeed, to an obtuser perception than Buckingham's, but that mediocrity will always find its little account in crushing rather than winning over genius, and is rendered almost as uncomfortable by an uncongenial coadjutor as by a strenuous opponent. Wentworth's conduct, at the last, was forced upon him by circumstances :—but his energetic support of the Petition of Rights was only the completion of a series of hints, all of which had been more or less intelligible ; and, even now, unwillingly understood as *this* was by the minister, it was yet more reluctantly acted upon, for by Buckingham's death alone, as we are informed, the "great bar" to

---

[1] Life of Laud, p. 194.   [2] Scrinia Reserata.

Wentworth's advancement was removed.[1]   It may be added, that, even in all these circumstances, when many steps were forced upon him, which his proud spirit but poorly submitted to, and wronged itself in submitting to, it is yet possible to perceive a quality in his nature which was afterwards more fully developed.   He was possessed with a rooted aversion, from the first, to the court flies that buzzed around the monarch, and as little inclined to suffer their good offices as to deprecate their hostility. The receipt, shortly after this, of divers ill-spelt and solemn sillinesses from the king, seems to have occasioned a deep and enduring gratitude in him, for the dispensing with a medium that had annoyed him.   "I do with infinite sense," writes he, "consider your majesty's great goodness, not only most graciously approving of that address of mine immediately to yourself, but allowing it unto me hereafter, which I shall rest myself upon as my greatest support on earth, and make bold to practise, yet I trust without importunity or sauciness."   The few attempts to ingratiate himself with the queen, which were ultimately forced on Wentworth by his declining fortunes, were attended with but faint success, and he appears to have impressed her, on the whole, with little beyond the prettiness of his hands, which she allowed to be "the finest in the world"[2]—to the prejudice of his head, which she was not so inclined to preserve.

In one word, what it is desired to impress upon the reader, before the delineation of Wentworth in his after years, is this—*that he was consistent to himself through-*

[1] Biog. Britt., vol. vii. p. 4179.

[2] This is told us by madame de Motteville, who repeats what Henrietta had said to her :—" Il était laid, mais assez agréable de sa personne ; et la reine, me contant toutes ces choses, s'arreta pour me dire qu'il avait les plus belles mains du monde."

out. I have always considered that much good wrath is thrown away upon what is usually called "apostacy." In the majority of cases, if the circumstances are thoroughly examined, it will be found that there has been "no such thing." The position on which the acute Roman thought fit to base his whole theory of Æsthetics—

> " Humano capiti cervicem pictor equinam
> Jungere si velit, et varias inducere plumas,
> Undique collatis membris, ut turpiter atram
> Desinat in piscem mulier formosa supernè,
> Spectatum admissi risum teneatis, amici?" &c.

—is of far wider application than to the exigencies of an art of poetry; and those who carry their researches into the moral nature of mankind, cannot do better than impress upon their minds, at the outset, that in the regions they explore, they are to expect no monsters— no essentially discordant termination to any "mulier formosa supernè." Infinitely and distinctly various as appear the shifting hues of our common nature when subjected to the prism of CIRCUMSTANCE, each ray into which it is broken is no less in itself a primitive colour, susceptible, indeed, of vast modification, but incapable of further division. Indolence, however, in its delight for broad classifications, finds its account in overlooking this; and among the results, none is more conspicuous than the long list of apostates with which history furnishes us. It is very true, it may be admitted, that when we are informed by an old chronicler that, "at this time, Ezzelin changed totally his disposition,"—or by a modern biographer that, "at such a period, Tiberius first became a wicked prince,"—we examine too curiously if we consider such information as in reality regarding other than the act done, and the popular inference recorded ; beyond which it was no part of the writer to inquire. But such historians as these value themselves materially on their dispensation of good or evil fame ; and as the "complete change," so dramatically recounted, has commonly no mean influence on the nature of their award, the observations I have made may be of service to the just estimate of their more sweeping conclusions.

Against all such conclusions I earnestly protest in the case of the remarkable personage whose ill-fated career we are now retracing. Let him be judged sternly, but in no unphilosophic spirit. In turning from the bright band of patriot brothers to the solitary Strafford—"a star which dwelt apart"—we have to contemplate no extinguished splendour, razed and blotted from the book of life. Lustrous, indeed, as was the gathering of the lights in the political heaven of this great time, even that radiant cluster might have exulted in the accession of the "comet beautiful and fierce," which tarried a while within its limits ere it "dashed athwart with train of flame." But it was governed by other laws than were owned by its golden associates, and—impelled by a contrary, yet no less irresistible force, than that which restrained them within their eternal orbits—it left them, never to "float into that azure heaven again."

Before attending Wentworth to his presidency in the North, we may stop to consider one of those grand features in his character, on which many subordinate considerations depend, and a proper understanding of which ought to be brought, as a first requisite, to the just observation of his measures.

I cannot believe Wentworth to have been the vain man popular opinion has pronounced him, nor discover in him any of that overweening and unwarranted self-confidence, which friends no less than foes have laid to his charge. An arrogance, based on the supposed possession of pre-eminent qualities which have no existence, is one thing; and the calm perception of an undoubted superiority, is another. Wentworth, indeed, "stood like a tower"—but that unshaken confidence did not "suddenly scale the light." Its stately proportions were slowly evolved; its eventual elevation unavoidable, and amply vindicated. We have met with no evidences of a refractory or self-sufficient disposition in the youth of Wentworth? His studies at Cambridge had a prosperous issue, and he ever remembered his college life with affection. "I am sorry to speak it, but truth will out," writes he to Laud concerning an episcopal delinquent, "this Bishop is a St. John's man—of Oxford, I mean, not Cambridge; our Cambridge panniers never brought such a fairing to the market."[1] His deep esteem for his tutor,

[1] Strafford Papers, vol. i. p. 189. Laud makes merry upon this happy phrase of the lord deputy's. The passages are characteristic of the correspondence, and therefore worth quoting. "And so your Lordship," he writes, "is very sorry to tell the truth, but only that it will out. A St. John's man you say he is, and of Oxford—your Cambridge panniers never brought such a fairing to the market. Yes, my good lord, but it hath; for what say you of dean Palmer? Who, besides his other virtues, sold all the lead off from the church at Peterburgh; yet he was brought in your Cambridge panniers; and so was bishop Howland too, who used that bishoprick, as well as he did the deanary. I must confess this man's baseness hath not many fellows, but his bribery may have store. And I pray, is that ever a whit the less fault, because it is gentleman-like for hundreds and thousands? Whereas this man deals for twenty shillings and less. I hope you will not say so, and if you do not, then I pray examine your Cambridge panniers again, for some say such may be found there, but I for my part will not believe it, unless your lordship make me." Wentworth appears to have contested this point in Laud's own humour. The bishop retorts by asking him what his "Jonnism," means. "Now you are merry again. God hold it. And what? Dr. Palmer acted like a king? Be it so. But he was another card in the pack. As for bishop Howland, you never

Greenwood, reflects honour on both parties. I have said that it was originated by good services performed, and so, perhaps, it is necessary to limit all Strafford's likings —all, except the fatal one which cost him life, his liking for the weak and unworthy king, which had its origin in that abstract veneration for power, which (or rather, as he afterwards too late discovered, the semblance of which) we have just seen him by some practices beneath his nature, climbing up to, and in the exercise of which, we are to view him hereafter. But his esteem for Greenwood, whatever its origin, was not to have been provoked by truckling sycophancy. Nothing of that sort would have succeeded in impressing its object with so profound a respect as dictates the following paragraph in an interesting letter to his nephew and ward, sir W. Savile. "In these, and all things else, you shall do passing well to consult Mr. Greenwood, who hath seen much, is very well able to judge, and certainly most faithful to you. If you use him not most respectively, you deal extreme ungrateful with him, and ill for yourself. He was the man your father loved and trusted above all men, and did as faithfully discharge the trust reposed in him, as ever in my time I knew any man do for his dead friend, taking excessive pains in settling your estate with· all possible cheerfulness, without charge to you at all. His

---

heard of him. What? Nor of Jeames his wife neither? Good Lord, how ignorant you can be when you list. Yea but you have taken St. John's Ox. *Flagrante crimine,* and I put you to your memory. Is it so? Come on then : you know there is a cause in the Star-Chamber ; some were to answer, and they brought their answers ready written. If the bishop of Lincoln sent them ready for his turn, hath he not an excellent forge? What if this appear? I hope you will not then say I put you to your memory. 'Tis now under examination, and is not this if, &c. *flagrante crimine ?* Go brag now."

advice will be always upright, and you may safely pour your secrets into him, which, by that time you have conversed a little more abroad in the world, you will find to be the greatest and noblest treasure this world can make any man owner of; and I protest to God, were I in your place, I would think him the greatest and best riches I did or could possess."[1] In the same letter, Wentworth assures this youth — "you cannot consider yourself, and advise and debate your actions with your friends too much; and, till such time as experience hath ripened your judgment, it shall be great wisdom and advantage to distrust yourself, and to fortify your youth by the counsel of your more aged friends, before you undertake anything of consequence. It was the course that I governed myself by after my father's death, with great advantage to myself and affairs; and yet my breeding abroad had shown me more of the world than yours hath done, and I had natural reason like other men; only I confess I did in all things distrust myself, wherein you shall do, as I said, extremely well, if you do so too."[2] There is no self-sufficiency here!

Wentworth's method of study has been transmitted to us by sir George Radcliffe, and I quote it in strong corroboration of the view which has been urged. "He writ," Radcliffe assures us, "as well as he spoke: this perfection he attained, first, by reading well penned authors in French, English, and Latin, and observing their expressions; secondly, by hearing of eloquent men, which he did diligently in their sermons and publick speeches; thirdly, by a very great care and industry, which he used when he was young, in penning his epistles

---

[1] Papers, vol. i. p. 170.
[2] Ibid. p. 169.

and missives of what subject soever; but above all, he had a natural quickness of wit and fancy, with great clearness of judgement, and much practice, without which his other helps, of reading and hearing, would not have brought him to that great perfection to which he attained. I learned one rule of him, which I think worthy to be remembered : *when he met with a well penned oration or tract upon any subject or question, he framed a speech upon the same argument, inventing and disposing what seemed fit to be said upon that subject, before he read the book ; then reading the book, compare his own with the author, and note his own defects, and the author's art and fulness ;* whereby he observed all that was in the author more strictly, and might better judge of his own wants to supply them."[1]   Now this early habit of confronting, so to speak, the full grown wits of other men—of satisfying himself of his own precise intellectual height by thoroughly scanning the acknowledged stature of the world's giants—is as much removed from a rash assumption as from the nervous apprehension of mediocrity.

Wentworth's temper was passionate; and it is curious and instructive, in the present view of his character, to mark the steps he took in relation to this. I have already spoken of his extreme cautiousness; of the select council that canvassed his business, suggested his measures, and revised his correspondence; of his deference to advice, and indeed, submission to reproof, from his assured friends. " He was naturally exceeding choleric," says sir George Radcliffe, "an infirmity with which he had great wrestlings; and though he kept a watchfulness over himself concerning it, yet it could not be so prevented, but sometimes upon sudden occasions

---

[1] Papers, vol. ii. p. 435.

it would break. He had sundry friends that often admonished him of it; and he had the great prudence to take in good part such admonitions: nay, I can say that I, one of his most intimate friends, never gained more upon his trust and affection, than by this freedom with him, in telling him of his weaknesses. For he was a man and not an angel, yet such a man as made a conscience of his ways, and did endeavour to grow in virtue and victory over himself, and made good progress accordingly." This " good progress " brought him eventually to a very efficient self-control. In cases where he would seem to have exceeded it, and to have been transported beyond decency and prudence, it would be hasty to assume, as Clarendon and other writers have done, that it was in mere satisfaction of his will. These writers, it will not be difficult to show, have not that excuse for the failure of their principles in Wentworth's person. The truth was that, as in the case of Napoleon and other great masters of the despotic art, anger was one of the instruments of his policy. He came to know when to be in a passion, and flew into a passion accordingly. " You gave me a good lesson to be patient," he writes to old secretary Cooke, " and indeed my years and natural inclinations give me heat more than enough, which however, I trust, more experience shall cool, and a watch over myself in time altogether overcome; in the mean space, in this at least it will set forth itself more pardonable, because my earnestness shall ever be for the honour, justice, and profit of my master; and *it is not always anger, but the misapplying of it, that is the vice so blameable, and of disadvantage to those that let themselves loose thereunto.*" [1]

In the same despatch to the secretary from which I

---

[1] Strafford Papers, vol. i. p. 87.

have taken the above, he had observed, immediately before,—" Nor is it one of my least comforts that I shall have the means to resort to so wise and well affected a friend to me as I esteem yourself, and to a servant that goes the same way to my master's ends that I do; and therefore let me adjure you, by all the interests that I may or would have in you, that as you will (I am sure) assist me when I am right, so by your sensible and grave counsel, reduce me when I may happen to tread awry."[1] And thus, from the first, is Wentworth found soliciting the direction of others in all important conjunctures; not, indeed, with the vague distress of one unprovided with expedients of his own, and disposed to adopt the first course that shall be proposed, but with the calm purpose of one decided on the main course to be pursued, yet not unwilling that it receive the corroboration, or undergo the modification, of an experienced adviser. This has been occasionally illustrated in the business of his nomination by the king for the office of sheriff, where, having already chosen his party, he submits his determination to his father-in-law, the earl of Clare, whose answer has been quoted. I have mentioned also his practice of transmitting duplicates of his despatches on all urgent occasions to Laud, Cooke, and Cottington.

No passage, indeed, in the career of Wentworth proves him to have been a vain man. His singular skill is never satisfied, without an unremitting application of means to any desired end, and the neglect of no circumstance, the most minute and apparently trivial, that may conduce to its success. Would he ensure his own return for a county, and smuggle in a ministerial candidate under the wing of his own popularity?—He proceeds as though his personal

---

[1] Strafford Papers, vol. i. p. 87.

merits could in no way influence the event, and all his hopes are founded on the activity of his friends, which he leaves no stone unturned to increase. *In one and the same day*, sir Thomas Gower, high sheriff of York, is informed that—" Being, at the entreaty of some of my best friends, resolved to try the affections of my country-men in the next election of knights for the shire, I could do no less than take hold of this fit occasion to write unto you these few lines. Wherein I must first give you thanks for the good respect you have been pleased to show towards me, to some of my good friends who moved you for your just and equal favour at the time of the election ; which, as I will be found ready to deserve and affectionately to requite, so must I here solicit you for the continuance of your good purposes towards me ; and lastly desire to understand from you, what day the county falls out upon (which is to be the next after the receipt of the writ), that so I may provide myself and friends to give our first voices for Mr. Secretary, and the second for myself."—Sir Henry Bellasis assured that—" Presently upon my return from London, I find by Mr. Carre, how much I am beholden unto you for your good affection. In truth I do not desire it out of any ambition, but rather to satisfy some of my best friends, and such as have most power over me. Yet, if the country make choice of me, surely I will zealously perform the best service for them that my means or understanding shall enable me unto. And having thus far upon this occasion declared myself, must take it as a great testimony of affection in them that shall afford me their voices, and those of their friends for Mr. secretary Calvert in the prime, and myself in the second place. Particularly am I hereby to give you therefore thanks, and will so settledly lodge this favour in my heart, that I will not fail to remember and deserve it. *In my next letters I will likewise let Mr. Secretary know your good respect and kindness towards him, whereof I dare assure you he will not be unmindful.* The election day will fall out very unhappily upon Christmas-day; but it is irremediless, and therefore must be yielden unto. If you will please to honour me with the company of yourself and friends upon that day at dinner, I shall take it as a second and especial favour: in retribution whereof you shall find me still conversant, as occasion shall be ministered, in the unfeigned and constant offices of your very assured and affectionate friend."—Sir Henry Savile instructed that—" I have received your two letters, and in them both find matter to thank you for your respect and kindness towards me. The later of them I received just the afternoon I came out of town, *but I write effectually to Mr. Secretary for a burgess-ship for you at Richmond, in regard I knew my lord of Cumberland was partly engaged: but I will amongst them work out one, or I will miss far of my aim.* So soon as I hear from Mr. Secretary, I will give you further certainty herein; in the mean time, methinks it were not amiss if you tried your ancient power with them of Aldborow, which I leave to your better consideration, and in the mean time not labour the less to make it sure for you elsewhere, if these clowns chance to fail you. The writ, as I hear, is this week gone to the sheriff; so the next county day, which must without hope of alteration be that of the election, falls to be Christmas-day, which were to be wished otherwise; but the discommodity of our friends more upon that day than another makes the favour the greater, our obligation the more, and therefore I hope they will the rather dispense with it. If the old knight should but endanger it, 'faith, we might be reputed men of small power and esteem in the country! but the truth is, I fear him not. If your health serve you, I shall wish your company at York, and that yourself and friends would eat a Christmas pie with me there: I tell you there would be a hearty welcome, and I would take it as an especial favour, so value it, and as such an one remember it."—Sir Matthew Boynton reminded that—" The ancient and near acquaintance that hath been betwixt us causeth me to rank you in the number of my friends; and being moved by my friends to stand second with Mr. secretary Calvert for knight of the shire at this next parliament, I assure myself I might confidently address myself unto you for the voices of yourself and friends in the election, which falls out unfortunately to be upon Christmas-day. But as the trouble of my friends thereby will be the greater, so doth it add to my obligation. I hope likewise to enjoy your company and friends that day at dinner. You shall be in no place better welcome."— And Christopher Wandesford given notice that—" the writ will be delivered by Mr. Radcliffe within these two days to the sheriff, to whom I have written, giving him thanks for his kindness, desiring the continuance thereof. And now, lest you should think me forgetful of that which concerns yourself, I hasten to let you know that I have got an absolute promise of my lord Clifford, *that if I be chosen knight, you shall have a burgess-ship (reserved for me) at Appleby, wherewith I must confess I am not a little pleased, in regard we shall sit there, judge, and laugh together.*"

The reader will remember that all these, with many other letters, are written and despatched on the same day. No apology is necessary for the length at which

I quote them; since, in rescuing them from false and distorted arrangement, much misconception is prevented, and a very valuable means of judgment furnished on Wentworth's general conduct.

He goes on to let sir Thomas Fairfax know, that—"I was at London much intreated, and, indeed, at last enjoined, to stand with Mr. secretary Calvert for to be knight of this shire the next parliament, both by my lord Clifford and himself; which, after I had assented unto, and despatched my letters, I perceived that some of your friends had motioned the like to Mr. Secretary on your behalf, and were therein engaged, which was the cause I writ no sooner unto you. Yet, hearing by my cousin Middleton that, he moving you in my behalf for your voices, you were not only pleased to give over that intendment, but freely to promise us your best assistance,—I must confess I cannot forbear any longer to write unto you how much this courtesy deserves of me; and that I cannot choose but take it most kindly from you, as suitable with the ancient affection which you have always borne me and my house. And presuming of the continuance of your good respect towards me, I must entreat the company of yourself and friends with me at dinner on Christmas-day, being the day of the election, where I shall be most glad of you, and there give you further thanks for your kind respects."—And thus reports progress to Mr. Secretary himself:—"May it please you, sir, the parliament writ is delivered to the sheriff, and he by his faithful promise deeply engaged for you. I find the gentlemen of these parts generally ready to do you service. Sir Thomas Fairfax stirs not; but sir John Savile, by his instruments exceeding busy, intimating to the common sort under hand, that yourself,

being not resiant in the county, cannot by law be chosen, and, being his majesty's secretary and a stranger, one not safe to be trusted by the country;—but all this according to his manner so closely and cunningly as if he had no part therein; neither doth he as yet further declare himself than only that he will be at York the day of the election;—and thus finding he cannot work them from me, labours only to supplant you. I endeavour to meet with him as well as I may, and omit nothing that my poor understanding tells me may do you service. My lord president hath writ to his freeholders on your behalf, and seeing he will be in town on the election day, it were I think very good he would be pleased to show himself for you in the Castle-yard, and that you writ unto him a few lines, taking notice you hear of some opposition, and therefore desire his presence might secure you of fair carriage in the choice. *I have heard, that when sir Francis Darcy opposed sir Thomas Lake in a matter of like nature, the lords of the council writ to sir Francis to desist. I know my lord chancellor is very sensible of you in this business; a word to him, and such a letter, would make an end of all.* Sir, pardon me, I beseech you, for I protest I am in travail till all be sure for you, which imboldens me to propound these things, which notwithstanding I most humbly submit to your judgment. When you have resolved, be pleased to dispatch the bearer back again with your answer, which I shall take care of. There is not any that labours more heartily for you than my lord Darcy. Sir, I wish a better occasion wherein to testify the dutiful and affectionate respects your favours and nobleness may justly require from me."
—Sir Arthur Ingram is then apprised, in a letter which is full of character, that, " as touching the election, we now

grow to some heat; sir John Savile's instruments closely
and cunningly suggesting under hand Mr. Secretary's
non-residence, his being the king's servant, and out of
these reasons by law cannot, and in good discretion
ought not, be chosen of the country; whereas himself is
their martyr, having suffered for them; the patron of the
clothiers; of all others the fittest to be relied on; and
that he intends to be at York the day of the election,—
craftily avoiding to declare himself absolutely.   And thus
he works, having spread this jealousy, that albeit I
persuade myself generally they would give me their prime
voice, yet in good faith I think it very improbable we
shall ever get the first place for Mr. Secretary; nay, I
protest we shall have need of our strength to obtain him
a second election: so as the likeliest way, so far as I am
able to judge, to secure both, will be for me to stand for
the prime, and so cast all my second voices upon him,
which, notwithstanding, we may help by putting him first
in the indenture.   I am exceeding sorry, that the foulness
and length of the way put me out of hope of your
company; and therefore I pray you, let us have your
advice herein by the bearer.   Your letter to your friends
in Halifax admits some question, because you desire
their voices for Mr. Secretary and myself the rather for
that sir John Savile stands not; so, say they, if he stand,
we are left to our liberty.   You will therefore please to
clear that doubt by another letter, which, delivered to
this messenger, I will get sent unto them.   I fear greatly
they will give their second voice with sir John.   Mr.
Leech promised me he would procure his lord's letter to
the freeholders within Hallomshire and the honor of
Pontefract; that my cousin Lascells, my lord's principal
agent in these parts, should himself labour Hallomshire;

Mr. Banister, the learned steward of Pontefract, do the like there; and both of them be present at the election, the better to secure those parts. I hear not any thing of them. I pray you, press Mr. Leech to the performance of his promise; letting him know sir John Savile's friends labour for him, and he declares in a manner he will stand; and get him to send the letters by this my servant. I desire likewise he would intreat my cousin Lascells, that he would take the pains to come over, and speak with me the Monday before Christmas-day here at my house. Sir, you see how bold I am to trouble you, and yet I must desire you would be pleased to afford me the commodity of your house for two nights, to entertain my friends. I shall, God willing, be most careful that nothing be impaired, and shall number this amongst many other your noble courtesies, which have inviolably knit me unto you."—Sir Thomas Dawney is solicited to the same effect, and sir Henry Slingsby informed that— "the certainty I have of sir John Savile's standing, and the various reports I hear of the country people's affection towards Mr. Secretary, makes me desirous to know how you find them inclined in your parts. For this wapentake, as also that of Osgodcross and Staincross, I certainly persuade myself, will go wholly for us. In Skyrack I assure myself of a better part, and I will perform promise with Mr Secretary, bringing a thousand voices of my own besides my friends. Some persuade me, that the better way to secure both, were for me to stand prime, cast all my second voices on Mr. Secretary, and put him first into the indenture. I pray you consider of it, and write me your opinion; *I would not lose substance for such a toyish ceremony.* There is danger both ways: for if Mr. Secretary stand first, it is much to be feared, the country will not stand for him firm and intire against sir John. *If I be first chosen, which I make no question but I could, then is it to be doubted, the people might fly over to the other side, which, notwithstanding, in my conceit, of the two is the more unlikely: for, after they be once settled and engaged for me, they will not be so apt to stir. And again, it may be so suddenly carried, as they shall have no time to move.* At a word, we shall need all our endeavours to make Mr. Secretary, and therefore, sir, I pray you gather up all you possibly can. I would gladly know how many you think we may expect from you. My lord Clifford will be at Tadcaster upon Christmas-eve, about one of the clock: if that be your way, I am sure he would be glad yourself and friends would meet him there; *that so we might go into York the next day, vote, and dine together,* where you shall be most heartily welcome."—Sir Thomas Fairfax is again moved very earnestly to make—" all the strength of friends and number you can to give their voices for us at the next election, falling to be upon Christmas-day; the rather, because *the old gallant of Hooley* intends certainly to stand, whom indeed, albeit I should lightly weigh, were the matter betwixt him and me, yet I doubt Mr. Secretary (if his friends stand not closely to him) being not well known in the country. Sir, you have therefore hereby an opportunity offered to do us all an especial favour, which shall bind us to a ready and chearful requital, when you shall have occasion to use any of us. My lord Clifford will be, God willing, at Tadcaster upon Christmas-eve about one of the clock, where I assure myself he will much desire that yourself and friends will be pleased to meet him, *that so we may go into York together;* and myself earnestly intreat the company of yourself and them the next day at dinner, which I shall esteem as a double favour."—And his cousin Thomas Wentworth advertised that, "being, as you know, engaged to stand with Mr. Secretary Calvert to be knights for this parliament, and sir John Savile our only opponent, I must make use of my friends and intreat them to deal thoroughly for us, in regard the loss of it would much prejudice our estimations above. In which number I esteem yourself, one of my best and fastest friends. The course my lord Darcy and I hold is, *to intreat the high constables to desire the petty constables to set down the names of all freeholders within their townships, and which of them have promised to be at York and bestow their voices with us, so as we may keep the note as a testimony of their good affections, and know whom we are beholden unto,* desiring them further to go along with us to York on Sunday, being Christmas-eve, or else meet us about two of the clock at Tadcaster. I desire you would please to deal effectually with your high constables, and hold the same course, that so we may be able to judge what number we may expect out of your wapentake. As I no ways doubt of your uttermost endeavours and pains in a matter of this nature, deeply touching my credit, so will I value it as a special testimony of your love towards me. I hope you will take the pains to go along with us, together with your friends, to York, *that so we may come all in together,* and take part of an ill dinner with me the next day; where yourself and friends shall be right heartily welcome." [1]

It is not necessary to recall attention to the political principle, or the party views, which are evidenced in

---

[1] These various letters will be found in the Strafford Papers.

these letters[1]; but how singular and complete is the illustration they afford, of Wentworth's practice of letting slip no method, however ordinary, of compassing his designs! Is he interested, either, in the success of a lawsuit?—we find that—" he spent eight years' time, besides his pains and money, in soliciting the business and suits of his nephews sir George and sir William Savile, going every term to London about that only, without missing one term in thirty, as I verily believe. And all this merely in memory of the kindness which had passed betwixt him and his brother-in-law sir George Savile, then deceased."[2] And so with all things that interested him.

To this head, then, the reader is asked to refer many proceedings, which, hitherto, have been cited in proof of an excessive vanity. They were rather the suggestions of a mind well aware of the influence of seeming trifles on the accomplishment of important purposes. The pompous enumeration of his heraldic honours in the preamble to his patent of nobility, and the " extraordinary pomp" with which he was created Viscount and president of the North, were no unnecessary precaution against the surprise and disdain of an insolent herd of courtiers, and were yet ineffectual wholly to restrain their sarcasms.[3] The unexampled splendour of his after progress to the opening of the Irish parliament was, no doubt, well

---

[1] The beginning of electioneering tactics is also curiously discernible in them.

[2] Radcliffe's Essay.

[3] " The duke of Buckingham himself flew not so high in so short a revolution of time. He was made a viscount with a great deal of high ceremony upon a Sunday, in the afternoon, at Whitehall. My lord Powis, who affects him not much, being told that the heralds had fetched his pedigree from the blood royal, viz. from John of Gaunt, said, ' *Dammy, if ever he comes to be king of England, I will turn rebel.*'"—*Epistolæ Howellianæ*, No. 34. edit. 1650. .

calculated to " beget an awful admiration " in the minds
of a body of men whose services he was then preparing
to obtain by far more questionable means ;—and his
fierce resentment of the slightest infringement of the
etiquette he had succeeded in establishing, his minute
arrangements with respect to the ceremony he conceived
necessary to the powers he was entrusted with, have their
censure on other grounds than any intrinsic absurdity
they evince. It seems to me to be high time, in cases
of this sort, to shift our censure to the grosser absurdity
of the principles which require such means for their
support. Ceremony in the abstract—the mere forms of
etiquette, sinking through their own emptiness, sustaining
no purpose, and unsustained by none—Wentworth regarded with a more supreme scorn than they were held
in by any of his prudish opponents among his own party.
"I confess," writes he on one occasion, "this matter of
PLACE I have ever judged *a womanly thing*, and so love
not to trouble myself therewith, more than needs must."
He cares not, moreover, submitting cheerfully throughout
to the king's unworthy arrangement,—that himself should
gather "golden opinions" by a liberal bestowment of
honours in Ireland on the more troublesome of his
suitors, while to his deputy was confided the ungracious
task of interposing a veto on the royal benefaction, and
receiving, in his own person, the curses of the disappointed.[1] Against the bitterness of their discontent,
Wentworth had his unfailing resource. " I shall not
neglect," he writes, " to preserve myself in good opinion
with this people, in regard I become thereby better able
to do my master's service ; longer than it works to that
purpose, I am very indifferent what they shall think, or

---

[1] See Strafford Papers, vol. i. p. 140.

can say, concerning me."   Not the less scruple had he
in complaining of the king's arrangement, when it was
tortured to purposes he had never contemplated, and he
discovered that the character of his government was
become that of an iron rule, wherein reward had no
place, even for its zealous supporters.[1]   For the foolish
gravity of the luckless king had continued to pen epistle
upon epistle, disposing of the most subordinate posts in
the army, as well as the higher dignities of the church.
The system, in the first instance, however, was one which
a proud man, certainly, might submit to, but a vain man
would hardly acquiesce in.

I resume the progress of Wentworth's fortunes.   His
elevation became an instant subject of general remark ;
and it is not difficult to discover, that, in his native
county, where he was best known, the surprise excited
by so sudden a change, after such violent opposition, was
balanced by a greater surprise, on the other hand, that

---

[1] One instance, out of the many which strikingly illustrate Wentworth's character in this respect, may be subjoined. Lord Newburgh
had procured from the king a promise of promotion for a young man
in the Irish army—which the lord deputy felt would be disadvantageous to the public service.   Here are·some passages of his
remonstrance :—" For if I be not favoured so far, as that I may be
able to make myself friends, and draw unto myself some dependence,
by the expectance men may have from me in these places, that so I
may have assistance and cheerful countenance from some, as I have
already purchased the sour and bent brow of some of them ; I foresee, I shall have little honour, comfort, or safety amongst them.
For a man to enforce obedience by punishment only, and be deprived
all means to reward some—to be always in vinegar, never to communicate of the sweet—is, in my estimation of it, the meanest, most
ignoble condition any free spirit can be reduced unto. . . . . The
conclusion therefore is, I am confident his majesty will not debar
me of what (be it spoken under favour) belongs to my place, for all
the solicitation of the pretty busy lord Newburgh, who, if a man
should move his majesty for anything in the gift of the chancellor of
the duchy, would as pertly cackle, and put himself in the way of
complaint, as if he had all the merit and ability in the world to serve
his master."—*Strafford Papers,* vol. i. pp. 136—142.

the honour should have been delayed so long. "Give me leave to inform you," writes sir Richard Hutton[1], in a passage which is expressive of both these feelings, "that your late conferred honour is the subject of much discourse here in Yorkshire, which, I conceive, proceeds from the most, not out of any other cause than their known worth in you, which is thought merited it much sooner and greater; but this is only to entertain you a little longer; for I know that your actions are not justly liable to any censure, I am sure not to mine; for, being yours, it speaks them good to me, if not the best." The character of the important office entrusted to Wentworth included much that was especially grateful to him :— enlarged by his desire, it presented power almost unlimited; freedom at the same time from the little annoyances of the court; and the opportunity of exhibiting his genius for despotic rule in his own county, where personal friends might witness its successes, and old adversaries, should the occasion offer, be made the objects of its triumph. To crown his cause of satisfaction, the duke of Buckingham, who had still hung darkly over his approach to a perfect confidence and favour, was removed by the knife of Felton. Secret congratulations passed, within a few days after this event, between Wentworth and Weston. Every thing seemed to favour his entrance into power, and a light rose upon the future. "You tell me," writes his friend Wandesford to him, "God hath blessed you much in these late proceedings. Truly, I believe it, for by these circumstances we know, we may guess at them we know not."[2] This friend was not forgotten. Though so recently one of the active

---

[1] Strafford Papers, vol. i. p. 47.
[2] Ibid. p. 49.

managers of the impeachment against Buckingham, he was at once received into favour, and Wentworth waited his opportunity to employ the services of others, equally dear and valuable, while he did not fail to improve his opportunities of intercourse among his new associates. Laud was the chief object of his concern in this respect, for he had observed Laud's rising influence with the king.

Wentworth wisely deferred his departure to the North until after the dissolution of parliament. The powers that awaited him there, increased by his stipulations, I have described as nearly unlimited. The council of York, or of the North, whose jurisdiction extended over the counties of York, Northumberland, Cumberland, and Westmoreland, over the cities of York and Hull, the bishopric of Durham, and the town of Newcastle-upon-Tyne[1], included within itself the powers of the courts of common law, of the chancery, even of the star chamber. It had originated in the frequent northern rebellions which followed Henry VIII.'s suppression of the lesser monasteries. Before the scheme for the suppression of the greater monasteries was carried into effect, it was judged expedient, in consequence of such disturbances, to grant a commission to the bishop of Llandaff and others, for the purpose of preserving the peace of these northern counties. This commission was, to all appearances, simply one of oyer and terminer; but a clause had been inserted in it, towards the conclusion, authorising the commissioners to hear all causes, real and personal, when either or both of the parties laboured under poverty[2], and to decide according to sound discretion.

---

[1] Rushworth, vol.i . p. 162.

[2] "Quando ambæ partes, vel altera pars, gravata paupertate fuerit."—*Rushworth*, vol. ii. p. 162.

This latter licence, however, was soon afterwards declared by all the judges to be illegal; and the power of hearing real and personal causes at all was rarely acted upon up to the second year of Elizabeth's reign, when it also was declared to be illegal, since causes regarding property, whether real or personal, could only be decided by the laws of the land. It was reserved for James to issue, over these decisions, a new commission, "very differing," says Clarendon, "from all that went before." The commissioners were no longer ordered to inquire "per sacramentum bonorum et legalium hominum," or to be controlled by any forms of law, but were referred merely to secret instructions, which, for the first time, were sent down to the council. This at once reduced the whole of the North to an absolute subjection, and that so flagrant, that the judges of the court of common pleas had the decent courage to protest actively against it, by issuing prohibitions on demand to the president and council; and James himself was obliged to have the instructions inrolled, that the people might, in some measure, be able to ascertain by what rules their conduct was to be regulated.[1]

One of Wentworth's first announcements, in succeeding to this enormous power, the very acceptance of which was a violation of the vital principles and enactments of the petition of right, was to declare that he would lay any man by the heels who ventured to sue out a prohibition in the courts at Westminster.[2] His excuse for such a course of proceeding was afterwards boldly avowed.[3]

---

[1] An interesting account of the origin and practices of this council of York was given by Hyde (lord Clarendon) in the long parliament. The speech is reported by Rushworth, vol. ii. pp. 162—165.

[2] Rushworth, vol. ii. p. 159.

[3] In his answers to the charges of his impeachment. See Rushworth, vol. ii. p. 161

" It was a chaste ambition, if rightly placed, to have as much power as may be, that there may be power to do the more good for the place where a man serves." Now Wentworth's notion of good went straight to the establishment of absolute government; and to this, his one grand object, from the very first moment of his public authority, he bent every energy of his soul. He devoted himself, night and day, to the public business. Lord Scroop's[1] arrears were speedily disposed of, an effective militia was embodied and disciplined, and all possible means were resorted to for an increase of revenue. The fines on recusants, the compositions for knighthood, and the various exactions imposed by government, were rigorously enforced by him. At the same time his hand, though heavy, was equal, and the reports of his government were, in consequence, found to be very various. The complainants contradicted each other. "Your proceeding with the recusants," writes Weston, "is here, where it is well understood, well taken, tho' there be different rumours. For, it is said, that you proceed with extreme rigour, valuing the goods and lands of the poorest at the highest rates, or rather above the value, without which you are not content to make any composition. This is not believed, especially by me, who know your wisdom and moderation : and your last too gave much satisfaction even to those who informed me, when they saw thereby, that you had compounded with none but

---

[1] His predecessor in the government of York, afterwards earl of Sunderland. Wandesford speaks of him with great contempt, in a letter to Wentworth : "Your predecessor, like that candle hid under a bushel, while he lived in this place, darkened himself and all that were about him, and dieth towards us (excuse me for the phrase) like a snuff unmannerly left in a corner."—*Strafford Papers*, vol. i. p. 49.

to their own contentment." [1] Cottington, the chancellor of the exchequer, had expressed more characteristically, some days before, the approbation of the court. " For the business of the recusants, my lord treasurer sent immediately your letter to the king (who is in his progress), from whom he received a notable approbation both of your intentions and proceedings, as he himself will tell your lordship in his own letters; for you are his mistress, and must be cherished and courted by none but himself." So early did the king deem it expedient to exhibit, that peculiar sense of his minister's service. When the minister had bound himself up inextricably with the royal cause, it was thought to be less expedient !

In such a course as this which Wentworth had now entered on, it is quite clear, that to have permitted the slightest disregard of the authority assumed, must have proved fatal. I cannot see any thing unnatural, therefore, in his conduct to Henry Bellasis, and in several other personal questions which at present come under notice. Nothing is apparent in it at variance with the system to be worked out, nothing outrageous or imprudent, as his party have been at some pains to allege. These matters are not to be discussed in the abstract. Despotism is the gist of the question; and if the phrase "unnatural" is to be used, let it fall upon that. The means employed to enforce it, are obliged, as a matter of necessity, to partake of its own nature, or it would not for an instant be borne. One of Wentworth's first measures had been to claim for himself, as the representative of absolute royalty, the most absolute reverence and respect. On the occasion of a "solemn meeting," however, this young man Bellasis, the son of the lord

---

[1] Strafford Papers, vol. i. p. 52.

Faulconberg, manifested a somewhat impertinent disregard of these orders, entered the room without " showing any particular reverence" to the lord president, remained there with his hat on, and as Wentworth himself passed out of the meeting "with his hat off, the king's mace-bearer before him, and all the rest of the company uncovered, Mr. Bellasis stood with his hat on his head, looking full upon his lordship without stirring his hat, or using any other reverence or civility." In a man of rank, this was the less to be overlooked. Bellasis was ordered before the council board, where he pleaded that his negligence had arisen from accident, that his look was turned the other way, that he was not aware of the lord president's approach, till he had passed, and, finally, that he meant no disrespect to the lord president's dignity.   He was required to express, in addition, his sorrow for having given offence to "lord Wentworth."   He refused to do this ; but at last, after a month's imprisonment in the Gate-house, was obliged to submit.[1]   Other cases of the same description occurred. A barrister at law, something disaffected to the lord president's jurisdiction, expiated his offence in a lowly submission on his knees[2]; and a punishment fell on sir David Foulis, heavier and more terrible, in proportion to Wentworth's sense of the conduct that had provoked it.

Sir David Foulis was a deputy lieutenant, a justice of the peace, and a member of the council of York. Holding this position in the county, he had, on various occasions, made very disrespectful mention of the council of York ; had thrown out several invidious insinuations

---

[1] See the proceedings before the council board, Rushworth, vol. ii. p. 88.

[2] See Rushworth, vol. ii. p. 160.

against its president; and had shown much activity and zeal in instigating persons not to pay the composition for knighthood, which he considered an illegal and oppressive exaction.[1] Wentworth immediately resolved to make him a signal example; and the extraordinary perseverance, and unscrupulous measures, by dint of which he at last secured this, are too singularly illustrative of his character, to be passed over in silence. An information was immediately ordered to be exhibited in the star chamber against sir David Foulis; against his son, who had shared in his offence; and against sir Thomas Layton, the high sheriff of the county, who had sanctioned and assisted the disaffection. Some necessary delays put off the hearing of the cause till after Wentworth's departure to Dublin. But one of the last things with which he busied himself previous to his departure, was the making sure of the issue. He wrote from Westminster to the lord treasurer, (one of the judges that were to try it!) who was then in Scotland—"I have perused all the examinations betwixt me and Foulis, and find all the material parts of the bill fully proved, so as I have him soundly upon the hip; but I desire it may not be spoken of, for albeit I may by order of the court see

---

[1] Foulis had, in less important matters, equally sought to baffle the authority of the lord president. I find the following passage in a letter to Wentworth, from sir William Pennyman, one of his watchful retainers :—"There was a constable under sir David Foulis (who, by reason of some just excuse as was pretended, appeared not) that refused to pay twelve pence to captain Philips, and it was thus discovered. I bid one of the townsmen lay down twelve pence, and the constable should pay him again. He answered, That the constable told him, that sir David Foulis had commanded him, that if any were demanded he should pay none ; and of this I thought it but my part to acquaint your lordship ; not that I would aggravate any thing against sir David Foulis, for it might only be some misprision in the constable, but that your lordship might know of the least passage which may have relation or reflection upon yourself."

them, yet he may not, till the end of the next term."[1]
Weston did not receive this hint at first very cordially;
but Cottington, another of the judges, wrote to him a
week or two after he had quitted London,—"We say
here that your lordship's cause against Foulis shall come
to hearing this term, and I inquire much after it."
Wentworth, though then much distracted by sickness
and affairs, acted eagerly on this intimation, and sent
over a special messenger to Cottington, with a short brief
of the strong points of the case, written out by himself,
and an extremely characteristic letter. He says boldly,
—"I must wholly recommend myself to your care of me
in this, which I take to concern me as much, and to have
therein as much the better, as I ever had in any other
cause all the days of my life; so I trust a little help will
serve the turn."   It is clear, in point of fact, that Wentworth felt that much of his authority, in so far as personal
claims sustained it—or, in other words, that much of his
probable success or non-success in the new and desperate
assumptions, by which alone his schemes of government
could be carried on—was concerned in the extent of
punishment awarded in the present case, and the corresponding impression likely to be created. He omits no
consideration in his letter, therefore, that is in any way
likely to influence Cottington. He points out particularly
how much the "king's service" is concerned, and that
the arrow was "shot at him" in reality. "The sen-
tencing of this man," he continues, "settles the right of
knighting business bravely for the crown, for in your
sentence you will certainly declare the undoubted right
and prerogative the king hath therein by common law,
statute law, and the undeniable practice of all times;

[1] Strafford Papers, vol. i. p. 91.

and therefore I am a suitor by you to his majesty, that he would be graciously pleased to recommend the cause to the lords, as well in his own right, as in the right of his absent poor servant, and to wish them all to be there. *You* are like to begin the sentence, and I will be bold to tell you my opinion thereon. You have been pleased sometimes, as I sat by you, to ask me my conceit upon the cause then before us ;—admit me now to do it upon my own cause, for, by my troth, I will do it as clearly as if it concerned me not." An aggravation of every point in the case against Foulis and his son follows, with a curious citation of a number of precedents for a heavy punishment, and a strong personal appeal in behalf of his own character. " Much more I could say, if I were in the star chamber to speak in such a cause for my lord Cottington : but I will conclude with this,—that I protest to God, if it were in the person of another, I should in a cause so foul, the proof so clear, fine the father and the son, sir David and Henry Foulis, in 2000*l.* apiece to his majesty, and in 2000*l.* apiece damages to myself for their scandal ; and they both to be sent down to York, and there publicly at York assizes next, to acknowledge *in the face of the whole country*, the right his majesty hath to that duty of knightings ; as also the wrong he hath done me ; humbly craving pardon of his majesty, and expressing his sorrow so to have misrepresented his majesty's most gracious proceedings, even in that course of compounding, where the law would have given him much more, as also for so falsely slandering and belying me without a cause. For sir Thomas Layton, he is a fool, led on by the nose by the two former, nor was I willing to do him any hurt ; and so let him go for a coxcomb as he is ; and when he comes home, tell his neighbours, it

was well for him he had less wit than his fellows." [1]   As
the hearing approached more nearly, Wentworth, regard-
less of the equivocal reception Weston had formerly given
him, wrote again to the lord treasurer.   "My lord, I have
to be heard this term a cause between sir David Foulis
and me in the star chamber; and a very good one, if I
flatter not myself exceedingly: I do most earnestly
beseech your lordship's presence, and that I may taste of
the ordinary effects of your justice and favour towards
me your faithful servant, albeit here removed in another
kingdom." [2]   Scarcely a member of that considerate
court did he fail to solicit as earnestly.

How could the honest judges fail to perform, all that
had been so asked of them?   Foulis was degraded from
his various offices; fined 5000*l.* to the king, 3000*l.* to
Wentworth; condemned to make a public acknowledgment of the most abject submissiveness "to his majesty
and the lord viscount Wentworth, not only in this court,
but in the court of York, and likewise at the open assizes
in the same county;" and, finally, committed to the
Fleet during his majesty's pleasure!   His son was also
imprisoned and heavily fined.   Layton, the "fool," was
presented with his acquittal.   Wentworth's gratitude at
this result overflowed in the most fervent expressions to
his serviceable friends.   Cottington was warmly thanked.
"Such are your continued favours towards me," he wrote
to Laud, "which you were pleased to manifest so far in
the star chamber, in that cause betwixt sir David Foulis
and me, not only by your justice, but by your affection

[1] Strafford Papers, vol. i. pp. 145, 146. A more remarkable
opportunity was reserved for him, on the occasion of his own impeachment, to express his contempt of this sir Thomas Layton. See
Rushworth, vol. viii. p. 151.

[2] Strafford Papers, vol. i. p. 143.

too, as indeed, my lord, the best and greatest return I can make, is to pray, I may be able to deserve," &c.   A long despatch to Cooke included an expression of the "obligation put upon me by the care you expressed for me in a suit this last term, which came to a hearing in the star chamber, betwixt sir D. Foulis and me, and of the testimony your affection there gave me, much above my merit.   Sir, I humbly thank you," &c. &c.   A still more important and weighty despatch to Weston closed with—"I do most humbly thank your lordship for your noble presence and justice in the star chamber; being the business indeed, in my own estimation, which more concerned me than any that ever befel me, hitherto, in my whole life."   And to his cousin the earl of Cleveland he thus expressed himself:—"I understand my cause in the star chamber hath had a fair evening: for which I am ever to acknowledge and reverence the justice of that great court to an absent man.   Your lordship hath still been pleased to honour me with your presence, when any thing concerned me there: and believe me, if ever I be absent from the place where I may serve you, it shall be most extremely against my will.   I see it must still be my fortune to work it out in a storm, and I find not myself yet so faint, as to give over for that, or to abandon a good cause, be the wind never so loud or sour."   One characteristic circumstance remains to be added.   All the various letters and despatches in which the passages I have quoted are to be found, together with others to various noble lords, *bear the same date.*[1]   No one of those who had served Wentworth, was left to speak of thanks that he only had received.[2]

[1] See the Strafford Papers, vol. i. pp. 189. 194. 202. 204. &c. &c.
[2] I may conclude the mention of this Foulis affair by quoting a characteristic note from one of Wentworth's voluminous private

In relief from this painful exhibition, of a false public principle tyrannizing over private morals and affections, I turn to present the somewhat redeeming aspect of those uncontrolled regards which Wentworth could yet suffer himself to indulge. In consequence of incessant application[1] to the duties of his office, he was now able to pass little of his time at the family seat; but he seems to have been anxious that his children, William, and the little lady Anne, should, for health's sake, continue to reside there. He had entrusted them accordingly to the charge of sir William Pennyman, a person bound to his service by various strong obligations.[2] The lady Arabella,

---

despatches to the Rev. Mr. Greenwoode. After instructions of various sorts respecting his personal affairs in Yorkshire, which occupy eight closely printed folio pages, the lord deputy subjoins :—
"One word more I must of necessity mention, that is, the business betwixt me and sir David Foulis. How this stands I know not : but I pray you inform yourself what lands I have received the rents of by virtue of the extent, and what money Richard Marris has received towards my 3000*l.* damages and costs of suit ; and that you will cause a perfect and half year's account to be kept of all the disbursements and receipts concerning this matter in a book precisely by itself. I beseech you set this business in a clear and certain course, for you may be sure, if any advantage or doubt can be raised, I shall be sure to hear of it."—*Strafford Papers*, vol. i. p. 488. Letter from Dublin, dated Nov. 1635.

[1] His friends were constantly, but vainly, warning him of the dangers he incurred by this. "I long," writes his friend Mainwaring to him, "to hear of my lady's safe delivery, and of your lordship's coming up. . . Your lordship must give me leave to put you in mind of your health, for I hear you take no recreation at all."—*Strafford Papers*, vol. i. p. 54.

[2] This person afterwards played his part at the impeachment. It may be worth while to quote a passage from one of his letters, written at the period referred to in the text, in illustration of the means which Wentworth employed to engage, as deeply as possible, the devotion of men who promised to be useful to him. "For my own part," writes Pennyman to the lord president, "I hope shortly to pay my composition, and I wish I could as easily satisfy your debt, and compound with your lordship, as I can with the king. But it is a thing impossible. My best way, I think, is to do like the painter, who, when after a great deal of pains he could not describe

then on the eve of confinement, remained with Wentworth. Pennyman appears to have had careful instructions to write constant accounts of the children, and it is interesting to observe the sort of details that were thought likely to prove most welcome to their father. " Now," he says, " to write that news that I have, which I presume will be most acceptable, your lordship's children are all very well, and your lordship need not fear the going forward of your building, when you have so careful a steward as Mrs. Anne. She complained to me very much of two rainy days, which, as she said, hinder'd her from coming down, and the building from going up, because she was inforced to keep her chamber, and could not overlook the workmen."[1] This important little maiden, then between three and four years old, had certainly inherited the spirit of the Wentworths! " Mr. William and Mrs. Anne," Pennyman writes on another occasion, "are very well. They were not a little glad to receive their tokens, and yet they said, they would be more glad to receive your lordship and their worthy mother. We all, with one vote, agreed in their opinion, and wished, that your lordship's occasions might be as swift and speedy in their despatch as our thoughts and desires are in wishing them."[2] At the commencement of 1631, Wentworth's second son was born. This child, Thomas Wentworth, after eight months of uncertain

---

the infinite sorrow of a weeping father, presented him on a table with his face covered, that the spectators might imagine that sorrow which he was not able to express. My debt, like his sorrow, is not to be described, much less my thanks and acknowledgments. Yet give me leave to tell your lordship, that there is not one alive that more honours you than your lordship's most faithful and indebted servant."—*Strafford Papers*, vol. i. p. 56.

[1] Strafford Papers, vol. i. p. 55.   [2] Ibid. p. 57.

health, died.   At about this time the services of the lord president seem to have been urgently required in London, and Weston wrote to him entreating his immediate presence.[1]   The health of the lady Arabella, however, who was again near the period of confinement, was now an object of deep anxiety to Wentworth, and he remained with her in Yorkshire.   In October, a second daughter, the young Arabella, was born to him, and within the same month, on a Tuesday morning, says Radcliffe, "his dear wife, the lady Arabella died.[2]   I took this earl out of bed, and carried him to receive his last blessing from her."[3]   Wentworth deeply felt her loss, and never, at any time, through his after life, recalled her beauty, her accomplishments, or her virtue, without the most tender enthusiasm.

Some days after this sad event, Wentworth received intelligence from his friend and relation, sir Edward Stanhope, of certain intrigues which, during his absence, had been moving against him in the court at London. "I received your letter," he writes back, "by which I perceive you have me in memory, albeit God hath taken

---

[1] "I hope," writes the lord treasurer, "this bearer will find you well, well disposed, and the better, enduring so prudently as I hear you do, the loss of your younger son.   We are glad here to hear you are in so good a temper, and that you receive it as a seasoning of human felicity, which God often sends where he loves best ; but you need none of my philosophy ; and therefore this is only to remember you of being here in the beginning of the term, according to your promise, and I intreat you to think it necessary to make haste.   We want you now for your counsel and help in many things."—*Strafford Papers*, vol. i. p. 58.

[2] Essay.   Mr. Mac-Diarmid and other writers have fallen into the error of supposing that she died after the birth of the last boy.

[3] Radcliffe here alludes, "by *this* earl," to the boy William, who was earl of Strafford when his essay was written.   Mr. Brodie whimsically turns it into sir George Radcliffe carrying Wentworth himself out of bed to receive his wife's last blessing.   Brit. Emp. vol. iii. p. 129.

from me your noblest cousin, the incomparable woman and wife my eyes shall ever behold.' I must confess this kindness works with me much. After some allusions to Stanhope's intelligence, he proceeds: " Yet truly, I cannot believe so ill of the propounders, both because in my own nature I am the man least suspicious alive, and that my heart tells me, I never deserved but well of them, indeed passing well. It is impossible it should be plotted for my ruin ; sure at least impossible I can think so ; and if there can be such mischief in the world, then is this confidence given me as a snare by God to punish me for my sins yet further, and to draw me yet more immediately and singly to look up to him, without leaving me any thing below to trust or look to. The worst sure that can be is, with honour, profit, and contentment, to set me a little further off from treading upon any thing themselves desire,—which granted, I am at the height of my ambitions, brought home to enjoy myself and friends, to leave my estate free and plentiful to your little cousin, and which is more than all this, quietly and in secret to serve my Maker, to commune with him more frequently, more profitably, I trust, for my soul than formerly."[1]

Of short duration was this composed attitude of mind ! The ink was scarcely dry upon his letter when he reappeared in his court at York, pursued with startling energy some of his most resolute measures, and re-assured his master in London of the invaluable nature of his services, by sundry swellings of the royal revenue. Money, the main nerve that was to uphold the projected system, was still the grand object of Wentworth's care, and money he sent to Charles. The revenue, which, on his succeeding to the presidency of York, he had found

[1] Strafford Papers, vol. i. p. 61.

no more in amount than 2000*l.* a year, he had already raised to an annual return of 9500*l.*[1]

, Still, however, intriguers were busy against him, and a rumour was conveyed by them to Weston's ear, that he had resolved to use his notoriously growing influence with the king, to endeavour to win for himself the staff of the lord treasurer. The trusty Wandesford discovered this, and despatched the intelligence to Wentworth. The next courier from Yorkshire brought a packet to Weston. " Let shame and confusion then cover me," ran the characteristic letter it enclosed, " if I do not abhor the intolerable anxiety I well understand to wait inseparably upon that staff, if I should not take a serpent as soon into my bosom, and,—if I once find so mean a thought of me can enter into your heart, as that to compass whatever I could take most delight in, I should go about beguilefully to supplant any ordinary man (how much more then impotently to catch at such a staff, and from my lord treasurer)—if I leave not the court instantly, betake myself to my private fortune, reposedly seek my contentment and quiet within my own doors, and follow the dictamen of my own reason and conscience, more according to nature and liberty, than in those gyves, which now pinch and hang upon me. Thus you see how easily you may be rid of me when you list, and in good faith with a thousand thanks : yet be pleased not to judge this proceeds out of any wayward weary humour in me neither; for, my endeavours are as vigorous and as cheerful to serve the crown and you as ever they were, nor shall you ever find them to faint or flasquer. I am none of those soft tempered spirits : but I cannot endure to be mistaken, or suffer my purer and more intire affections to be soiled,

[1] Strafford Papers, vol. i. pp. 89, 90.

or in the least degree prejudiced, with the loathsome and odious attributes of covetousness and ambitious falsehood. Do me but right in this. Judge my watches to issue (as in faith they do) from clearer cisterns. I lay my hand under your foot, I despise danger, I laugh at labour. Command me in all difficulties, in all confidence, in all readiness. No, no, my lord," continued Wentworth, lapsing into the philosophic tone he could assume so well, "No, no, my lord! they are those sovereign and great duties I owe his majesty and your lordship, which thus provoke me beyond my own nature rather to leave those cooler shades, wherein I took choicest pleasure, and thus put myself with you into the heat of the day, than poorly and meanly to start aside from my obligations, convinced in myself of the most wretched ingratitude in the whole world. God knows how little delight I take in the outwards of this life, how infinitely ill satisfied I am with myself, to find daily those calm and quiet retirements, wherein to contemplate some things more divine and sacred than this world can afford us, at every moment interrupted thorough the importunity of the affairs I have already. To heaven and earth I protest it, it grieves my very soul!"[1] Weston's suspicions, which, had he known Wentworth better, would never for a moment have been entertained, could not but. sink before such language as this; and the lord president's speedy arrival in London, exploded every hostile attempt that still lingered about the court against him.

Charles was now remodelling his counsels. The extraordinary success of Wentworth's northern presidency had inspired him with new hopes; his coffers had been filled without the hated help of the house of commons ;

---

[1] Strafford Papers, vol. i. pp. 79, 80.

and that prospect of independent authority which he earnestly entertained, no longer seemed distant or hopeless. A conclusion of peace with France and Spain favoured the attempt. He offered lord Wentworth the government of Ireland. His favourite scheme was to deliver up the three divisions of the kingdom to the superintendence of three favourite ministers, reserving to himself a general and not inactive control over all. Laud was the minister for England, and the affairs of Scotland were in the hands of the marquess of Hamilton. Ireland, accepted by Wentworth, completed the proposed plan.

The condition of Ireland, at this moment, was in the highest degree difficult and dangerous. From the conquest of Henry the second up to the government of Essex and Mountjoy, her history had been a series of barbarous disasters. The English settlers, in a succession of ferocious conflicts, had depraved themselves below the level of the uncivilized Irish; for, instead of diffusing improvement and civilization, they had obstructed both. The system of government was in consequence become the mere occasional and discretionary calling of a parliament by the lord deputy for the time, composed entirely of delegates from within the English pale, whose duty began and closed in the sanctioning some new act of oppression, or the screening some new offender from punishment. One glimpse of a more beneficial purpose broke upon Ireland in the reign of Henry the seventh, during the government of sir Edward Poynings, who procured a decree from the parliament, that all the laws theretofore enacted in England should have equal force in Ireland. With the determination of destroying, at the same time, the discretionary power that had been used, of summoning and dismissing parliaments at pleasure,

and of passing sudden laws for the purpose of occasional
oppressions, sir Edward Poynings procured the enactment
of his famous bill, that a parliament should not be
summoned above once a year in Ireland, nor even then,
till the propositions on which it was to decide had been
seen and approved by the privy council of England.
But the native Irish chiefs had been too fiercely hardened
in their savage distrust of the English to reap any advantage from these measures. They retreated to their
fastnesses, and only left them to cover the frontier with
outrage and bloodshed.

Lord Mountjoy at last subdued them, released the
peasantry from their control, and framed a plan of
impartial government. In the course of the ensuing
reign new settlements of English were accordingly formed,
the rude Irish customs were discountenanced, the laws
of England every where enforced, courts of judicature
established after the English model, and representatives
from every part of the kingdom summoned to the parliament. When England herself, however, began to groan
under oppressions, Ireland felt them still more heavily,
and was flung back with a greater shock. The arbitrary
decrees of Charles's privy council, military exactions, and
martial law, were strangling the liberties of Ireland *in
their very birth.* Bitter, too, in its aggravation of other
grievances, was Irish theological discord. The large
majority of papists, the sturdy old protestants of the
pale, the new settlers of James, presbyterians, and
puritans,—all were in nearly open warfare, and the
penalties enforced against recusants were equally hateful
to all. The rigour of the church courts, and the
exaction of tithes, kept up these discontents by constant
exasperation.

Such was the state of affairs when Charles sent lord Falkland to Dublin. His lordship soon found that his government was little more than the name of one. The army had gradually sunk to 1350 foot and 200 horse; which mean force, divided into companies, was commanded by privy counsellors, who, managing to secure their own pay out of the receipts of the exchequer, compounded with the privates for a third or fourth part of the government allowance! Insignificant in numbers, such management had rendered the soldiers ten times more inefficient, and, utterly wanting in spirit or conduct, often, indeed, the mere menial servants of the officers, they excited only contempt. Over and over again lord Falkland detailed this state of things to Charles, and prayed for assistance; but the difficulties in England, and the deficiencies in the Irish revenue, united to withhold it. At last, however, warned by imminent dangers that threatened, the king announced his resolution to augment the Irish forces to 5000 foot and 500 horse, and, unable to supply the necessary charge from an empty treasury, he commanded the new levies to be quartered on the different towns and counties, each of which was to receive a certain portion of the troops, for three months in turn, and to supply them with the required necessaries. Alarmed by this project,—and justly considering a great present sacrifice, with some chance of profit, better than to be burthened with a tax of horrible uncertainty, which yet gave them no reasonable reliance for the future,—the Irish people instantly offered the king a liberal voluntary contribution, on condition of the redress of certain grievances. Catholics and protestants concurred in this, and delegates from both parties laid the proposal before the king himself, in

London. The money they offered first; in the shape of
a voluntary contribution of 100,000*l.*, the largest sum
ever yet returned by Ireland, and to be paid by instalments of 10,000*l.* a quarter. Their list of grievances
they produced next; desiring relief from the exactions of
courts of justice, from military depredations, from trade
monopolies, from the religious penal statutes, from retro-
spective inquiries into defective titles beyond a period of
sixty years [1], and, finally, praying that the concessions
should be confirmed by an Irish parliament. Some of
these conditions were intolerable to Charles. A parliament was at all times hateful to him, and scarcely less
convenient than the absence of parliaments, to a prince
who desired to be absolute, was the privilege of increasing
the royal revenue, and obliging the minions of royalty,
by discovering old flaws in titles. Glorious had been
the opportunity of escheating large possessions to the
crown, or of passing them over to new proprietors!
Yet here was a present offer of money, an advantage
not to be foreborne — whereas, so convenient was
Charles's moral code, an assent to obnoxious matters
was a thing to be withdrawn at the first convenient
opportunity, and evaded at any time. The "graces,"
as the concessions were called, were accordingly promised to be acceded to; instalments of the money
were paid; and writs were issued by lord Falkland
for a parliament.

The joyful anticipations raised in consequence soon
received a check. The writs were declared void by the
English council, in consequence of the provisions of

[1] It had been usual to dispossess proprietors of estates, for defects
in their tenures as old as the original conquest of Ireland! No man
was secure at his own hearth-stone. See Leland, vol. ii. pp. 466
—468.

Poynings's law[1] not having been attended to by lord Falkland, who was proved to have issued the writs on his own authority, without having previously transmitted to England a certificate of the laws to be brought forward in the proposed parliament, with reasons for enacting them, and then, as he ought to have done, waited for his majesty's licence of permission under the great seal. Still the people thought this a casual error, and they waited in confidence of its remedy. The Roman catholic party, meanwhile, encouraged by the favourable reception of their delegates at court, and elated by a confidence of protection from the queen, proceeded to act at once in open defiance of the penal statutes. They seized churches for their own worship, thronged the streets of Dublin with their processions, erected an academy for the religious instruction of their youth, and reinforced their clergy by supplies of young priests from the colleges of France and Spain. The extreme alarm of the protestants at these manifestations, induced lord Falkland at last to issue a proclamation, prohibiting the Roman catholic clergy from exercising any control over the people, and from celebrating their worship in public. The Roman catholics, incensed at this step, now clamoured for the promised graces and parliament; the protestants had too many reasons to join them in the demand; and both parties united in declaring that payment of the contribution, under present circumstances, was an intolerable burthen. In vain lord Falkland offered to accept the payment in instalments of 5000*l.*, instead of 10,000*l.*, a year; the discontents daily increased, and, in the end, drove the lord deputy from power. Lord Falkland, the

---

[1] These provisions had received additional ratification by subsequent statutes, the 3d and 4th of Philip and Mary.

object of censure that should have fallen elsewhere, returned to England.

A temporary administration, consisting of two lords justices; the one, lord chancellor, viscount Ely, and the other, lord high treasurer, the earl of Cork; was formed. Both these noblemen were zealously opposed to the Roman catholics, and instantly, without waiting the king's orders, commenced a rigorous execution of the penal statutes against recusants. An intimation from England of the royal displeasure, threw some shadow over these proceedings, but not till the opposition they had strengthened had succeeded in suppressing the academy and religious houses which had been erected by the Roman catholics in Dublin. To complete the difficulties of the present state of affairs, the termination of the voluntary contribution now fast approached, and the temper of all parties left any hope of its renewal more than desperate.

Imminent, then, was the danger which now beset the government of Ireland. Without the advantage of internal strength, it had no prospect of external aid. The treasury in England could not afford a farthing to increase the army, the money designed for that purpose had been swallowed up in more immediate necessities, and the army sank daily into the most miserable inefficiency. Voluntary supply was out of the question, and compulsory exactions, without the help of soldiers, still more ridiculously vain. In the genius of the lord president of the north, Charles had one hope remaining.[1]

---

[1] Ample authorities for this rapid summary of Irish affairs will be found in Leland's History, vol. ii. p. 107. to the end, and vol. iii. pp. 1—10. ; edition of 1733. I have also availed myself of Mr. Mac-Diarmid's account, Lives of British Statesmen, vol. ii. pp. 125—135.

Wentworth received his commission in the early months of 1632. He resolved to defer his departure, however, till he had informed himself fully of the state of his government, and fortified himself with all the authorities that should be needful. The energy, the prudence, the various powers of resource, with which he laboured to this end, are only to be appreciated by an examination of the original documents, which still remain in evidence of all.[1] They were most extraordinary. The first thing he did was to procure an order from the king, in restriction of the authority of the government of lords justices, during his own absence from Dublin.[2] In answer, then, to various elaborate congratulations from the officers of the Irish government, he sent back cold, but peremptory, requests for information of their various departments. The treasury necessities, and means of supply, were his primary care. The lords justices declared that the only possible resource, in that respect, was to levy rigorously the penalties imposed by statute on the Roman catholics, for absence from public worship. The cabinet in London, . powerless of expedient, saw no chance of avoiding this, when lord Cottington received from York one of Wentworth's vigorous dispatches.

" Now, my lord," reasoned the new lord deputy, " I am not ignorant that what hath been may happen out again, and how much every good Englishman ought, as well in

---

[1] See the Strafford Papers, vol. i. pp. 61—97.

[2] Id. ibid. p. 63. After intimating to the lords justices Wentworth's appointment, the royal order proceeds :—" We have, therefore, in the mean time thought fit hereby to require you not to pass any pardons, offices, lands, or church livings by grant under our great seal of that our kingdom ; nor to confer the honour of knighthood upon any, or to dispose of any company of horse or foot there : only you are required in this interim to look to the ordinary administration of civil justice, and to the good government of our subjects and army there."

reason of state as conscience, to desire that kingdom were well reduced to conformity of religion with us here —as, indeed, shutting up the postern gate, hitherto open to many a dangerous inconvenience and mischief, which have over-lately laid too near us, exhausted our treasures, consumed our men, busied the perplexed minds of her late majesty and all her ministers. Yet, my lord, it is a great business, hath many a root lying deep, and far within ground; which would be first thoroughly opened before we judge what height it may shoot up unto, when it shall feel itself once struck at, to be loosened and pulled up; nor, at this distance, can I advise it should be at all attempted, *until the payment for the king's army be elsewhere and surelier settled, than either upon the voluntary gift of the subjects, or upon the casual income of the twelvepence a Sunday.* Before this fruit grows ripe for gathering, the army must not live *præcario,* fetching in every morsel of bread upon their swords' points. Nor will I so far ground myself with an implicit faith upon the all-foreseeing providence of the earl of Cork, as to receive the contrary opinion from him in *verbo magistri;* when I am sure that if such a rush as this should set that kingdom in pieces again, I must be the man that am like to bear the heat of the day, and to be also accountable for the success, not he. Blame me not, then, where it concerns me so nearly, both in honour and safety, if I much rather desire to hold it in suspence, and to be at liberty upon the place to make my own election, than thus be closed up by the choice and admission of strangers, whom I know not, how they stand affected, either to me or the king's service. Therefore let me beseech you to consult this business seriously with his majesty and with my lord treasurer. Admit me here, with all submission, to express myself upon this point; and finally, be pleased to draw it to some present resolution, which, the shortness of time considered, must instantly be put in action. I do conceive, then, what difficulties, nay, what impossibility soever, the council of Ireland hath pretended, *that it is a very easy work to continue the contribution upon the country for a year longer, which will be of infinite advantage to his majesty's affairs; for we look very ill about us, if in that time we find not the means either to establish that revenue in the crown, or raise some other equivalent thereunto.* And this we gain, too, without hazarding the public peace of the subject by any new apprehensions, which commonly accompany such fresh undertakings, especially being so general as is the twelvepence upon the absentees." The despatch then went on to suggest, that the very representations of the lords justices might be used for the purpose of dispensing with their propositions,—and to draw out, for the instruction of the council, a succinct plan of effecting this.[1]

Distrustful, notwithstanding, of the energy of Cottington and his associates, Wentworth followed his despatch in person, arrived in London[2], prevailed with the council to enter into his design, and had a letter immediately sent off to the lords justices, bitterly complaining of all the evils they had set forth, of the impossibility of raising voluntary supplies, and the consequent necessity of exacting the penalties. "Seeing," added the king, by Wentworth's dictation, "Seeing you conceive there is so

[1] See Strafford Papers, vol. i. pp. 75—77.
[2] This is evident from a subsequent despatch to Cottington, in which he reminds him that the resolution I am about to describe was taken finally "in presence of the treasurer, your lordship, the secretary Cooke, and myself." Vol. i. p. 74.

much difficulty in the settlement of the payments, and considering the small hopes you mention in your letters of further improvement there, *we must be constrained, if they be not freely and thankfully continued, to streigthen our former graces vouchsafed during those contributions, and make use more strictly of our legal rights and profits* to be employed for so good and necessary a work." Leaving this letter, with other secret instructions, to work their effects, Wentworth next despatched a private and confidential agent to Ireland, himself a Roman catholic, to represent to his brethren personally, and in secret, the lord deputy's regard for them, his willingness to act as a mediator and his hope that a moderate voluntary contribution might be accepted in release of their heavy fines;—in one word, he sent this person "a little to feel their pulse underhand."[1] "The instrument I employed," Wentworth afterwards wrote to Cottington, "was himself a papist, and knows no other than that the resolution of the state here is set upon that course [of exacting the recusant fines], and that I do this privately, in favour and well-wishing, to divert the present storm; which else would fall heavy upon them all; being a thing framed and prosecuted by the earl of Cork; which makes the man labour it in good earnest, taking it to be a cause *pro aris et focis*." The first thing this agent discovered and communicated to his employer, was that his temporary representatives, the lords justices, were seeking to counteract his purpose, and had utterly neglected the instructions of the last letter that had been despatched to them from the king. With characteristic energy, Wentworth seized this incident for a double purpose of advantage.

[1] See Strafford Papers, vol. i. pp. 73, 74.

There would be little hazard in supposing that their lordships of Ely and Cork were indebted to the extraordinary letter from which I shall quote the opening passages, for the strongest sensation their official lives had known. "Your lordships," wrote Wentworth, "heretofore received a letter from his majesty, directed to yourselves alone, of the 14th April last; a letter of exceeding much weight and consequence; a letter most weightily and maturely consulted, and ordered by his majesty himself; a letter that your lordships were expressly appointed you should presently cause to be entered in the council book, and also in the signet office; to the end there might be public and uniform notice taken of his majesty's pleasure so signified by all his ministers, and others there, whom it might concern. How is it, then, that I understand this letter hath, by your lordships' order, lain ever since (and still doth, for anything I know) sealed up in silence at the council table? Not once published or entered, as was precisely directed, and expected from your lordships! copies denied to all men! and yet not so much as the least reason or colour certified over hither for your neglect, or (to term it more mildly) forbearance, to comply with his majesty's directions in that behalf! Believe me, my lords, I fear this will not be well taken, if it come to be known on this side, and in itself lies open enough to very hard and ill construction, reflecting and trenching deeper than at first may be apprehended. *And pardon me, my lords, if in the discharge of my own duty I be transported beyond my natural modesty and moderation, and the respects I personally bear your lordships, plainly to let you know I shall not connive at such a presumption in you, thus to evacuate my master's directions ; nor contain myself in silence, seeing them before my face so slighted, or at least laid aside, it seems, very little regarded.* Therefore I must, in a just contemplation of his majesty's honour and wisdom, crave leave to advise you forthwith to mend your error by entering and publishing that letter as is commanded you, or I must, for my own safety, acquaint his majesty with all; and I pray God the keeping it close all this while, be not, in the sequel, imputed unto you as a mighty disservice to his majesty, and which you may be highly answerable for."[1] The next communication from his popish agent, informed Wentworth that the omissions complained of had been repaired, and, further, that all parties had agreed to "continue on the contribution as now it is," till his coming. The deputy was thus left to complete, without embarrassment, his already meditated financial projects; and the lords justices, with their friends, had leisure to consider, and amene themselves to, the new and most peremptory lord, who was shortly to appear amongst them !

Ireland was hereafter to be the scene of an absolute government,—the government of a comprehensive mind, but directed to a narrow and mistaken purpose. The first grand object of Wentworth's exertions, was to be accomplished in rendering the king's power uncontrollable. Beyond this other schemes arose. The natural advantages of Ireland, worked to the purpose of her own revenue, might be further pressed to the aid of the English treasury,—and a scheme of absolute power successfully established in Ireland, promised still greater service to the royalist side in the English struggle.

The union of singular capacity with the most determined vigour which characterized every present move-

---

[1] Strafford Papers, vol. i. p. 77.

ment of Wentworth, while it already, in itself, seemed a forecast of vast though indefinable success, left the king no objection to urge against any of the powers he demanded. The following stipulations were at once assented to. They are all characteristic of ·Wentworth, of his sagacity no less than his ambition. They open with the evident assumption that the debts of the Irish establishment will soon be settled, and with consequent cautious exceptions against the rapacity of those numerous courtiers, who waited, as Wentworth well knew, to pounce upon the first vacant office, or even the first vacant shilling. The lord deputy demanded—

" That his majesty may declare his express pleasure, that no Irish suit, by way of reward, be moved for by any of his servants, or others, before the ordinary revenue there become able to sustain the necessary charge of that crown, and the debts thereof be fully cleared.— That there be an express caveat entered with the secretaries, signet, privy-seal, and great seal here, that no grant of what nature soever, concerning Ireland, be suffered to pass till the deputy be made acquainted, and it hath first passed the great seal of that kingdom, according to the usual manner.—That his majesty signify his pleasure, that especial care be taken hereafter, that sufficient and credible persons be chosen to supply such bishopricks as shall fall void, to be admitted of his privy council, to sit as judges, and serve of his learned council there ; that he will vouchsafe to hear the advice of his deputy before he resolve of any in these cases ; and that the deputy be commanded to inform his majesty truly and impartially, of every man's particular diligence and care in his service there, to the end his majesty may timely and graciously reward the well deserving, by calling them home to better preferments here.—That no particular complaint of injustice or oppression be admitted here against any unless it appear the party made his first address to the deputy.—That no confirmation of any reversion of offices within that kingdom be had, or any new grant of a reversion hereafter to pass. —That no new office be erected within that kingdom before such time as the deputy be therewith acquainted, his opinion first required, and certified back accordingly.—That the places in the deputy's gift, as well of the civil as the martial list, be left freely to his dispose; and that his majesty will be graciously pleased not to pass them to any upon suit made unto him here."[1]

Lord Wentworth further required and obtained, in the shape of supplementary private propositions, the following :—

"That all propositions moving from the deputy touching matters of revenue may be directed to the lord treasurer of England, without acquainting the rest of the committee for Irish affairs.[2]—That the address of all other dispatches for that kingdom be, by special direction of his majesty, applied to one of the secretaries

---

[1] I have already alluded to the limitation under which this proposition was acceded to by the king. Charles was to make the grants conditionally to the applicants, and Wentworth was to concede or refuse them as the good of the service required. "Yet so too," stipulated the king, "as I may have thanks howsoever ; that if there be any thing to be denied, you may do it, not I."—*Strafford Papers*, vol. i. p. 140.

[2] Reasons are subjoined to each proposition. As a specimen I quote from the few lines appended to the above :—"Thus shall his majesty's profits go more stilly and speedily to their ends without being unseasonably vented as they pass along ; and the deputy not only preserved but encouraged to deliver his opinion freely and plainly upon all occasions, when he is assured to have it kept secret and in few and safe hands."

singly.[1]—That the lord viscount Falkland be required to deliver in writing in what condition he conceives his majesty's revenue and the government of that kingdom now stand, together with a particular of such designs for advancing his majesty's service, as were either unbegun or unperfected by him when he left the place, as also his advice how they may be best pursued and effected."

Not even content with these vast and extraordinary powers and precautions, lord Wentworth engaged for another condition—the most potent and remarkable of all—that he was to consider them changeable on the spot whenever the advancement of his majesty's affairs required. "Your lordship may rest assured," writes secretary Cooke, "that no mediation shall prevail with his majesty to exempt the lord Balfour from the rest of the opposers of the contributions, but that he will be left with the rest to the censure of your justice. *And I am persuaded, that in this and all the rest of your proceedings for his service, his princely resolution will support you, if the rest of your friends here do their duties in their true representation thereof unto him.* As your speedy passage for Ireland is most necessary for that government, so your safety concerneth his majesty's honour no less than your own. It is therefore found reasonable, ·that you expect captain Plumleigh, who, with this fair weather, will come about in a short time, (so as it may be hoped) he will prevent your coming to that port, where you appoint to come aboard. *Your instructions (as you know) as well as the establishment are changeable upon occasions for advancement of the affairs.* And as

---

[1] "This I will have done by secretary Cooke," so written by the king himself upon the original paper.

you will be careful not to change without cause, so when you find it necessary, his majesty will conform them by his wisdom to that he findeth fit upon your advice. For my service in any thing that may tend to further your noble ends, besides the duty of my place and trust, the confidence you repose in me, and the testimony you give thereof, are so obligatory, that I must forget myself much, if you find not my professions made good. For the Yorkshire business, in the castigation of those mad men and fools [1] which are so apt to fall upon you, that course which yourself, the lord Cottington, and Mr. attorney resolve upon, is here also taken, that prosecution may be made in both courts. I find your vice-president a young man of good understanding and counsellable, and very forward to promote his majesty's service. [2] The secretary is also a discreet well-tempered man." [3]

---

[1] These "mad men and fools" were "sir John Bouchier and his complices," who soon received their most unjust judgment. This passage will serve to prove the value of Wentworth's answer to this matter, also urged against him afterwards on his impeachment. "For the sentence against sir John Bouchier, the defendant was not at all acquainted with it, being then in Ireland !"—See *Rushworth*, vol. ii. p. 161. It is to be observed at the same time that the commons had not the advantage of the present evidence.

[2] Edward Osborne had been finally chosen by Wentworth. A passage in the following extract from a letter of sir William Pennyman's shows that the latter had been previously thought of for the office :—"My servant can best satisfy your lordship of the good health of Mr. William and Mrs. Anne, for he saw them both before his journey ; they have been very well, and I trust will continue so. I am most willing, I wish I could say able too, to be your lordship's vice-president, but the defect of this must be supplied with the surplusage of the other."

[3] Strafford Papers, vol. i. p. 93. The allusion to lord Balfour, with which the above despatch opens, requires explanation. Wentworth, who had already possessed himself of the most intimate knowledge of the state of parties and disputes in his new government, had written thus some days before to Cooke :—"I have sent here likewise unto you a letter from the lords justices, together with all the examinations taken of the lord Balfour, and the rest which

Wentworth, notwithstanding his new dignities, had resolved not to resign the presidency of Yorkshire.   And here we see, in the midst of his extraordinary preparations for his Irish government, he had yet found time to prosecute every necessary measure that had a view to the security of his old powers in the north.   We gather from this letter of the secretary their general character. He celebrated his departure by some acts of vigorous power, and he wrung from the council of London such amplifications even of his large and unusual presidential commission, as might compensate for the failure of personal influence and energy consequent on his own departure.[1]   He pressed more especially for the settle-

---

refused the contribution in the county of Fermanagh, by all which you will find plainly how busy the sheriff and sir William Cole have been in mutinying the country against the king's service; and I beseech you acquaint his majesty therewithal, and for the rest leave it to me when I come on the other side, and believe me, I will teach both them and others better grounds of duty and obedience to his majesty than they have shown in this wanton and saucy boldness of theirs.   And so much the more careful must we be to correct this peccant humour in the first beginnings, in regard this is a great revenue, which his majesty's affairs cannot subsist without; so that we must either continue that to the crown, or get something from that people, of as much value another way; wherein I conceive it most necessary to proceed most severely in the punishment of this offence, which will still all men else for a many years after; and, therefore, if the king or yourself conceive otherwise, help me in time, or else I shall be sure to lay it on them soundly.   My lord Balfour excuseth his fault, and will certainly make means to his majesty for favour, *wherein under correction, if his majesty intend to prosecute the rest, I conceive it is clearly best for the service to leave him entirely to run a common fortune,* as he is in a common case with the rest of those delinquents.''—*Strafford Papers,* vol. i. p. 87.

[1] The obtaining of such a commission formed one of the articles of his after impeachment, and his answer was, that he had never sat as president after the articles were framed.   But he did not deny that the power they vested was exercised by his vice-president, on the lord-president's behalf, and consequently with the full responsibility of the latter.   His instrumentality in obtaining these instructions, indeed, was not directly proved; but it was proved

ment of a dispute with lord Faulconberg by a peremptory punishment of the latter : "for this you know," he wrote to the secretary, "is a public business, and myself being to leave this government for a while, desirous to settle and establish this council in their just powers and credits,

---

that on one occasion "the president fell upon his knees and desired his majesty to enlarge his powers, or that he might have leave to go home and lay his bones in his own cottage."—*Rushworth*, vol. ii. p. 161. The commission was granted immediately after. Its most terrible article was that which in every case, in distinct terms, wrested from the subject the privilege of protection in Westminster Hall, and cut him off from any share in the rights, poor and confined as they were, of the rest of his fellow subjects. During Wentworth's absence in Ireland, one judge of the exchequer, Vernon, dared to move in defiance of these monstrous restrictions.' The lord deputy instantly wrote to Cottington, described Vernon's conduct, and thus proceeded :—"If this were not a goodly example in the face of a country living under the government of the president and council, for the respect and obedience due to the authority set over them by his majesty, of that awful reverence and duty which we all owe to his majesty's declared good will and pleasure under the great seal, I am much mistaken. I do, therefore, most humbly beseech this judge may be convented at the council board, and charged with these two great misdemeanors ; which if he deny, I pray you say openly in council I am the person will undertake to prove them against him, and withal affirm that by these strange extravagant courses he distracts his majesty's government and affairs more than ever he will be of use unto them, and that, therefore, I am a most earnest suitor to his majesty and their lordships, that he be not admitted to go that circuit hereafter ; *and, indeed, I do most earnestly beseech his majesty by you, that we may be troubled no more with such a peevish indiscreet piece of flesh. I confess I disdain to see the gownmen in this sort hang their noses over the flowers of the crown, blow and snuffle upon them, till they take both scent and beauty off them ; or to have them put such a prejudice upon all other sorts of men, as if none were able or worthy to be intrusted with honour and administration of justice but themselves."* This is surely a characteristic betrayal of Wentworth's interest in the powers of the new commission ! Some difficulties appear to have been encountered in the way of the course he proposed against this judge, for we find him at a subsequent date writing thus to the lord treasurer :—"If Mr. justice Vernon be either removed or amended in his circuit, I am very well content, being by me only considered as he is in relation to his majesty's service in those parts,—the gentleman otherwise unknown to me by injury or benefit."—See *Strafford Papers*, vol. i. pp. 129. 295.

which is fit for the king's service, *would fain see ourselves righted upon this arrogant lord, and so discipline all the rest upon his shoulders, as I might well hope they should exercise their jurisdiction in peace during the time of my absence.*"[1]   Lord Wentworth's fiercest prosecution of apparent personal resentments was, in all cases, the simple carrying out of that despotic principle in its length and breadth, and with reference to its ulterior aims, which had become the very law of his being. In this point of view only can they be justly or intelligibly considered. The cruelties associated with the name now about to be introduced, have their exaggeration, or their excuse, according as the feelings of the reader may determine—but, at all events, have their rational and philosophical solution—in this point of view alone.

The lord Mountnorris held at this time the office of vice-treasurer, which in effect was that of treasurer of Ireland. Clarendon observes of him, "He was a man of great industry, activity, and experience in the affairs of Ireland, having raised himself from a very private mean condition (having been an inferior servant to lord Chichester) to the degree of a viscount, and a privy counsellor, and to a very ample revenue in lands and offices; and had always, by servile flattery and sordid application, wrought himself into trust and nearness with all deputies at their first entrance upon their charge, informing them of the defects and oversights of their predecessors; and after the determination of their com-

---

[1] A note subjoined to this is too characteristic to be omitted :—
" There is like to be a good fine gotten of him [lord Faulconberg] for the king, *which, considering the manner of his life, were wonderous ill lost ; and lost it will be, if I be not here:* therefore I pray you let me have my directions with all possible speed."

mands and return into England, informing the state here,
and those enemies they usually contracted in that time,
of whatsoever they had done or suffered to be done
amiss; whereby they either suffered disgrace or damage,
as soon as they were recalled from those honours.   In
this manner he began with his own master, the lord
Chichester; and continued the same arts upon the lord
Grandison, and the lord Falkland, who succeeded; and,
upon that score, procured admission and trust with
the earl of Strafford, upon his first admission to that
government."[1]   This is quoted here, for the purpose of
introducing a letter of Wentworth's, which was written
at about this time, and which appears to me not only
to corroborate Clarendon's account, but (in opposition
to those who have urged, as Mr. Brodie[2], that Wentworth began his official connection with Mountnorris, by
" courting " the latter) to give at the same time the noble
vice-treasurer and informer-general fair warning, of the
character and intentions of the lord deputy he had there-
after to deal with.   Mountnorris had previously allied
himself with Wentworth by marriage with a near relative
of his deceased wife, the lady Arabella.   " I was not
a little troubled," runs Wentworth's letter, " when my
servant, returning from Dublin, brought back with him
the inclosed, together with the certainty of your lordship's
yet abode at West-Chester.   I have hereupon instantly
despatched this footman, expressly to find you out; and
to solicit you, most earnestly, to pass yourself over on
the other side : for besides that the monies which I
expect from you (which I confess you might some other
ways provide for), the customs there, you know how

---

[1] Hist. of Rebellion, vol. i. p. 175.
[2] Hist. of Brit. Empire, vol. iii. p. 70.

loose they lie ; our only confidence here being in you.'
Several other details are pressed with great earnestness.
"Therefore," he continues, "for the love of God, linger
no longer, but leaving your lady with my lady Cholmon-
deley, in case her present estate will not admit her to
pass along with you,—I will, God willing, not fail to
wait on her ladyship over myself, and deliver her safe to
you at Dublin :—the rather for that to tell your lordship
plainly, which I beseech you keep very private to yourself, it will be impossible for me to despatch the king's
business, and my own, and get hence before the end of
November at the soonest. My lord Ranelagh will be
here, I believe, within this day or two ; and, in regard of
his and my lord Dungarvan's being here before, I hold
it fit to communicate with your lordship the occasion,
which is this,—that there being a proposition made to
me for a marriage with my lord of Cork's daughter [1], I,

---

[1] This lady, whom Wentworth for excellent reasons declined
marrying, afterwards married George Goring, son of the earl of
Norwich. This was the lord deputy's management. Some eight
or nine months after he writes to the earl of Carlisle :—" Young Mr.
Goring is gone to travel, having run himself out 8000*l.*, which he
purposeth to redeem by his frugality abroad, unless my lord of Cork
can be induced to put to his helping hand, which I have undertaken
to solicit for him the best I can, and shall do it with all the power
and care my credit and wit shall anywise suggest unto me. In the
meantime his lady is gone to the bath to put herself in state to be
got with child, and when all things are prepared, she is like to want
the principal guest. Was ever willing creature so disappointed ?
In truth it is something ominous, if you mark it, yet all may do well
enough, if her father will be persuaded, and then if she be not as
well done to as any of her kin, Mr. Goring looseth a friend of me
for ever. You may say now, if you will, I put a shrewd task upon
a young man, there being no better stuff to work upon ; but it is
the more charity in us that wish it, and the most of all in him that
shall perform it *en bon et gentil cavalier.*" Such, I may remark, is
the (to him unusual) tone of levity, which he seldom failed to employ
in writing to this earl of Carlisle, whose wife, the famous countess,
had secretly become his mistress. This earl died in 1636. The
countess will be spoken of shortly. See also Strafford Papers, vol.
ii. p. 119.

that had no thought such a way, did nevertheless move a match, betwixt the young lord and my lord Clifford's daughter, which was by them accepted ; and so he comes now, I believe, to treat further of this matter with my lord Clifford. But this I must entreat you to keep private; with this, that albeit the house of Cumberland is to me, as all the world knows that knows me, in next esteem to my own family, yet be you well assured, this alliance shall not decline me from those more sovereign duties I owe my master, or those other faiths I owe my other friends." Some expressions of courtesy are then followed by this remarkable passage. " *It is enough said amongst honest men ; and you may easily believe me ; but look you, be secret and true to me, and that no suspicion possess you ; which else in time may turn to both our disadvantages.* For God's sake my lord, let me again press your departure for Ireland. And let me have 2000*l.* of my entertainment, sent me over with all possible speed; for I have entered fondly enough on a purchase here of 14,000*l.*, and the want of that would very foully disappoint me." It is clear to me in this, that Wentworth had resolved, from the first, to watch Mountnorris narrowly, and, on the earliest intimation of any possible renewal of his old treacheries, to crush him and them for ever.

Lady Mountnorris would possibly be startled in hearing from her lord, that the sorrowing widower of the lady Arabella was already speaking of the negotiation of another marriage. The entire truth would have startled her still more. Lord Wentworth had at this very time, though a year had not passed since the death of his last wife, whom he appears to have loved with fervent and continuing affection, "married Elizabeth, the daughter of sir Godfrey Rhodes, *privately.*"   Such is the statement of sir George Radcliffe.

Since Radcliffe wrote, however, some curious letters relating to this marriage have been discovered in the Thoresby museum. Sir George says that the marriage took place in October. I am now about to quote a letter which bears the date of October in the same year (the 30th), and which goes to prove that, supposing the statement in question correct, Wentworth must have sent the lady off to a distance from himself immediately after the ceremony. Nor is this the only singular circumstance suggested by this letter. Even sir George Radcliffe, probably, did not know all.

"Madam," Wentworth writes, "I have, in little, much to say to you, and in short terms to profess that which I must appear all my life long, or else one of us must be much to blame.   But, in truth, I have that confidence in you, and that assurance in myself, as to rest secure the fault will never be made on either side. *Well, then ; this little and this much, this short and this long, which I aim at, is no more than to give you this first written testimony, that I am your husband ; and that husband of yours, that will ever discharge those duties of love and respect towards you which good women may expect, and are justly due from good men to discharge them, with a hallowed care and continued perseverance in them : and this is not only much, but all which belongs me ; and wherein I shall tread out the remainder of life which is left me. More I cannot say, nor perform much more for the present ; the rest must dwell in hope until I have made it up in the balance, but I am and must be no other than your loving husband.*" A postscript [1]

---

[1] "If you will speak to my cousin Radcliffe for the paste I told you on for your teeth, and desire him to speak to Dr. Moore, in my

closes the letter, referring to some paste for the teeth, which proves that the lady was in London. Wentworth himself was at York, and, it is evident from his letters, had not quitted the county during the whole of that month. The lady's answer to this letter would seem to have been humbly affectionate, and to have conveyed to Wentworth a lowly but fervent expression of thankfulness—for that her new husband had promised not to cast her off as a deserted mistress! His reply (dated about a fortnight after his first letter) is in excellent spirit, and highly characteristic : — " Dear Besse," he begins, with the encouragement of tender words, "your first lines were wellcum unto me, and I will keep them, in regard I take them to be full, as of kindness, so of truth. *It is no presumption for you to write unto me; the fellowship of marriage ought to carry with it more of love and equality than any other apprehension. Soe I desire it may ever be betwixt us, nor shall it break of my parte.* Virtue is the highest value we can set upon ourselves in this world, and the chiefe which others are to esteem us by. That preserved, we become capable of the noblest impressions which can be imparted unto us. You succeed in this family two of the rarest ladies of their time. Equal them in those excellent dispositions of your mind, and you become every ways equally worthy

---

name, for two pots of it, and that the doctor will see it be good, for this last indeed was not so, you may bring me one down, and keep the other yourself." On the back of this letter, the following words are written, in a delicate female hand :—"Tom was borne the 17th of September, being Wednesday, in the morning, betwixt two and three o'clock, and was christened of the 7th of October, 1634." There is another letter of Wentworth's to lady Wentworth, dated from Sligo, in 1635, in the same museum, wherein he sends his blessing to "little Tom." This child died, but Elizabeth Rhodes afterwards bore lord Strafford a girl, who was yet an infant at her father's death.

of any thing that they had, or that the rest of the world can give.   And be you ever assured to be by me cherished and assisted the best I can, thorow the whole course of my life, wherein I shall be no other to you than I was to them, to wit, your loving husband, Wentworth." Still, however, Wentworth did not acknowledge her publicly; still he kept her, for some time, at a distance; and finally sent her over to Ireland, in the charge of sir George Radcliffe, some time before he himself quitted England. She arrived in Dublin with Radcliffe in January 1633[1], and was not joined by Wentworth till the July of that year, when his lordship at last ventured to acknowledge her.[2]   Laud, upon this, seems to have put some questions to the lord deputy, whose answer may be supposed, from the following passage in the archbishop's rejoinder, to have been made up of explanations and apologies, and a concluding hint of advice. "And now, my lord, I heartily wish you and your lady all mutual content that may be; and I did never doubt that you undertook that course but upon mature consideration, and you have been pleased to express to me a very good one, in which God bless you and your posterity, *though I did not write any thing to you as an examiner. For myself, I must needs confess to your lordship my weakness, that having*

---

[1] Radcliffe's Essay.

[2] His friends were instant in their congratulation, and, in a profusion of compliments, sought to intimate to his lordship,—that in this marriage of one so far beneath him in rank and consideration, he had only furnished another proof of his own real and independent greatness.   There is something pleasanter in the earl of Leicester's note, who simply regrets that he "had not the good fortune to be one of the throng that crowded to tell you how glad they were that you had passed your journey and landed safely in your government, or (which I conceive a greater occasion of rejoycing with you) that you were happily and healthfully arrived in the arms of a fair and beloved wife."—*Strafford Papers*, vol. i. p. 157.

been married to a very troublesome and unquiet wife before, I should be so ill advised as now, being about sixty, to go marry another of a more wayward and troublesome generation." [1]   There will not be any further occasion to remark upon the early circumstances of this marriage, which in its subsequent results presented nothing of a striking or unusual description, but I shall here add, for the guidance of the reader in his judgment of these particulars of Wentworth's conduct, some few considerations which in justice ought not to be omitted.

Lord Wentworth was a man of intrigue, and the mention of this is not to be avoided in such a view of the bearings of his conduct and character as it has been here attempted, for the first time, to convey.   It is at all times a delicate matter to touch upon this portion of men's histories, partly from the nature of the subject, and partly from a kind of soreness which the community feel upon it, owing to the inconsistencies between their opinions and practices, and to certain strange perplexities at the heart of those inconsistencies, which it remains for some bolder and more philosophical generation even to discuss.   Meantime it is pretty generally understood, that fidelity to the marriage bed is not apt to be most prevalent where leisure and luxury most abound; and, for the same reason, there is a tendency in the richer classes to look upon the licences they take, and to talk of them with one another, and so by a thousand means to increase and perpetuate the tendency,—of which the rest of society have little conception, unless it be, indeed, among the extremely poor.   For similar effects result from being either above or below a dependence upon other people's opinions.   When it was publicly brought

---

[1] Strafford Papers, vol. i. p. 125.

out, therefore, that Wentworth, as well as gayer men of the court, had had his "levities," as the grave lord chancellor Clarendon calls them,—it naturally told against him with the more serious part of the nation; not, however, without some recoil, in the opinions of candid observers, against the ingenuousness of those who told it,—because the latter, as men moving in the same ranks themselves, or on the borders of them, must have known the licence secretly prevailing, and probably partook of it far more than was supposed. Lady Carlisle, one of the favourites of Wentworth, subsequently became the mistress of Pym himself. Lord Clarendon, backed with the more avowed toleration, or, rather, impudent unfeelingness, which took place in the subsequent reign, not only makes use of the term just quoted in speaking of intrigue, but ventures, with a sort of pick-thank chuckle of old good-humour, to confess that, in his youth, he conducted himself in these matters much as others did, though with a wariness proportionate to his understanding. "*Caute,*" says he, in the quotation popular at the time, and used by Wentworth himself, "*si non caste.*"

We are also to take into consideration, that if the court of Charles the First had more sentiment and reserve than that of his heartless son, it was far from being so superior to courts in general in this respect, as the solemn shadow which attends his image with posterity naturally enough leads people to conclude. The better taste of the poetry-and-picture-loving monarch did but refine, and throw a veil over, the grosser habits of the court of his father James. Pleasure was a Silenus in the court of James. In that of Charles the Second, it was a vulgar satyr. Under Charles the First, it was still of the breed, but it was a god Pan, and the muses piped among his nymphs.

Far from wondering, therefore, that Wentworth, notwithstanding the gravity of his bearing and the solemn violence of his ambition, allowed himself to indulge in the fashionable licence of the times, it was to be expected that he would do so, not only from the self-indulgence natural to his will in all things, but from the love of power itself, and that he might be in no respect behindhand with any grounds which he could furnish himself with, for having the highest possible opinion of his faculties for ascendancy. As nine-tenths of common gallantry is pure vanity, so a like proportion of the graver offence of deliberate seduction is owing to pure will and the love of power,—the love of obtaining a strong and sovereign sense of an existence not very sensitive, at any price to the existence of another. And thus, without supposing him guilty to that extent, might the common gallantries of the *recherché* and dominant Strafford, be owing greatly to the pure pride of his will, and to that same love of conquest and superiority, which actuated him in his public life.

A greater cause for wonder might be found in the tenderness with which he treated the wives to whom he was unfaithful, and especially the one, this Elizabeth Rhodes, who was comparatively lowly in birth. But so mixed a thing is human nature, as at present constituted, that the vices as well as virtues of the man might come into play in this very tenderness, and help to corroborate it;—for, in addition to the noble and kindly thoughts which never ceased to be mixed up with his more violent ones, he would think that the wife of a Wentworth was of necessity a personage to be greatly and tenderly considered on all occasions,—and even his marriage into an obscure family would be reconciled to his pride, by the instinct which leads men of that complexion to think it equally difficult for themselves to be lowered by anything they choose to do, and for the object of their attention not to be elevated by the same process of self-reference.

Nor,—to quit this delicate subject, which I could not but touch on, to assist the reader, with what has gone before, to a proper judgment of facts that are yet to be mentioned,—and which, in truth, contains matter for the profoundest reflection of those who might choose to consider it by itself,—will it be thought extraordinary by such as have at all looked into the nature of their fellow creatures, that a man like Wentworth should have treated his wives tenderly, at the very times at which he was most unfaithful to them. For, whether influenced by love or by awe, they do not appear to have offended him at any time by their complaints, or even to have taken notice of his conduct; and they were in truth excellent women, worthy of his best and most real love; so as to render it probable that his infidelities were but heats of will and appetite, never, perhaps, occasioning even a diminution of the better affections, or, if they did, ending in the additional tenderness occasioned by remorse. It is a vulgar spirit only that can despise a woman for making no remonstrances; and a brutal one, that can ill treat her for it. A heart with any nobleness left in it, keeps its sacredest and dearest corner for a kindness so angelical; and Wentworth's pride had enough sentiment to help his virtues to a due appreciation of the generosity, if it existed; or to give it the benefit of supposing that it would have done so, in favour of such a man as he, beloved by wives of so sweet a nature.

The lord Wentworth was of a tall and graceful person, though much sickness had early bent an originally sensitive frame, which continued to sink more rapidly in after-life under the weight of greater cares. Habitual pain had increased the dark hue and deep contractions of a brow, formed and used to " threaten and command," and no less effective in enforcing obedience, than the loud and impressive voice that required it. He alludes to this sportively in a letter to the earl of Exeter, wherein he writes, " *This bent and ill favoured brow of mine was never prosperous in the favour of ladies ; yet did they know, how perfectly I do honour, and how much I value, that excellent and gracious sex, I am persuaded I should become a favourite amongst them ; tush, my lord, tush, there are few of them know how a gentle a garçon I am.*"[1] Happy, as it is evident, is the opposite consciousness, out of which such pleasant complaining flows ! Whereupon lord Exeter rejoins with justice, in a passage which may serve to redeem his lordship amply from the stupidity that is wont to be charged to him,—" My lord, I could be angry with you, were you not so far off, for wronging of your bent brow, as you term it in your letter ; *for, you*

---

[1] Strafford Papers, vol. i. p. 178. 180. His letters to lord Exeter and his wife are all very pleasant, and, in their deep sense of personal attentions during illness, touching. "Be not so venturesome on my occasion," he writes, dissuading Exeter from a winter journey to discharge such offices of friendship, "be not so venturesome on my occasion, till this churlish season of the year be past, and the spring well come on. There is old age in years as well as in bodies, January and February are the hoar hairs of the year, and the more quietly, the more within doors we keep them, we with the year grow the sooner young again in the spring."—"To neither of you," he concludes, "with this new year I can wish any thing of new, but that you may tread still round the ancient and beaten paths of that happiness you mutually communicate the one with the other."

had been cursed with a meek brow and an arch of white hair upon it, never to have governed Ireland nor Yorkshire so well as you do, where your lawful commands have gotten you an exact obedience. Content yourself with *that brave commanding part of your face, which showeth gravity without dullness, severity without cruelty, clemency without easiness, and love without extravagancy.*" An ungallant consolation under female displeasure follows :—— " And if it should be any impeachment unto your favour with that sex you so much honour, you should be no loser ; for they that have known them so long as I have done, have found them nothing less than *diabolos blancos* " —which lady Exeter judges fit to dispense with in a postscript :—" I cannot consent to the opinion of the lord that spake last, neither do I believe that it was his own, but rather vented as a chastisement to my particular. To your lordship all our sex in general are obliged, myself infinitely, who can return you nothing but my perpetual well wishes, with admiration of your vertues, and my heartiest desire that all your imployments and fortunes may be answerable." [1] Wentworth, indeed, had not needed this assurance, under a remark which May's happy quotation,

> " Non formosus erat, sed erat facundus Ulysses,
>   Et tamen æquoreas torsit amore Deas,"

has long since shown to be uncalled for. The intense passion of a Mirabeau or a Strafford will hardly make shipwreck for the want of a " smooth dispose."

Wentworth had much wronged his " bent brow," and he knew that he had wronged it. It was sufficiently notorious about the court, that whenever it relaxed in

---

[1] Strafford Papers, vol. i. p. 241.

favour of any of the court dames, its owner was seldom left to hope in vain. The lady Carlile[1], the lady Carnarvon, the young lady Loftus, were not, if written letters and general rumours deserve trust, the only evidences of this.

Sad indeed were the consequences of Wentworth's casual appearances in the queen's withdrawing room! " Now if I were a good poet," writes the lord Conway to the lord deputy himself, " I should with Chaucer call upon Melpomene—

[1] This extraordinary woman, whom Dryden called the " Helen of her country," and from whom Waller borrowed a compliment for Venus, (" the bright Carlile of the court of heaven,") played a conspicuous part in the public affairs of the time. " She was thought to be as deeply concerned in the counsels of the court, and afterwards of the parliament, as any in England." After the death of Strafford she had become the mistress of Pym. Yet her passions were not extreme ! Sir Toby Mathews lets us into her character :—" She is of too high a mind and dignity, not only to seek, but almost to wish, the friendship of any creature : *they whom she is pleased to chuse, are such as are of the most eminent condition, both for power and employments ;* not with any design towards her own particular, either of advantage or curiosity ; *but her nature values fortunate persons as virtuous.*" The writer of Waller's life (the countess was aunt to the poet's Sacharissa), in the Biographia Britannica, says that several letters of hers are printed in the " Strafford Papers." This is a mistake, but we find frequent allusions to her throughout the correspondence. If any one wished to know of Wentworth's health, they applied to lady Carlile. " I hope you are now recovered of your gout, which my lady of Carlile told me you had." (ii. 124.) If any one wanted favour at court they wrote to Wentworth to bespeak the interest of lady Carlile. We find even Laud, for a particular purpose, condescending to this :—" I will write to my lady of Carlile," Wentworth writes back, " as your grace appoints me. In good sadness I judge her ladyship very considerable ; for she is often in place, and is extreamly well skilled how to speak with advantage and spirit for those friends she professeth unto, which will not be many. There is this further in her disposition, she will not seem to be the person she is not, an ingenuity I have always observed and honoured her for." (Papers, vol. ii. p. 120.) And again, out of many I could put before the reader :—" I have writ fully to my lady of Carlile, and am very confident, if it be in her ladyship's power, she will express the esteem she hath your lordship in, to a very great height." (Vol. ii. p. 138.)

K

> To help me to indite
> Verses that weepen as I write.

My lady of Carnarvon, *being well in the favour and belief of her father and husband*, came with her husband to the court, and it was determined she should have been all this year at London, her lodgings in the Cock-pit; *but my lord Wentworth hath been at court, and in the queen's withdrawing-room was a constant looker upon my lady, as if that only were his business*, for which cause, as it is thought, my lord of Carnarvon went home, and my lord chamberlain preached often of honour and truth. One of the sermons, I and my lady Killegrew, or my lady Stafford, which you please, were at; it lasted from the beginning to the end of supper, the text was, that . . . . When supper was ended, and we were where we durst speak, my lady Killegrew swore by G—d, that my lord chamberlain meaned not any body but her and my lord of Dorset. *But my lady Carnarvon is sent down to her husband, and the night before she went was with her father in his chamber till past twelve, he chiding and she weeping*, and when she will return no man knows; if it be not till her face do secure their jealousy, she had as good stay for ever. *Some think that my lord Wentworth did this rather to do a despight to her father and husband, than for any great love to her.*" [1]

[1] Strafford Papers, vol. ii. p. 47. Lord Conway's letters to Wentworth are extremely amusing. They record with particular care the unlucky courtships of Vandyke :—"It was thought," he writes on one occasion to the lord-deputy, "that the lord Cottington should have married my lady Stanhope; I believe there were intentions in him, but the lady is, as they say, in love with Carey Raleigh. *You were so often with sir Anthony Vandike, that you could not but know his gallantries for the love of that lady;* but he is come off with a coglioneria, for he disputed with her about the price of her picture, and sent her word, that if she would not give the price he demanded, he would sell it to another that would give more. This week every

Sir George Radcliffe, indeed, in his Essay, observes on this head :—"He was defamed for incontinence, wherein I have reason to believe that he was exceedingly much wronged. I had occasion of some speech with him about the state of his soul several times, but twice especially, when I verily believe he did lay open unto me the very bottom of his heart. Once was, when he was in a very great affliction upon the death of his second wife ; and then for some days and nights I was very few minutes out of his company :—the other time was at Dublin, on a Good Friday (his birth-day), when he was preparing himself to receive the blessed sacrament on Easter day following. At both these times, I received such satisfaction, as left no scruple with me at all, but much assurance of his chastity. I knew his ways long and intimately, and though I cannot clear him of all frailties, (for who can justify the most innocent man?) yet I must give him the testimony of conscientiousness in his ways, that he kept himself from gross sins, and endeavoured to approve himself rather unto God than unto man, to be religious inwardly and in truth, rather than outwardly and in shew." What has been quoted from lord Conway's letter, however,—and, were it necessary to my purpose, many letters more, and of stronger meaning, are to be produced,—does not come within Radcliffe's rebuke of the "defamation" employed against Strafford. The only tendency of what sir George says, therefore, is to confirm the charge in its warrantable view, (with which alone I have dwelt upon it,) of illus-

---

one will be at London ; the queen is very weary of Hampton Court, and will be brought to bed at St. James's ; then my lady of Carlile will be a constant courtier ; her dog hath lately written a sonnet in her praise, which Harry Percy burnt, or you had now had it."

trating duly private conduct and character.   Far different was Pym's great object when, instancing in the house of commons, as Clarendon informs us, "some high and imperious actions done by Strafford in England and Ireland, some proud and over-confident expressions in discourse, and some passionate advices he had given in the most secret councils and debates of the affairs of state, he added some lighter passages of his vanity and amours, that they who were not inflamed with anger and detestation against him for the former, might have less esteem and reverence for his prudence and discretion."[1]

These words may recall me to the actual progress of Strafford's life and thoughts. Prudence and discretion —whatever his great associate of the third parliament might afterwards think right, or just, or necessary to his fatal purposes, to urge—still, so far as they may be associated in a grand project of despotism, eminently characterised every movement of lord Wentworth. The king had now become extremely anxious for his departure, which the winding up of certain private affairs alone delayed."[2] On the completion of these he arrived in

---

[1] Clarendon, Hist. of Rebellion, vol. i. p. 137.

[2] A note from Radcliffe's Essay will show that the energetic method and despatch which made the difficulties of the public business sink before him, were no less serviceable in the conduct of his private affairs. "In the managing of his estate and domestical affairs, he used the advice of two friends, Ch. Gr. and G. R., and two servants, Richard Marris his steward, and Peter Man his solicitor. Before every term they met, and Peter Man brought a note of all things to be considered of; which being taken into consideration one by one, and every one's opinion heard, resolution was had and set down in writing, whereof his lordship kept one copy and Peter Man another: at the next meeting, an account was taken of all that was done in pursuance of the former orders, and a new note made of all that rested to be done, with an addition of such things as did arise since the last meeting, and were requisite to be consulted of. His whole accounts were ordered to be made up twice every year, one half ending the 20th of September, the other

London, for the purpose of setting sail immediately. Here, however, he was unexpectedly delayed by the necessity of waiting the arrival of a man of war; for so dangerously was the Irish Channel at that time infested with pirates, that the lord deputy could not venture to pass over without convoy. "The winds fall out so contrary," he writes in answer to the secretaries, who, with the king and court, were engaged in a progress, "that the king's ship cannot be gotten as yet forth of Rochester river; but so soon as we can speed it away, and I have notice from captain Plumleigh that he is ready for my transportation, I will not stay an hour; desiring extremely now to be upon the place where I owe his majesty so great an account, as one that am against all non-residents, as well lay as ecclesiastical." Wentworth took care, at the same time, to avail himself of some opportunities offered him by this delay. He completed some pending arrangements; secured finally the close counsel and assistance of Laud[1]; established a private

---

the 20th of March; *for by that time the former half year's rents were commonly received, or else the arrears were fit to be sought after; it being no advantage either to the tenant or landlord to suffer arrears to run longer.*"

[1] A few months after his departure, Laud was created archbishop of Canterbury. Wentworth had foreseen this. "One advantage your lordship will have," writes lord Falkland in a somewhat pettish letter, "that I wanted in the time of my government, an archbishop of Canterbury to friend; who is withal a person of especial power to assist you in that part which shall concern the church government; the third and principal member of the kingdom;—for the translation of the late archbishop into heaven, and of the late bishop of London unto the see of Canterbury, makes that no riddle, being so plain." The sort of stipulations for mutual service which passed between the lord deputy and Laud, may be gathered from two out of twenty requests of the latter which reached Dublin castle before Wentworth himself had arrived there. They are equally characteristic of the sincerity and atrocity of the bigotry of Laud. "I humbly pray your lordship, to remember what you have promised me concerning the church at Dublin, which hath for divers years been used for a stable

and direct correspondence with the king himself for the sanction of his more delicate measures; instructed a gossiping person, a hired retainer of his own, the rev. Mr. Garrard, to furnish him, in monthly packets of news, with all the private scandal and rumours and secret affairs of the court, and of London generally; and obtained the appointment of his friends Wandesford and Radcliffe to official situations, and to seats in the privy council, reserving them as a sort of select cabinet of his own, with whom every thing might be secretly discussed.[1]   These things settled, he now himself became anxious for his departure, which, with some further delay, and not without some personal loss [2], he at last accomplished.

---

by your predecessors, and to vindicate it to God's service, as you shall there examine and find the merits of the cause." And again: —"There is one Christopher Sands, who, as I am informed, dwells now in Londonderry, and teaches an English school there, and I do much fear he doth many things there to the dishonour of God, and the endangering of many poor souls. For the party is a Jew, and denies both Christ and his Gospel, as I shall be able to prove, if I had him here. I humbly pray your lordship that he may be seized on by authority, and sent over in safe custody, and delivered either to myself or Mr. Mottershed, the register of the high commission, that he may not live there to infect his majesty's subjects." Vol. i. pp. 81, 82.

[1] He found great advantage in this; and a few months after his arrival in Dublin wrote to the lord treasurer some strenuous advice, suggested by his experience,—"that too many be not taken into counsel on that side, and that your resolutions, whatever they be, be kept secret; for, believe me, there can be nothing more prejudicial to the good success of those affairs than their being understood aforehand by them here. So prejudicial I hold it, indeed, that on my faith there is not a minister on this side that knows any thing I either write or intend, excepting the Master of the Rolls and sir George Radcliffe, for whose assistance in this government, and comfort to myself amidst this generation, I am not able sufficiently to pour forth my humble acknowledgments to his majesty. Sure I were the most solitary man without them, that ever served a king in such a place." Vol. i. pp. 193, 194., &c. Wandesford's office was that of Master of the Rolls.

[2] "They write me lamentable news forth of Ireland," he informs the secretary in one of his last letters before his departure, "what

Lord Wentworth arrived in Dublin in July, 1633. His very arrival, it is justly said, formed a new era in the government of Ireland. He ordered the ceremonial of the British court to be observed within the castle; a guard, an institution theretofore unknown, was established; and the proudest of the Irish lords were at once taught to feel the "immense distance" which separated them from the representative of their sovereign.[1]

---

spoil is done there by the pirates. There is one lyes upon the Welch coast, which it seems is the greatest vessel, commanded by Norman: another is a vessel of some sixty tuns, called the Pickpocket of Dover, lyes in sight of Dublin: and another lyes near Youghall:—who do so infest every quarter, as the farmers have already lost in their customs a thousand pounds at least, all trade being at this means at a stand. The pirate that lyes before Dublin took, on the 20th of the last month, a bark of Liverpool, with goods worth 4000*l.*, and amongst them as much linen as cost me 500*l.* ; and in good faith I fear I have lost my apparel too ; which if it be so, will be as much loss more unto me, besides the inconvenience which lights upon me, by being disappointed of my provisions upon the place. By my faith, this is but a cold welcome they bring me withal to that coast, and yet I am glad at least that they escaped my plate ; but the fear I had to be thought to linger here unprofitably, forced me to make this venture, where now I wish I had had a little more care of my goods, as well as of my person." Vol. i. p. 90.

[1] See Strafford Papers, vol. i. pp. 200, 201. In the various orders he procured, he invariably distinguished between the demands of his place, and the courtesies due to his person. In this despatch to Cooke, a number of minute instructions are prayed for, which were instantly granted. Among others, he demanded "instructions to call upon the nobility and others to attend the deputy upon all solemn processions to church, and such like. This is not so well observed as it ought, and they grow generally more negligent than is fit they were, *not truly I trust in any distaste to me, for to my person they give as much respect as I desire from them ; but I know not how, in point of greatness, some of them think it too much perchance to be tied to any thing of duty, rather desirous it might be taken as a courtesy.* It would do therefore very well, his majesty were graciously pleased by letter to signify what the attendance is he requires at their hands." These he specifies accordingly, with a vast quantity of laborious and ceremonious regulations, adding, "I confess I might, without more, do these things ; but where I may seem to take any thing to myself, I am naturally modest, and should be extreme unwilling to be held supercilious or imperious amongst

An extract from the lord deputy's first despatch, written about a week after his arrival, and 'duplicates of which he forwarded at the same time, with his customary zeal, to Cooke and Cottington, is too characteristic to be omitted. " I find them in this place," he writes, "a company of men the most intent upon their own ends that I ever met with, and so as those speed, they consider other things at a very great distance. I take the crown to have been very ill served, and altogether impossible for me to remedy, *unless I be intirely trusted,* and lively assisted and countenanced by his majesty, which I am bold to write unto your lordship once for all, not for any end of my own, but singly for his majesty's service. Besides, what is to be done must be speedily executed, *it being the genius of this country to obey a deputy better upon his entrance than upon his departure from them;* and therefore I promise your lordship I will take my time : for whilst they take me to be a person of much more power with the king, and of stronger abilities in myself, than indeed I have reason either in fact or right to judge myself to be, I shall, it may be, do the king some service ; *but if my weakness therein once happen to be discovered amongst them in this kingdom, for the love of God, my lord, let me be taken home;* for I shall but lose the king's affairs, and my own time afterwards ; and my unprofitableness in the former, I confess, will grieve me much more than any prejudice which may happen to my

---

them ; so as I cannot do therein as I both could and would, where I were commanded. Therefore, if these be held duties fit to be paid to his majesty's greatness, which is alike operative, and to be reverenced thorough every part of his dominions, I crave such a direction in these as in the other, that so they may know it to be his pleasure ; *other wise I shall be well content they may be spared, having in truth, no such vanity in myself as to be delighted with any of these observances."*

own particular by the expense of the latter. The army I conceive to be extremely out of frame; an army rather in name than in deed, whether you consider their numbers, their weapons, or their discipline. And so in truth, not to flatter myself, must I look to find all things else, so as it doth almost affright me at first sight, yet you shall see I will not meanly desert the duties I owe my master and myself: howbeit, without the arm of his majesty's counsel and support, it is impossible for me to go through with this work; and therein I must crave leave to use your lordship only as my mediator, so often as I shall have occasion. I send your lordship the original herein inclosed, of the offer for this next year's contribution, and to the secretary but the copy; judging it might be thought fitter for your lordship to present it to his majesty than the other. You will be pleased to send it me safely back, there being many particulars contained therein; of which I shall be able to make very good use hereafter, if I do not much mistake myself." [1]

Wentworth, in fact, extraordinary as were the powers with which he had been invested, had still reason for distrust in the weakness and insincerity of the king; and thus sought to impress upon his council, as the first and grand consideration of all, that unless unlimited authority was secured to him, he could, and would, do nothing. One thing, he saw at once, stood in the way of his

---

[1] Strafford Papers, vol. i. pp. 96, 97. In the lord treasurer's copy of this despatch is the following characteristic note on a money transaction in which Weston thought he had been somewhat sharply dealt with :—"Your lordship is pleased to term my last letter you received in Scotland an angry one ; but by my troth your lordship, under favour, was mistaken ; for I neither was, nor conceived I had cause to be, angry ; only I was desirous you might truly understand the state of my accounts, without any other thought at all." Secure of Laud's influence, Wentworth had become careless of Weston.

scheme of government. In the old time, whilst Ireland continued to be governed only as a conquered country, the lord deputy and council had used their discretion in superseding the common law courts, and assuming the decision of private civil causes. During the weaker governments which succeeded, however, this privilege was surrendered; and lord Falkland himself had confirmed the surrender, by an express prohibition. The common law, and its authority, had in consequence gained some little strength at the period of Wentworth's arrival. He had not rested many days in his state chair, before this prohibition was suspended, and the old privilege restored.[1] At all risks, even the most fatal, Wentworth silenced the objectors in both countries. He had visions before him which they dared not to contemplate! Their notion of government was one of sordid scheming: not the less was the subject to be wronged, but the more should the instruments of wrong avoid the responsibility of it; they saw nothing but their own good, and sought to prevent nothing save their own harm. Wentworth was a despot, but of a different metal. He shrunk from no avowal, in shrinking from no wrong;

---

[1] "I find that my lord Falkland was restrained by proclamation, not to meddle in any cause betwixt party and party, which certainly did lessen his power extremely; I know very well the common lawyers will be passionately against it, who are wont to put such a prejudice upon all other professions, as if none were to be trusted, or capable to administer justice, but themselves; *yet how well this suits with monarchy, when they monopolise all to be governed by their year-books, you in England have a costly experience;* and I am sure his majesty's absolute power is not weaker in this kingdom, where hitherto the deputy and council-board have had a stroke with them." Such is an extract from a remarkable despatch to Cooke, which fills nearly ten closely printed folio pages, written soon after the lord deputy's arrival, and filled with reasoning of the most profound and subtle character, in reference to his contemplated schemes and purposes. See Vol. i. p. 194.

and, confident of the plans he proposed to execute, felt that the individual injury he inflicted at present would be redeemed and forgotten in the general prosperity of the future. "These lawyers," he writes to the lord marshal, "would monopolise to themselves all judicature, as if no honour or justice could be rightly administered but under one of their bencher's gowns. *I am sure they little understand the unsettled state of this kingdom, that could advise the king to lessen the power of his deputy, indeed his own, until it were brought into that stayed temper of obedience and conformity with that of England, or at least till the benches here were better provided with judges, than God knows as yet they are.* Therefore, if your lordship's judgment approve of my reasons, I beseech you, assist me therein, or rather the king's service, *and I shall be answerable with my head.*"[1] Equal in all his exactions, he had suspected also from the first, that the great complainants against his government would be men of rank; and now, in further organisation of his powers, procured an order from the king, that none of the nobility, none of the principal officers, "none of those that hath either office or estate here," should presume to quit the kingdom without the licence of the lord deputy.[2] When his use of this power was afterwards spoken against, he silenced the objectors by a stern and sarcastical reference to one of the graces they had themselves solicited, which seemed indeed to warrant the authority, but had been proposed with a far different purpose, that of preventing men of large fortunes from deserting their estates, and wasting their revenues abroad !

Wentworth called his first privy council. The mem-

---

[1] Strafford Papers, vol. i. p. 223.
[2] Ibid. p. 362., and see p. 348.

bers of this body had hitherto borne great sway in the government of the island[1], greater, indeed, than the lords deputies themselves,—and they were now, for the first time, to see their authority broken, and their rank and influence set at scorn.   Only a select number of them were summoned, a practice usual in England[2], but in Ireland quite unheard of.   But the mortifications reserved for those that had been honoured by a summons, were almost greater than were felt by the absent counsellors !   Having assembled at the minute appointed, they were obliged to wait several hours upon the leisure of the deputy, and when he arrived at last, were treated with no particle of the consideration which deliberative duties claim.

Wentworth laid before them a provision for the immediate necessities of government, and more especially for the maintenance of the army.   The views of the lord deputy, somewhat more reaching than their own, startled them not a little.   Sir Adam Loftus, the son of the lord chancellor, broke a sullen silence by proposing that the voluntary contribution should be continued for another year, and that a parliament should, meantime, be prayed

[1] The lords justices were the chief leaders of this body.   Wentworth, in one of his despatches, had written thus :—"On Thursday seven-night last in the morning, I visited both the justices at their own houses, which albeit not formerly done by other deputies, yet I conceived it was a duty I owed them, being as then but a private person, *as also to show an example to others what would always become them to the supreme governor, whom it should please his majesty to set over them.*"   This was a subtle distinction, which their lordships did not afterwards find they had much profited by.

[2] "I desire," Wentworth had demanded of Cooke, "that the orders set down for the privy council of England might be sent unto us, with this addition, that no man speak covered save the deputy, and that their speech may not be directed one to another, but only to the deputy ; as also, taking notice of their negligent meetings upon committees, which, indeed, is passing ill, to command me straitly to cause them to attend those services as in duty they ought."

for. "After this followed again a long silence," when the lord deputy called on sir William Parsons, the master of the wards, to deliver his opinion. It was unfavourable. "I was then put to my last refuge," says Wentworth, "which was plainly to declare that there was no necessity which induced me to take them to counsel in this business, *for rather than fail in so necessary a duty to my master, I would undertake, upon the peril of my head, to make the king's army able to subsist, and to provide for itself amongst them without their help.* Howbeit, forth of my respect to themselves I had been persuaded to put this fair occasion into their hands, not only to express their ready affections and duties to his majesty, and so to have in their own particular a share in the honour and thanks of so noble a work; but also that the proposition of this next contribution might move from the protestants, as it did this year from the papists, and so these no more in show than substance to go before those in their cheerfulness and readiness to serve his majesty; . . . so as my advice should be unto them, to make an offer under their hands to his majesty of this next year's contribution, with the desire of a parliament, in such sort as is contained in their offer, which herewith I send you enclosed. They are so horribly afraid that the contribution money should be set as an annual charge upon their inheritances, as they would redeem it at any rate, *so as upon the name of a parliament thus proposed, it was something strange to see how instantly they gave consent to this proposition,* with all the cheerfulness possible, and agreed to have the letter drawn, which you have here signed with all their hands."[1]

[1] Strafford Papers, vol. i. pp. 98, 99. With characteristic purpose Wentworth subjoins to this despatch a private note to Cooke:—

A "parliament!" This word, Wentworth knew, would sound harshly in the ear of Charles, who had, by this time, prohibited its very mention in England. But he saw, from what had occurred in the council, in what consideration the mere name was held there; and he saw, moreover, abroad among the nation, a feeling in favour of it, which might, by a bold movement, be even wrested to the purpose of tyranny, but could never, with any safety to that cause, be altogether avoided.

Nor was this aspect of affairs forced upon Wentworth by necessity alone. He had certainly entered Ireland with one paramount object,—that of making his master "the most absolute prince in Christendom," in so far as regarded that "conquered country." Wealthier he meant her to become, even in the midst of his exactions; but a slave he had resolved to make her, in so far as the popular control was to be admitted over her government. Yet it has been shown that Wentworth was not a vain man, that he was ever ready to receive the suggestions of the occasion and the time, and it is clear that he entered Ireland by no means assured of being able to carry his purposes into effect by the simple and straightforward

---

"I should humbly advise that in some part of your next letter you would be pleased to give a touch with your pen concerning sir Adam Loftus, such as I might show him, for he deserves it; and it will encourage the well affected, and affright the other, when they shall see their actions are rightly understood by his majesty; and also some good words for the lord chancellor, the lord Cork, the lord of Ormond, and the lord Mountnorris; and chiefly to express in your despatch that his majesty will think of their desire for a parliament, and betwixt this and Christmas give them a fair and gracious answer, for the very hope of it will give them great contentment, and make them go on very willingly with their payments." Had none of these men afterwards thwarted him in his great despotic projects, Wentworth would have sought every means of covering them with rewards —to which he recognised no stint or measure, when called for by his notion of public service.

machinery of an absolute despotism. The king might
see in parliaments nothing but an unnecessary obstruction
to the free exercise of his royal will, and might have
directed Wentworth to "put them off handsomely," or
otherwise. But Wentworth had impressions of his own,
which were not to be so got rid of. These parliaments
—which had been only hurriedly glanced at by the
averted eye of Charles, on some occasion when he had
been forced to "come at the year's end with his hat in
his hand," and to whom the notion they had conveyed
was simply the strengthening his conviction that "such
assemblies were of the nature of cats, they ever grew
cursed with age" — these parliaments were known
thoroughly, and were remembered profoundly, by Wentworth. He had been conversant with the measures, and
connected with the men. He had been the associate of
Pym, and had spoken and voted in the same ranks with
Eliot. Such an experience might be abhorred, but could
not be made light of; and that mighty power, of which
he had been the sometime portion, never deserted the
mind of Wentworth. He boldly suffered its image to
confront him, that he might the better resist its spirit and
divert its tendency.

When he arrived in Ireland, therefore, he was quite
prepared for the mention of parliament—even for the
obligation of granting it. He had not watched human
nature superficially, though, unfortunately, he missed
of the final knowledge. He would have retained that
engine whose wondrous effects he had witnessed, and
had even assisted in producing. He would have compelled it to be as efficient in the service of its new master,
as of late in withstanding his pleasure. And Wentworth could not but feel, probably, that the foundation

for so vast a scheme as his, which was to embody so many far-stretching assumptions, might be not unsafely propped at the first with a little reverence of authority.[1] He would set up a parliament, for instance, which should make itself "eminent to posterity as the very basis and foundation of the greatest happiness and prosperity that ever befell this nation,"—by the extraordinary and notable process of being forced to confirm the king's claim to unlimited prerogative! That "way of parliaments," it is evident from many passages in his despatches, he could not but covet,—even while he spoke of leaving "such forms," and betaking himself to "his majesty's undoubted privilege." Power, indeed, was the great law of Wentworth's being; but from all this it may be fairly supposed, that even over the days of his highest and most palmy state lingered the uneasy fear that he might, after all, have mistaken the nature of power, and be doomed as a sacrifice at last to its truer, and grander, and more lasting issues. The fatal danger he frequently challenged—the "at peril of my head," which so often occurs in his despatches—must have unpleasantly betrayed this to his confederates in London.

A parliament then, he acknowledged to himself, must

---

[1] On one occasion, it may be remarked, when the attorney-general in England much wished, as he fancied, to strengthen the famous Poynings' act by an abolition of certain incidents attached to it, Wentworth opposed him in an elaborate argument. I quote a remarkable passage from the despatch:—"Truly I am of opinion, that in these matters of form it is the best not to be wiser than those that went before us, but '*stare super vias antiquas.*' *For better it is to follow the old track in this particular, than question the validity of all the statutes enacted since Poynings' act; for if this which is done in conformity thereunto be not sufficient to warrant the summons of this present parliament, they were all those parliaments upon the same grounds unlawfully assembled, and consequently all their acts void; which is a point far better to sleep in peace, than unnecessarily or farther to be awakened.*" Vol. i. p. 269.

ultimately be summoned in Ireland. But he was cautious in communicating this to the English council. "My opinion as touching a parliament," he writes to Cooke, "I am still gathering for, but shall be very cautious and cunctative in a business of so great weight, naturally distrusting my judgment, and more here, where I am in a sort yet a stranger, than in places where I had been bred, versed, and acquainted in the affairs and with the conditions of men ; so as I shall hardly be ready so soon to deliver myself therein as formerly I writ; but, God willing, I shall transmit that and my judgment upon many other the chief services of his majesty betwixt this and Christmas. I protest unto you it is never a day I do not beat my brains about them some hours, well foreseeing that the chief success of all my labours will consist much in providently and discreetly choosing and saddening my first ground : for if that chance to be mislayed or left loose, the higher I go the greater and more sudden will be the downcome."[1] Some short time, however,

---

[1] Strafford Papers, vol. i. p. 134. More genuine and characteristic still was a letter he enclosed by the same messenger to lord Carlisle :—"I am yet ingathering with all possible circumspection my observations, where, upon what, and when, to advise a reformation, and to set myself into the way of it, under God's good blessing, and the conduct of his majesty's wisdom. I shall, before it be long, be ripe to return the fruit of my labours to be examined and considered on that side, and then rightly disposed to set them on work and pursue them here with effect, taking along with me those two great household gods, which ought always to be reverenced in the courts, and sway in the actions, of princes,—honour and justice. These counsels, I confess, are secret ones, *it being one of my chiefest cares to conceal my intentions from them all here,* as they with the same industry pry into me, and sift every corner for them ; and this I do, to the end I might, if it be possible, win from them ingenuous and clear advice, *which I am sure never to have, if they once discover how I stand affected ; for then it is the genius of this place to soothe the deputy, be he in the right or wrong, till they have insinuated themselves into the fruition of their own ends, and then at after to accuse him, even of those things wherein themselves had a principal share, as well*

L

after the date of this letter, he forwarded an elaborate despatch to the secretary for the consideration of the king. In this despatch he insisted very strongly on the wide distinction between English and Irish parliaments which had been planted by the act of Poynings [1], he

---

in the counsel as in the execution. God deliver me from this ill sort of men, and give me grace so far to see into them beforehand, as that neither my master's service or myself suffer by them. My lord, I ever weary you when I begin, and judge how I should have troubled you, if the wind had stood oftener for England." The earl of Strafford had melancholy and disastrous proof of the truth of that account by Wentworth, "of the genius of that place." Some of the men who hunted him most fiercely to the scaffold were men that had been willing instruments of his worst power in Ireland.

[1] The origin of this act has been already adverted to. The popular leaders in England declaimed strongly against Wentworth's interpretation of it. If measures were produced, they maintained, of sufficient weight to satisfy the king and council, the intention of the law was fulfilled; for, they argued, it was never designed to preclude the members of parliament, when once assembled, from introducing such other topics as they might deem expedient for the general welfare. Wentworth, on the other hand, strenuously contended that the express letter of the law was not to be thus evaded; that the previous approbation of the king and council was distinctly required to each proposition; and that no other measures could ever be made the subject of discussion. Surely, however, looking at the origin of the measure, the popular is the just construction. The act was designed, with a beneficial purpose, to lodge *the initiative power* of parliament in the English council, as a protection against the tyranny of lords and deputies. But once establish this power, and the restraint was designed to terminate. Great was the opportunity, however, for Wentworth, and he made the most of it. Poynings' act was his shield. "I am of opinion," he writes to Cooke, "there cannot be any thing invaded, which in reason of state ought to be by his majesty's deputy preserved with a more hallowed care, than Poynings' act, and which I shall never willingly suffer to be touched or blemished, more than my right eye." Vol. i. p. 279. Again, when the English attorney proposed something which the lord deputy feared might work against the stability of the Poynings' bill, Wentworth described it, "A mighty power gotten by the wisdom of former times; and it would be imputed to this age, I fear, as a mighty *lacheté* by those that shall still succeed, should we now be so improvident as to lose it; and, for my own part, so zealous am I for the prerogatives of my master, so infinitely in love with this in especial, that my hand shall never be had as an instrument of so

dwelt on the exigencies of the state, and alleged various powerful reasons in that regard. He claimed also the permission to issue the writs instantly; for if they were deferred till the voluntary contribution should again be about to terminate, they would appear, he argued, to issue from necessity, the parliament would be emboldened to clog their grants with conditions, "and conditions are not to be admitted with any subjects, much less with this people, where your majesty's absolute sovereignty goes much higher than it is taken (perhaps) to be in England." A detailed plan succeeded his many and most emphatic reasons, which unquestionably "clenched" them. The parliament that was to be summoned, Wentworth pledged himself should be divided into two sessions,—the first of which should be exclusively devoted to the subject of supplies; while the second, which might be held six months afterwards, should be occupied with the confirmation of the "graces," and other national measures, which his majesty so fearfully apprehended. Now the parliament, Wentworth reasoned, would, in its first session, in all probability, grant a sufficient supply for the expenditure of three years, and this once secured, the "graces" might be flung over if necessary. Further, the lord deputy pledged himself that he would procure the return of a nearly equal number of protestants and catholics to the house of commons, in order that both parties, being nearly balanced against each other, might be more easily managed. He proposed, moreover, to obtain qualifications for a sufficient number of military officers, whose situations would render them dependent on propitiating the pleasure of the lord deputy. Then,

---

fatal a disservice to the crown, as I judge the remittal or weakening this power would be."

he urged, with the parties nearly equal, they might easily be kept in an equal condition of restraint and harmlessness,—since the catholics might be privately warned, that if no other provision was made for the maintenance of the army, it would be necessary to levy on them the legal fines; while all that was necessary to keep the protestants in check, would be to hint to them that, until a regular revenue was established, the king could not let go the voluntary contributions, or irritate the recusants by the enforcement of the penal statutes. "In the higher house," Wentworth concluded, "your majesty will have, I trust, the bishops wholly for you; the titular lords, rather than come over themselves, will put their proxies into such safe hands as may be thought of on this side; and in the rest, your majesty hath such interest, what out of duty to the crown, and obnoxiousness in themselves, as I do not apprehend much, indeed any, difficulty amongst them."

The whole of this extraordinary document is given in an appendix to this volume [1], and the reader is requested to turn to it there.

Let him turn afterwards to the dying words of its author, and sympathise, if he can, with the declaration they conveyed, that "he was so far from being against parliaments, that he did always think parliaments in England to be the happy constitution of the kingdom and nation, and the best means, under God, to make the king and his people happy." In what sense these words were intended, under what dark veil their real object was concealed, the reader may now judge. It is uplifted before him. Those five sections by which Charles is "fully persuaded to condescend to the present

[1] See Appendix I. p. 279.

calling of a parliament,"—the notice of the villanous juggle of the "two sessions," with which the wretched people are to be gulled,—the chuckling mention of the advantage to be taken of "the frightful apprehension which at this time makes their hearts beat,"—the complacent provision made for the alternative of their "starting aside,"—the king who is to be able, and the minister who is to be ready, "to chastise such forgetfulness," and "justly to punish so great a forfeit as this must needs be judged to be in them,"—all these things have long ago been expiated by Wentworth and his master; but their damning record remains against those, who would proclaim that expiation to have been unjustly demanded.

Overwhelmed by his minister's project, Charles at last yielded.[1] Still, even while, reluctantly, he consented, he could not see altogether clearly the necessity for "these things being done these ways," and all the assurances of the lord deputy could not prevent Charles bidding him, "as for that hydra, take good heed; for you know, that here I have found it as well cunning as malicious. It is true, that your grounds are well laid, and, I assure you, that I have a great trust in your care and judgment; yet my opinion is, *that it will not be the worse for my service, though their obstinacy make you to break them, for I fear that they have some ground to demand more than it is fit for me to give.* This I would not say, if I had not confidence in your courage and dexterity; that, in that case, you would set me down there *an example what to do here.*"

Wentworth now issued his writs for a parliament to be instantly held in Dublin, and great joy prevailed among

<hr>

[1] Strafford Papers, vol. i. p. 231.

the people. The privy council were summoned, in conformity with the provisions of the law of Poynings, to
deliberate on the propositions to be transmitted to
England as subjects for discussion in the session. "To
gain this first entrance into the work," Wentworth
observes, "I thought it fit to intrust it in this manner
with a committee, not only to expedite the thing itself
the more, but also better to discover how their pulses
beat, wherein I conceived they would deliver themselves
more freely, than if I had been present amongst them
myself." Soon, however, while the lord deputy waited
without, he was rejoined by his trusty counsellors
Wandesford and Radcliffe, with the news that their
associates were restive; that they were proposing all
sorts of popular laws as necessary to conciliate the
houses; and that, as to subsidies, they quite objected to
transmitting a bill with blanks to be filled up at discretion,
and were of opinion that the amount should be specified,
and confined within the strictest limits of necessity. "I
not knowing what this might grow to," writes Wentworth,
"went instantly unto them, where they were in council,
and told them plainly I feared they began at the wrong
end, thus consulting what might please the people in a
parliament, when it would better become a privy council
to consider what might please the king, and induce him
to call one." The imperious deputy next addressed
them in a very long and able speech, pressed upon them
the necessities of the nation, and the only modes of
arresting them. "The king therefore desires," he continued, "this great work may be set on his right foot,
settled by parliament as the more beaten path he covets
to walk in, *yet not more legal than if done by his prerogative royal, where the ordinary way fails him.* If this

people then can be so unwise as to cast off his gracious proposals, and their own safety, it must be done without them ; and for myself, as their true friend, I must let them know, that I cannot doubt, but they will altogether save me the trouble, hasten in their advice, and afford their best means for the fulfilling these his so good intentions. That as a faithful servant to my master I shall counsel his majesty to attempt it first by the ordinary means ; disappointed there, where he may with so much right expect it, *I could not in a cause so just and necessary deny to appear for him in the head of that army, and there either persuade them fully his . majesty had reason on his side, or else think it a great honour to die in the pursuit* of that, wherein both justice and piety had so far convinced my judgment, as not left me wherewithal to make one argument for denying myself unto commands so justly called for and laid upon me." In conclusion, Wentworth gave them a still more characteristic warning :—
" Again I did beseech them to look well about, and be wise by others' harms. They were not ignorant of the misfortunes these meetings had run in England of late years. That therefore they were not to strike their foot upon the same stone of distrust, which had so often broken *them.* For I could tell them, as one that had, it may be, held my eyes as open upon those proceedings as another man, that what other accident this mischief might be ascribed unto, there was nothing else that brought it upon us, but the king's standing justly to have the honour of trust from his people, and an ill-grounded narrow suspicion of theirs, which would not be ever entreated, albeit it stood with all the reason and wisdom in the world. This was that spirit of the air that walked in darkness betwixt them, abusing both, whereon if once

one beam of light and truth had happily reflected, it had vanished like smoke before it!"[1]

The council could not hold to one of their purposes in the presence of such overawing energy—"whereupon they did, with all cheerfulness, assent unto the council; professed they would entirely conform themselves unto it; acknowledged it was most reasonable this kingdom should defray itself; that they would not offer the pardon, or any other act that might bear the interpretation of a condition; that they would send over no other laws but such as I should like; nay, if I pleased, they would send over the bill of subsidy alone."[2]

Another obstruction remained, which was as fiercely and immediately disposed of. The council had ventured

[1] See Strafford Papers, vol. i. p. 236—241., for the despatch, in which these things are all most happily described. Laud, in a subsequent letter, gives Wentworth some account of the way in which the despatch had been received. I extract one amusing passage:—"The next day, at Greenwich, your despatch to secretary Coke was read to the committee, the king present, order given for us to meet, and for speed of our answer to you. If speed be not made to your mind, I am not in fault, and I hope you will have all things in time. Every body liked your carriage and discourse to the council, but thought it too long, *and that too much strength was put upon it; but you may see what it is to be an able speaker.* Your old friend says, he had rather see you talk something into the exchequer, but he pleases himself extremely to see how able Brutus is in the senate-house! And wot you what? When we came to this passage in your despatch, 'Again, I did beseech them to look well about, and to be wise by others' harms, they were not ignorant of the misfortunes these meetings had run in England of late years,' &c. *Here a good friend of yours interposed, 'quorum pars magna fui.'* I hope you will charge this home upon my lord Cottington; he hath so many Spanish tricks, that I cannot tell how to trust him for any thing but making of legs to fair ladies."—*Strafford Papers,* vol. i. pp. 255, 256.

[2] Strafford Papers, vol. i. p. 255. To this Wentworth shrewdly subjoins,—"But I, not thinking it fit it should come so singly from the king without some expression of care for the good government of his people, have caused it to be accompanied, as you will receive it, by this express."

to suggest to the lord deputy the existence of an ancient custom, whereby the lords of the pale claimed the right of being consulted respecting the projected measures, but which Wentworth had at once silenced by "a direct and round answer." Four days after this, however, the earl of Fingal, on behalf of his brother peers, obtained an interview, and, as the deputy described, "very gravely, and in a kind of elaborate way, told me," &c. &c. It is simply necessary to add, that so peremptory and supremely contemptuous was Wentworth's reception of these traditionary claims, that the lord Fingal was fain to escape from his presence with a submissive apology.[1]

Nothing remained now but the elections. Some difficulty attended them at the first, but one or two resolute measures quelled it.[2] In July, 1634, an

[1] See the deputy's own account, Strafford Papers, vol. i. pp. 246, 247.

[2] "'The priests and Jesuits here,' writes Wentworth, in a very able despatch to Cooke, "are very busy in the election of knights and burgesses for this parliament, call the people to their masses, and there charge them, on pain of excommunication, to give their voice with no protestant. I purpose hereafter to question some of them :—being, indeed, a very insufferable thing for them thus to interpose in causes which are purely civil ; and of passing ill consequence, to warm and inflame the subjects one against another ; and, in the last resort, *to bring it to a direct party of protestant and papist, which surely is to be avoided as much as may be, unless our numbers were the greater.* A sheriff that, being set on by these fellows, carried himself mutinously in the election of burgesses for this town, we brought into the Castle Chamber upon an *ore tenus*, where, upon what he had set under his hand, we fined him 200*l.*, and 500*l.* more for his contempt in refusing to set his hand to another part of his examination, both at the council board and in open court, disabling him for ever bearing that office hereafter in this city. Which wrought so good an effect, as giving order presently for chusing of a new sheriff, and going on the next day with the election again, the voices were all orderly taken ; and the conformable proving the greater number, Catelin, the king's serjeant and recorder of this town, and alderman Barry, a protestant, were chosen ; the former whereof I intend to make the speaker, being a very able man for that purpose, and one I assure myself will in all

admirably balanced party of catholics and protestants assembled in the Irish house of commons.

With extraordinary pomp and ceremony[1] the lord deputy proceeded to meet them. His speech, however, was more startling than his splendour. He began by telling them that two sessions should be held; and that the first, "according to the natural order," should be devoted to the sovereign, and the second to the subject. " In demanding supplies," he continued, " I only require you to provide for your own safety; I expect, therefore, your contributions will be both liberal and permanent. That is, there must be a standing revenue (mark it well) provided by you to supply and settle the constant payments of the army. For it is far below my great master to come at every year's end, with his hat in his hand, to entreat that you would be pleased to preserve yourselves." Moreover, he told them that, if they expected constant protection without contributing towards it, they looked for more than had ever been the portion of a " conquered kingdom." A bitter warning succeeded this of the fate of English parliaments. "Take heed," he said, in a lesson from his own patriotic experiences, " take heed of private meetings and consults in your chambers, by design and privity aforehand to contrive how to discourse and carry the public affairs when you come into the houses. For, besides that they are in themselves unlawful, and punishable in a grievous measure, I never knew them in all my experience to do any good to the

---

things apply himself to his majesty's service."—*Strafford Papers*, vol. i. p. 260.

[1] " It was the greatest civility and splendour," writes Wentworth, " Ireland ever saw. A very gallant nobility and gentry appeared, far above that I expected." Vol. i. p. 276. See a programme in the Biog. Brit. vol. vii. pp. 4184, 4185.

public or to any particular man. I have often known them do much harm to both." With these were mingled some just entreatments. "Divide not nationally betwixt English and Irish. The king makes no distinction betwixt you, but reputes you all without prejudice, and that upon safe and true grounds, I assure myself, his good and faithful subjects. And madness it were in you, then, to raise that wall of separation amongst yourselves. If you should, you know who the old proverb deems likest to go to the wall; and, believe me, England will not prove the weakest. But, above all, divide not between the interests of the king and his people, as if there were one being of the king, and another being of his people." He concluded with a distinct statement, that their conduct during the session should be attended, according to its results, with punishment or reward."[1]

Not in words only, but equally in the manner of its delivery, did this speech proclaim the despotic genius of lord Wentworth. Here he resorted to all those arts which, as I have before remarked, are essentially necessary to the success of the despot; and illustrated, by conduct which to such superficial statesmen as my lord Cottington seemed vain and unnecessary, his profound knowledge of character. "Well," he writes to his more relying friend the archbishop of Canterbury,—"well, spoken it is since, good or bad I cannot tell whether; but sure, I am not able yet to help myself to a copy of it. But as it was, *I spake it not betwixt my teeth, but so loud and heartily, that I protest unto you I was faint withal at the present, and the worse for it two or three days after. It makes no matter, for this way I was assured they should have sound at least, with how little*

---

[1] Strafford Papers, vol. i. pp. 287—290.

weight soever it should be attended.   And the success was answerable.   For had it been low and mildly delivered, I might perchance have gotten from them, it was pretty well, —whereas this way, filling one of their senses with noise, and amusing the rest with earnestness and vehemence, they swear (yet forgive them, they know not what they say!) it was the best spoken they ever heard in their lives.   Let Cottington crack me that nut now." [1]

Secure of his measures, Wentworth demanded at once the enormous grant of six subsidies.[2]   With the view, at the same time, of preventing the possibility of the parties communicating in any way with each other, and so cutting from beneath them every ground of mutual reliance, he introduced the proposition to the house on the second day of their meeting.   Ignorant of each other's sentiments—incapable of any thing like a plan of opposition—nothing was left for protestants and catholics but to seek to rival each other, as it were, in the devotion of loyalty.   The subsidies were voted unconditionally [3], and one voice of profound respect for the lord deputy rose from all.[4]   Not less successful was his management

[1] Strafford Papers, vol. i. p. 273.

[2] He had great difficulty in inducing the privy council to accede to this.   At last he prevailed—" Sir Adam Loftus," as he writes to Cooke, " first beginning the dance, which is now the second time he hath done the king passing good service in this kind." Vol. i. p. 259.   Not a single service did lord Wentworth ever receive, without acknowledging it strongly to the king, accompanied by the special naming of those who had so served him.

[3] These were the first "settled subsidies" that had ever been paid in Ireland.   See Papers, vol. i. p. 307.

[4] See Strafford Papers, vol. i. pp. 277—279.   One restive member there was, and one only.   This was sir Robert Talbot ; who, having mentioned Wentworth without a sufficiently awful respect, was instantly expelled, and committed to custody till, on his knees, he begged pardon of the deputy.   Commons' Journ. vol. i. p. 116. Leland, vol. iii. p. 18.   One case may be added to this of a very different character, in proof that, when Wentworth saw the means

of the convocation of Irish clergy, which had been summoned with parliament, and from whom eight subsidies were ultimately procured. Fortified with his money bills, and just as the session was on the eve of closing, Wentworth turned with contempt to the proceedings of the house of lords.[1] Here had been oppo-

---

of advancing the public service, even at the cost of some personal consideration, he did nor care to waive the latter. Among the proclamations he had issued to regulate the parliamentary sitting, he expressly forbade the entrance of any member of either house with his sword, and all obeyed this except the young earl of Ormond, who told the usher of the black rod that he should have no sword of his except through his body. Equally resolute was his answer to the fiery questioning of the lord deputy himself,—quietly producing his majesty's writ, which had called him tc parliament "cinctum cum gladio," or "per cincturam gladii." The doubt then occurred to the deputy, of the superior value of young Ormond's service to his enmity; and, after consultation with "his two friends, sir George Radcliffe and Mr. Wandesford," the youth was taken into favour. I am obliged to Mr. Crofton Croker for the favour of this note, which I find in a manuscript translation he has been good enough to lend me, of the Irish portion of the travels of a gasconading coxcomb of a Frenchman, Sieur de la Boullaye-le-Gouz, who honoured the island with his company in 1644, and obliged the world with a most amusing account of his visit. This very Ormond was then viceroy, and the part he had himself played to lord Wentworth was curiously enough rivalled on this occasion by the illustrious Le Gouz. "I followed the train," observes our traveller, in Mr. Croker's happy translation, " in order to enter more freely into the castle, but at the door they ordered me to lay down my sword, which I would not do, saying that, being born of a condition to carry it before the king, I would rather not see the castle than part with my arms. A gentleman in the suite of the viceroy, *seeing from my gallant bearing that I was a Frenchman*, took me by the hand, saying, 'Strangers shall on this occasion be more favoured than residents,' and he brought me in. I replied to him, that his civility *equalled—that of the French towards his nation, when they met them in France!*"

[1] It was one of the strokes of the lord deputy's policy to aggravate every difference between the two houses. He describes, with singular sarcasm, in one of his despatches, a difference of this sort. "The commons would not confer with the lords, unless they might sit and be covered, as well as their lordships, which the other would by no means admit. For my part I did not lay it very near my heart to agree them, as having heretofore seen the effects which

sition—the positive enactment of various salutary regulations—the consideration of grievances ! ' "I let them alone," says one of his despatches, "till the last day that I came into the house to conclude the session ; but then, being very jealous lest in my time any thing might creep in, and grow upon the king's prerogative in this tender and important particular[1], I clearly declared they had therein proceeded further than they had warrant for . . . . . and did beseech their lordships to be better advised for the future, and not to exceed that power which was left them by that law, to wit,—a liberty only to offer by petition to the deputy and council such considerations as they might conceive to be good for the commonwealth, by them to be transmitted for laws, or staid, as to them should seem best; whereunto they condescended without any opposition."

The English ministers were rapt in delight and astonishment ! As the time approached, however, for the second session—the session of " graces "—a shadow fell over their congratulations. Bucklered with his law of Poynings, the lord deputy bravely reassured them. " For my own part," he wrote to Cooke—in the apt simile of an amusement which he was then, in the intervals of his bodily infirmities, ardently given to—" for my own part, I see not any hazard in it, considering that we have this lyme hound in our power, still to take off when we please ; which is not so easy with your parlia-

---

follow when they are in strict understanding, or at difference amongst themselves. I saw plainly that keeping them at distance I did avoid their joining in a petition for the graces."—*Strafford Papers,* vol. i. p. 279.

[1] The law of Poynings.

ments of England, where sometimes they hunt loose, forth of command, choose and give over their own game as they list themselves."[1] Further, however, to quiet the apprehensions of Charles, and induce him to suffer the continuance of parliament, Wentworth wrote to the king, telling him that the lord deputy and his council meant to take on themselves the whole responsibility and blame of refusing the obnoxious graces, while the whole merit of granting such as might be granted safely should be given to his majesty.[2]

Wentworth redeemed his pledge. It is unnecessary to describe the proceedings of that session at any length. Suffice it to say, that the arts and energy of the first session were redoubled to a greater success in the second. None of the obnoxious · graces were accorded. He openly told the parliament that he had refused even to transmit them to England, and asserted his right to do this under the law of Poynings.[3] For a time, the overbearing energy of his measures forced the members

---

[1] Strafford Papers, vol. i. p. 305. Wentworth preserved through life, notwithstanding his frightful illnesses, the most passionate fondness for hunting and hawking. It is curious to observe, in his accounts of these amusements, an occasional letting out of another object he may have had in them, besides that of personal enjoyment. They gave him an opportunity of display. "Your defeat of your hawking sport in Wiltshire," he writes at about this time to Cottington, " is nothing like to mine ; for (as the man you wot of said by the pigeons) here hath not been a partridge in the memory of man, so as having a passing high flying tarsell I am even setting him down, and to-morrow purpose, with a cast or two of sparhawks, to betake myself to fly at blackbirds, ever and anon taking them on the pate with a trunk. It is excellent sport, *there being sometimes* 200 *horse on the field looking upon us,* where the lord of Fonsail drops out of doors with a poor falconer or two ; and if sir Robert Wind and Gabriel Epsley be gotten along, it is a regale."—*Strafford Papers,* vol. i. p. 163.

[2] See Strafford Papers, vol. i. p. 328. And see the despatch to Cooke, vol. i. p. 338.

[3] See Strafford Papers, vol. i. p. 345. *et seq.*

to the silence of fear,—but this was broken by the catholic party, who, having suffered the most grievous wrong in the deception, at last made a feeble show of resistance. Wentworth instantly flung all his influence for the first time among the protestants, and precipitated the catholics into a trial of their strength, unadvised with each other, and utterly unprepared. They were at once defeated. The protestants then claimed their reward, and with an earnestness which was only finally subdued by the lord deputy's threats of worse terrors than those which their wrongs included.[1] He had nothing left now but to write one of his most pleasing despatches to his royal master, containing " at once a clear and full relation of the issue of this second session, which was, through the wayward frowardness of the popish party, so troublesome upon the first access, but is now recovered and determined by the good assistance of the protestants, with great advantage to your majesty, by those excellent and beneficial laws which, with much tugging, are gotten from them ; *and all the graces prejudicial to the crown laid also so sound asleep as I am confident they are never*

---

[1] " I roundly and earnestly told them I was very indifferent what resolution the house should fall upon, serving too just and gracious a master ever to fear to be answerable for the success of affairs in contingence, so long as I did sincerely and faithfully endeavour that which I conceived to be for the best. *That there were two ends I had my eye on, and the one I would infallibly attain unto,—either a submission of the people to his majesty's just demands, or a just occasion of breach, and either would content the king.* The first was undeniably and evidently best for them ; but could my master in his goodness consider himself apart from his subjects, or these become so ingrate, *I spake it confidently upon the peril of my head, a breach should be better for him than any supply they could give him in parliament.* And therefore I did desire that no man should deceive himself : my master was not to seek in his counsels, nor was he a prince that either could or would be denied just things." For the various incidents of this session, see Strafford Papers, vol. i. pp. 320, 321. 328. 339. 341. 343, 344, 345, 349. 353.

to be awakened more."[1]   In the next despatch he had the satisfaction of assuring his majesty, that the privilege of impeachment had been wrested both from lords and commons[2]; in the next, that certain troubles of the convocation had been most emphatically silenced[3]; and in the next, that his majesty was now, in the person of his humble deputy, the uncontrolled disposer of the destinies of Ireland! "So now I can say," wrote Wentworth at the close of a long despatch, which by the same messenger he had forwarded to Laud, and which contains a remarkable summary of the many important services he had rendered to the crown,—"*so now I can say the king is as absolute here as any prince in the whole world can be, and may be still, if it be not spoiled on that side.*   For, so long as his majesty shall have here a deputy of faith and understanding, and that he be preserved in credit, and independent upon any but the king himself, let it be laid, as a ground, it is the deputy's fault if the king be denied any reasonable desire."

This was grateful news to Laud.   Of all the suggesters

---

[1] In the same despatch (which see in Strafford Papers, vol. i. p. 341.) Wentworth urges upon the king the necessity of his surrendering matters of patronage and so forth more immediately into his lord deputy's hands :—" The fewer sharers in the service, the fewer there will be to press for rewards, to the lessening of your majesty's profit, and the more entire will the benefit be preserved for your crown ; *which must, in all these affairs, and shall, be my principal,* NAY, INDEED, MY SOLE END."

[2] See the case of sir Vincent Gookin, Papers, vol. i. pp. 349. and 393.   Wentworth established by this case, that, under Poyning's law, acts of judicature no less than of legislation, were prohibited, save by consent of the deputy and his council.

[3] See Strafford Papers, vol. i. pp. 342—345.   "I am not ignorant," subjoined Wentworth to this despatch, with a sort of involuntary forecast of an after reckoning, which he threw off in a self-deceiving jest,—" I am not ignorant that my stirring herein will be strangely reported, and censured on that side ; *and how I shall be able to sustain myself against your Prynnes, Pims, and Bens, with the rest of that generation of odd names and natures, the Lord knows.*"

of the infamous counsels of Charles, Laud and Wentworth were the most sincere :—Laud, from the intense faith with which he looked forward to the possible supremacy of the ecclesiastical power, and to which he was bent upon going, "thorough," through every obstacle ;—Wentworth, from that strong sense, with which birth and education had perverted his genius, of the superior excellence of despotic rule. Their friendship, in consequence, notwithstanding Wentworth's immense superiority in point of intellect [1], continued tolerably firm and steady, —most firm, indeed, considering the nature of their public connection. [2] The letters which passed between them partook of a more intimate character, in respect of the avowal of ulterior designs, than either of them, probably, chose to avow elsewhere ; and though many of their secrets have been effectually concealed from us by their frequent use of cyphers, sufficient remain to shadow forth the extremest purposes of both.

[1] It is amusing at times to observe the commissions to which Wentworth descended for the gratification of Laud, laughing at them secretly while he gravely discharged them. The archbishop himself, however, had an occasional suspicion of this ; and is to be seen at times insinuating, from beneath velvet words, a cat-like claw :—"I perceive you mean to build," he writes to the lord deputy on one occasion, "but as yet your materials are not come in ; but if that work do come to me before Christmas, as you promise it shall, I will rifle every corner in it : and you know, my good lord, after all your bragging, how I served you at York, and your church work there : *especially I pray provide a good riding house, if there be ever a decayed body of a church to make it in, and then you shall be well fitted, for you know one is made your stable already,* if you have not reformed it, of which I did look for an account according to my remembrances before this time." Vol. i. p. 156. Wentworth had forgotten one of his friend's first commissions, which the reader will recollect to have been quoted.

[2] A curious and instructive essay might be gleaned from the Strafford Papers, on the subject of the friendships of statesmen, or, rather say, of a king's advisers ; for the majority of these men did not deserve the name of statesmen.

Laud had to regret his position in England, contrasted with that of the Irish deputy. "My lord," he writes to Wentworth, speaking of the general affairs of church and state, "to speak freely, you may easily promise more in either kind than I can perform : for, as for the church, it is so bound up in the forms of the common law, that it is not possible for me, or for any man, to do that good which he would, or is bound to do. For your lordship sees, no man clearer, that they which have gotten so much power in and over the church will not let go their hold; they have, indeed, fangs with a witness, whatsoever I was once said in a passion to have. *And for the state, indeed, my lord, I am for Thorough ; but I see that both thick and thin stays somebody, where I conceive it should not ; and it is impossible for me to go thorough alone.* Besides, private ends are such blocks in the public way, and lie so thick, that you may promise what you will, and I must perform what I can, and no more."[1] To this Wentworth answers in a letter which is not preserved. Its import, however, may be gathered from this remarkable passage in Laud's rejoinder :—"I am very glad to read your lordship so resolute, and more to hear you affirm, that the footing of them which go thorough for our master's service is not now upon fee, as it hath been. But you are withal upon so many *ifs*, that by their help you may preserve any man upon ice, be it never so slippery. As, first, *if* the common lawyers may be contained within their ancient and sober bounds; *if* the word *Thorough* be not left out (as I am certain it is); *if* we grow not faint; *if* we ourselves be not in fault; *if* it come not to *peccatum ex te Israel; if* others will do their parts as thoroughly as you promise for yourself, and

---

[1] Strafford Papers, vol. i. p. 111.

justly conceive of me.   Now, I pray, with so many and such *ifs* as these, what may not be done, and in a brave and noble way?   But can you tell when these *ifs* will meet, or be brought together?"[1]   Satisfactory is the lord deputy's returning assurance :—" For the *ifs* your lordship is pleased to impute unto me, you shall hereafter have more positive doctrine.   I *know no reason, then, but you may as well rule the common lawyers in England, as I, poor beagle, do here ; and yet that I do, and will do, in all that concerns my master's service, upon the peril of my head.*   I am confident that the king, being pleased to set himself in the business, is able, by his wisdom and ministers, to carry any just and honourable action thorough all imaginary opposition, for real there can be none ; *that to start aside for such panic fears, fantastic apparitions, as a Prynne or an Eliot shall set up, were the meanest folly in the whole world ; that the debts of the crown taken off, you may govern as you please ; and most resolute I am that work may be done, without borrowing any help forth of the king's lodgings, and that is as downright* a peccatum ex te Israel *as ever was, if all this be not effected with speed and ease.*"[2]

Resolutely did the lord deputy, as I have shown, realise these principles,—and every new act of despotism which struck terror into Ireland shot comfort to the heart of Laud.   " As for my marginal note," exclaims the archbishop, " I see you deciphered it well, and I see you make use of it too,—do so still ; thorow and thorow. Oh that I were where I might go so too ! but I am

----

[1] Strafford Papers, vol. i. p. 155.

[2] Ibid. vol. i. p. 173. Following this passage, in the same letter, is language which it would be a gross outrage of decency to quote. The archbishop appears to have relished it exceedingly.

shackled between delays and uncertainties. You have a great deal of honour here for your proceedings. *Go on a God's name!*"[1] And on Wentworth went, stopping at no gratuitous quarrel that had the slightest chance of pleasing the archbishop, even to the demolishing the family tomb of the earl of Cork,—since his grace, among his select ecclesiastical researches, had discovered that the spot occupied by my lord of Cork's family monuments, was precisely that spot upon which the communion-table, to answer the purposes of heaven, ought to stand![2] To minister to their mutual purposes, Wentworth also introduced into Ireland the court of high commission, and wrested it to various notable purposes, political as well as religious.

The distinction between him and his confederate during all these proceedings is, nevertheless, to be discerned as widely as the difference of their respective intellects. Wentworth was a despot, but his despotism included many noble, though misguided, purposes. Even with this high commission court, unjustifiable as were the means, he unquestionably effected an increase to the respectability and usefulness of the clergy, and reformed the ecclesiastical courts,—while, at the same time, he never lost sight of the great present object of his govern-

---

[1] Strafford Papers, vol. i. p. 329.

[2] It would be impossible to notice in detail the various personal contests in which Wentworth engaged, though none of them passed, not even the most trifling, without illustrating, in a remarkable degree, the general features of his character. I may refer the reader respecting this affair of the earl of Cork to the Strafford Papers, vol. i. pp. 156. 200. 216. 222. 257. 298. 379. 459., and to vol. ii. p. 270. and p. 338. Lord Cork hit upon an ingenious plan of thwarting the lord deputy, though it failed in consequence of the superior influence of the latter. He wrote to the lord treasurer Weston, then notoriously jealous of Wentworth, and opposed to him and Laud, "entreating his favour, for that under this monument the bones of a Weston was entombed."

ment, that it should, "in the way to all these, raise, perhaps, a good revenue to the crown."[1] So, while Laud, in England, was, by a series of horrible persecutions, torturing and mutilating the puritans[2], the deputy of Ireland could boast with perfect truth that, "since I had the honour to be employed in this place, no hair of any man's head hath been touched for the free exercise of his conscience."[3]

It is also due to Wentworth to observe that, while, at this time, with a view to the furtherance of his general scheme of government, he conceived the vast and unattainable project of reducing all the people of Ireland to a conformity in religion, the measures by which he sought to accomplish that project were, many of them, conceived in the profoundest spirit of a large and wide-reaching policy. Theological strife he knew the useless

---

[1] Strafford Papers, vol. i. p. 187.

[2] "Mr. Prynne, prisoner in the Tower, who hath got his ears sewed on that they grew again as before to his head, is relapsed into new errors."—*Letter of his newsmonger, Gerrard, to Wentworth, Strafford Papers,* vol. i. p. 266. Again Prynne's ears expiated those "new errors." Laud's own notice in his diary (Nov. 1630.), of the punishment of Leighton, a Scotch divine, the father of bishop Leighton, is more horrible:—"Friday, Nov. 16., part of his sentence was executed upon him in this manner, in the new palace at Westminster, in term time. 1. He was severely whipped before he was put in the pillory. 2. Being set in the pillory, he had one of his ears cut off. 3. One side of his nose slit. 4. Branded on one cheek with a red-hot iron, with the letters S S. And, on that day sevennight, his sores upon his back, ear, nose, and face being not cured, he was whipped again at the pillory in Cheapside, and there had the remainder of his sentence executed upon him, by cutting off the other ear, slitting the other side of the nose, and branding the other cheek." Leighton was released, after ten years' captivity, by the Long Parliament, having by that time lost his sight, his hearing, and the use of his limbs.

[3] See his letter to Con, the popish resident, Strafford Papers, vol. ii. p. 112. His correspondences with this person are in all respects curious, and, to me, significant of a purpose which his death prevented the open disclosure of.

horrors of,—and he soon discovered, by his "experience of both houses," that "the root of all disorders in this kingdom is the universal dependence of the popish faction upon jesuits and friars." [1] He speedily declared his determination to the king himself. " I judge it, without all question, far the greatest service that can be done unto your crowns, on this side, to draw Ireland into a conformity of religion with England; which, indeed, would undoubtedly set your majesty in greater strength and safety, within your own dominions, than any thing now left by the great and happy wisdom of yourself and blessed father unaccomplished, to make us an happy and secure people within ourselves. And yet, this being a work rather to be effected by judgment and degrees than by a giddy zeal and haste, whenever it shall seem good in your wisdom to attempt it (for I am confident it is left as a means whereby to glorify your majesty's piety to posterity), there will, in the way towards it, many things fall continually in debate and consideration at the board, with which it will be very unfit any of the contrary religion be acquainted." [2]

Urged by the English council, he set about the great work. Undisguised was the astonishment of the archbishop, however, at the slow and gradual means proposed by the lord deputy. His grace had fancied that the trouts who had been so completely tickled out of their money [3] might be as easily tickled out of their religion, or any thing else. The lord Wentworth thought differently. " It will be ever far forth of my heart," he wrote,

---

[1] Strafford Papers, vol. i. pp. 431, 432.   [2] Ibid. p. 307.

[3] " Now fie upon it, if the salmon of that river be bad, yet your loss is the less, since you have so many trouts that may be tickled into anything, or anything out of them."—*Laud to Wentworth, Strafford Papers*, vol. i. p. 329.

in answer to urgent pressings of the question, accompanied with especial requests for the enforcing of fines for nonconformity, "to conceive that a conformity in religion is not above all other things principally to be intended. For, undoubtedly, till we be brought all under one form of divine service, the crown is never safe on this side; but yet the time and circumstances may very well be discoursed, and sure I do not hold this a fit season to disquiet or sting them in this kind; and my reasons are divers. This course alone will never bring them to church, being rather an engine to drain money out of their pockets, than to raise a right belief and faith in their hearts, and so doth not indeed tend to that end it sets forth. The subsidies are now in paying, which were given with an universal alacrity; and very graceful it will be in the king to indulge them otherwise as much as may be till they be paid. It were too much at once to distemper them, by bringing plantations upon them, and disturbing them in the exercise of their religion, so long as it be without scandal. And so, indeed, very inconsiderate, as I conceive, to move in this latter, till that former be fully settled, and by that means the protestant party become by much the stronger, which, in truth, as yet I do not conceive it to be. Lastly, the great work of reformation ought not, in my opinion, to be fallen upon, till all incidents be fully provided for, the army rightly furnished, the forts repaired, money in the coffers, and such a preparation in view as might deter any malevolent licentious spirit to stir up ill humour in opposition to his majesty's pious intendments therein; nor ought the execution of this to proceed by step or degrees, but all rightly dispersed, to be undertaken and gone through withal at once. And certainly in the mean time, the less you call the conceit of it into their memory, the better it will be for us, and themselves the quieter; —so, as if there were no wiser than I, *the bishops should be privately required to forbear these ecclesiastical censures till they understood further of his majesty's pleasure therein.*" [1]

Steadily he proceeded, as if already in the far, but not uncertain, distance, he saw the accomplishment of this extraordinary design. He began at what he conceived to be the root of the evil. The churches had fallen to ruin; the church revenues had been cut to pieces by long leases and fraudulent appropriations; and the offices of the church had been given into the hands of the ignorant,—since to such only the abject poverty of her means offered any of the inducements of service.[2] "Now," wrote Wentworth to the still precipitate archbishop, "to attempt the reducing of this kingdom to a conformity in religion with the church of England, before the decays of the material churches here be repaired, an able clergy be provided, that so there might be both wherewith to receive, instruct, and keep the people, *were as a man going to warfare without munition or arms.* It being, therefore, most certain *that this to be wished reformation must first work from ourselves,* I am bold to transmit over to your grace these few propositions, for the better ordering this poor church, which hath thus

---

[1] Strafford Papers, vol. ii. p. 49.

[2] The reader will be startled, probably, to hear the value of some of the Irish bishopricks in that day. "The old bishop of Kilfanora," writes Wentworth to Laud, "is dead, and his bishoprick one of those which, when it falls, goes a begging for a new husband, being not worth above fourscore pounds to the last man : yet *in the handling of an understanding prelate it might perchance grow to be worth two hundred pounds,* but then it will cost money in suit."—*Strafford Papers*, vol. ii. p. 172.

long laid in the silent dark. The best entrance to the cure will be, clearly to discover the state of the patient, which I find many ways distempered;—an unlearned clergy, which have not so much as the outward form of churchmen to cover themselves with, nor their persons any ways reverenced or protected; the churches unbuilt; the parsonage and vicarage houses utterly ruined; the people untaught thorough the non-residency of the clergy, occasioned by the unlimited shameful numbers of spiritual promotions with cure of souls, which they hold by commendams; the rites and ceremonies of the church run over without all decency of habit, order, or gravity, in the course of their service; the possessions of the church, to a great proportion, in lay-hands; the bishops farming out their jurisdictions to mean and unworthy persons:—" and so, through all the sources of the evil, in a despatch of elaborate learning and profound suggestion, the lord deputy proceeds, enforcing upon the archbishop, finally, that he must surrender his present hopes of any immediate result. " It would be a brainsick zeal and a goodly reformation truly," he exclaims, in a supplementary despatch of yet greater energy and earnestness, " to force a conformity to a religion, whereas yet there is hardly to be found a church to receive, or an able minister to teach, the people. No, no; let us fit ourselves in these two, and settle his majesty's payments for the army, discharge his debts, and then have with them and spare not! I believe the hottest will not set his foot faster or further on than I shall do. In the mean time, I appeal to any equal-minded man, whether they or I be more in the right."

Unparalleled were the confidence and self-possessed resource with which Wentworth's great schemes now ran side by side. At one and the same moment he forced the revenue by [which his projected buildings in the church were to be raised, and cleared away the obstructions which still covered the sites he had selected. The decision of ecclesiastical rights was removed by him from the courts of common law to the Castle-chamber; the earl of Cork was forced to restore an annual revenue of 2000*l.*, which had been originally wrested from the church; and, understanding that the bishop of Killala had been meddling with underhand bargains to defraud his see, he sent for him to the presence chamber, and told him, with open and bitter severity, that he deserved to have his surplice pulled over his ears, and to be turned out of the church on a stipend of four nobles a year ![1] His usual success followed these measures; lands and tithes came pouring into his hands; and he issued a commission for the repair of churches, and won for it a ready obedience.[2]

In the midst of his labours, Wentworth turned aside, for a moment, to prefer a personal suit to the king. Consideration in the eyes of those over whom he held so strict and stern a hand, was beyond all things valuable to him. It was, indeed, the very materiel of his scheme of government. He appears therefore to have felt at this time, that some sudden and great promotion from the king to himself would give his government an exaltation

---

[1] See the Strafford Papers, vol. i. pp. 151—156. 171. 380. &c.

[2] One or two of the most remarkable of the measures he projected incidental to this purpose of conformity, may be mentioned here. The reader must examine Wentworth's various despatches, if he desires to master the knowledge of them all. He took resolute steps to prevent the children of catholics from being sent to foreign convents for their education. He proposed the erection of a vast number of protestant schools throughout Ireland with large endowments and able teachers. He enforced the most rigorous penalties upon non-residence. See Papers, vol. i. p. 393.; vol. ii. p. 7.

in the eyes of that "wild and rude people," of infinite importance to its security. His claims upon the king were immeasurable, as his services had been admitted to be. He wrote to him, to solicit an earldom. "The ambition," he said, "which moves me powerfully to serve your majesty, as my obligations are above those that preceded in this imployment, suggests unto me an hope I may be more enabled in these restless desires of mine, if I might, before our meeting again in parliament, receive so great a mark of your favour as to have this family honoured with an earldom. I have chosen therefore with all humbleness to address these lines immediately to yourself, as one utterly purposed to acknowledge all to your princely grace, and without deriving the least of the privity of thanks elsewhere." A characteristic desire closed the letter, that "no other person know hereafter your majesty found it in your wisdom not fit to be done." [1]   And such *was* Charles's short-sighted and selfish wisdom ! He refused the request. It was sufficient for his purpose that Wentworth was now indissolubly bound to him, since the personal hatred his measures had already excited in the English popular party precluded the possibility of his return to *them.* Nor had Wentworth provoked the hatred of the popular party alone. Under his superior tyranny, the lords of petty despotism had been crushed [2], and incapable

---

[1] Strafford Papers, vol. i. pp. 301, 302.

[2] His inquiries into questionable titles and church grants had exploded many a little tyrant, though in this way much private wrong was done. The servants of the English court, however, could never exactly understand his policy in respect of opposition to the aristocracy, and especially his habit of sternly refusing any presents or conciliatory favours from them. I quote a characteristic passage from a despatch of the secretary Windebank.—"Though, while we had the happiness and honour to have your assistance here at the council board, you made many ill faces with your pen (*pardon, I*

oppressors had become the lord deputy's fiercest accusers of oppression. To please the king, moreover, he had taken upon himself the refusal of various offices to his more importunate courtiers, careless of the odium he provoked and scorned. To heap upon him any marks of personal favour, under such circumstances, was an act of courage and honesty which the weak monarch did not dare attempt. Such wretched tools as Buckingham were more to his personal liking, though less in the balance of his treasury! "I desire you not to think," he wrote, after refusing the lord deputy's suit, "that I am displeased with the asking, though for the present I grant it not. For, I acknowledge that noble minds are always accompanied with lawful ambitions. And be confident that your services have moved me more than it is possible for any eloquence or importunity to do. So that your letter was not the first proposer of putting marks of favour on you; and I am certain that you will willingly stay my time, now ye know my mind so freely; that I may do all things *a mi modo*."[1]

This refusal was sorely felt by Wentworth. Covering

---

beseech your lordship, the over free censure of your Vandyking), and worse oftentimes with your speeches, especially in the business of the lord Falconberg, sir Thomas Gore, Vermuyden, and others, yet I understand you make worse there in Ireland, and there never appeared a worse face under a cork upon a bottle, than your lordship hath caused some to make in disgorging such church livings as their zeal had eaten up. Another remarkable error of your lordship, which makes much noise here, is that you refuse all presents, for which in one particular you had your reward. *For, it is said, that a servant bringing you a present from his master, and your lordship refusing it, the servant likewise would have none of your reward. By this your lordship may perceive how circumspect you have reason to be of your ways, considering how many malicious eyes are upon you, and what interpretations they make of your actions."—Strafford Papers*, vol. i. p. 161.

[1] Strafford Papers, vol. i. p. 332.

their allusion to the king, he threw into his next despatch
to Cottington some expressions of uneasy regret. "I
spend more here than I have of entertainments from his
majesty, I suffer extreamly in my own private at home, I
spend my body and spirits with extream toil, I sometimes
undergo the misconstructions of those I conceived, should
not, would not, have used me so. . . . But I am resolved
to complain of nothing. I have been something unpros-
perous, slowly heard, and as coldly answered that way.
I will either subsist by the integrity of my own actions,
or I will perish."[1]

The lord deputy's relief was in the measures with
which his enterprising genius had surrounded him. I
have alluded to his repression of certain turbulences that
had arisen in the convocation:—he now, by his personal
influence, prevailed with the learned Usher to surrender
the ecclesiastical articles he had forwarded to Ireland,
and which were any thing but acceptable to Laud; he
forced upon the clergy a series of hateful metropolitan
canons; and, by a series of measures similar in spirit to
those which had subdued the parliament, he confounded
and subdued the restless parsons.[2] In an early despatch,
he had to boast of only one dissentient voice from a new
and most astounding "protestant uniformity"!

The Irish common lawyers now received some further
proofs of his care, with intelligible hints of his prospective
schemes. He presented them with the majority of the
English statutes that had been passed since the time of
Poynings, but exacted from them certain conditions, at
the same time, which soon enabled him to describe to
the king in the following terms his Irish ministers

---

[1] Strafford Papers, vol. i. p. 354.
[2] See Strafford Papers, vol. i. pp. 342—344.

of justice :—" Not declined to serve other men's un-warrantable purposes by any importunity or application ; never in so much power and estimation in the state and with the subject, as now, and yet contained in that due subordination to the crown as is fit ; ministring wholly to uphold the sovereignty ; carrying a direct aspect upon the prerogatives of his majesty, without squinting aside upon the vulgar and vain opinions of the populace." [1]

The army next engaged his attention. He supplied them with clothes, with arms, with ammunition ; he redeemed them from licentiousness [2], and strengthened them in numbers and in discipline. He completed several regiments of foot, collected together some most efficient cavalry, and, in a very short time, astonished the court in England by returns of a richly appointed and well marshalled force. They heard with still greater astonishment that the lord deputy himself could find time to visit the whole army, and to inspect every individual in it ! And he further declared to them, that he held himself ever ready to mount horse at a moment's warning, and lead a troop of his own, raised and ac-coutred at his own charge, to repress, by a sudden movement, any popular commotion. [3] Vainly, however,

---

[1] Strafford Papers, vol. ii. p. 18.

[2] "Whence it is that the soldier is now welcome in every place, where before they were an abomination to the inhabitants ; that by this means the army in true account may be said to be of double the strength it had been apprehended."—*Strafford Papers*, vol. ii. p. 17.

[3] "For myself, I had a dead stock in horses, furniture, and arms for my troop, that stood me in 6000*l.*, and all in readiness upon an hour's warning to march. Nor did I this out of vanity, but really in regard I did conceive it became me not to represent so great a majesty meanly in the sight of the people ; that it was of mighty reputation to the service of the crown, when they saw me in such a posture, as that I was upon an hour's warning able to put myself on horseback, and to deliver, in spight of all opposition, a letter in any part of the kingdom ; *and lastly, in regard men should see I would*

he strove to communicate energy enough to Charles to procure his seconding some wider schemes projected by him in reference to the army. The army was the key-stone of that vast building which the imagination of Wentworth had already raised in the distance. The army was to hang in potent control over every thing, to be "the great peace-maker betwixt the British and the natives, betwixt the protestant and the papist, and the chief securer, under God and his majesty, of the future and past plantations." But Wentworth was foiled, by the indolent envy of his English coadjutors, from realising the great desire he held, " that his majesty breed up and have a seminary of soldiers in some part or other of his dominions."[1]

Indolent envy and active opposition notwithstanding, —the general reputation of the lord deputy of Ireland increased daily. " Mr. secretary Cooke," wrote lord Cottington to him, " is so diligent and careful to give your lordship an account of all your dispatches and answers to them, as there is nothing for me to say, but that for ought I can discern every body else is so too. My lord marshal is your own, my lord of Canterbury your chaplain, secretary Windebank your man, the king your favourite, and I your good lord. In earnest you have a mighty stock of opinion amongst us, which must of necessity make you damnable proud, if you take not heed."[2] The lord treasurer Weston alone, the old pro-pitiator of the king's regards to the quondam supporter of the petition of rights, but now bitterly jealous of Wentworth's friendship with Laud, scarcely cared to

---

not exact so much duty from any private captain, as I did myself upon myself, being their general."—Strafford Papers, vol. ii. p. 18.

[1] Strafford Papers, vol. ii. p. 198.   [2] Ibid. vol. i. p. 430.

conceal his animosity.[1]   A fatal attack of illness, however, at this time removed Weston ; and the only alloy
which served to dash the secret satisfaction with which
the news of this event was received by Wentworth, was
the existence of very decided rumours that the vacant
staff would be offered to himself.[2]

I have already touched on the many objections which
Wentworth entertained to an office of this sort ; and he
now sought by every means, and with characteristic
energy, to prevent its being offered to him at all.   To
his friends who wrote to him urging its acceptance, he
peremptorily answered ; and, at the same time, by the
same messenger, forwarded various requests to several
of them, that they would take on themselves to intimate
in every quarter, as plainly as possible, their knowledge
of his objection to it.   In further promotion of this
object, he practised a very singular piece of deception.
His retained gossip, Mr. Garrard—who continued faithfully and regularly, in the absence of a newspaper, to
fulfil all the duties of one, and to retail to the deputy all

[1] " The truth is, I conceive my lord treasurer sometime before
his death wished me no good, being grown extreme jealous of my
often writing to my lord of Canterbury ; and myself out of a sturdi-
ness of nature not so gently passing by his unkind usage, as a man
of a softer and wiser temper might have done ;—for, I confess, I did
stomach it very much to be so meanly suspected (being as innocent
and clear of crime towards him as the day), considering that I had
upon my coming from court given him as strong a testimony of my
faith and boldness in his affairs, nay, indeed, a stronger, than any
other friend he had, durst, or at least would, do for him.   So as
finding myself thus disappointed of the confidence I had in his professions at our parting, I grew so impatient, as to profess even to
himself, I would borrow a being from no man living but my master,
and there I would fasten myself as surely as I could.   So as by his
death it is not altogether improbable, that I am delivered of the
heaviest adversary I ever had."—*Wentworth to the Earl of Newcastle, Strafford Papers*, vol. i. p. 411.   See also a letter of Laud's,
vol. i. p. 329.
[2] See Garrard's letter, in Strafford Papers, vol. i. pp. 388, 389.

the occurrences and scandal of the court and the city—
had given him from time to time most minute accounts
of the illness of Weston through its progressive stages,
and finally had reported his death.[1]   It was Wentworth's
policy, however, to convey to the court, that, so indifferent was he in respect of Weston's office, he had never
troubled himself to inquire the probable issue of his
illness, and, indeed, had never heard of it.   As soon,
therefore, as an official intimation of the occurrence was
sent to him from Cottington, we find him answering
thus !—" My very good lord, I was never more surprised
in my life than upon the reading of your last letter; *not
having had any notice of my lord treasurer's least indisposition before.*   And how it happens I know not, but I
am sure, I was never well since almost, and that Monday
night last I swooned twice before they could get off my
cloathes."[2]—And again, assuring lord Newcastle :—" Yet
I protest, I ever wished well to his person, and am
heartily sorry for his death, which was signified unto me
by my lord Cottington, *before I heard any thing of his
sickness, and took me in a manner by surprise.*"[3]

These precautions were successful.   Left settled in his
government of Ireland, he next sought, by every possible resource, to establish a permanent revenue.   In

[1] See Strafford Papers, vol. i. pp. 243. 374. 387. &c.
[2] Strafford Papers, vol. i. p. 393.
[3] Ibid. p. 411.   Cottington himself was a candidate for the office,
and never forgave Laud his disappointment, which the profits of the
mastership of the records were by no means sufficient to heal over.
The treasury was administered by commission for twelve months,
when it was placed by Laud, to the astonishment of all who were
still unacquainted with the archbishop's designs for the state
advancement of the church, in the hands of Juxon, bishop of
London.   Laud, recording the appointment in his Diary (March,
1636), observes that " No churchman had it since Henry VII.'s
time ;" and adds, " Now if the church will not hold themselves up
under God, I can do no more."

this pursuit he exhausted his industry, his energy, his genius. Under his superintendence, the produce of the customs rose, within four years, from 12,000*l.* a year to 40,000*l.*, and continued to advance rapidly. Nor were the means by which it was accomplished other than just and honourable. He improved the method of collection, protected the coasts, swept the channel and the harbours of pirates, and, in fine,—lifted the commerce and the shipping of Irèland into a rich prosperity, by freeing it from danger. "My humble advice," observes Wentworth, "for the increase of trade was, that his majesty should not suffer any act of hostility to be offered to any merchants or their goods within the channel, which was to be preserved and privileged, as the greatest of his majesty's ports, in the same nature and property as the Venetian state do their Gulf, and the king of Denmark his Sound :—and therefore I humbly besought his majesty and their lordships, that it might accordingly be remembred and provided for, in all future treaties with foreign princes." In completion of this scheme, the lord deputy struggled hard to rescue the trade of Ireland from several absurd restrictions and monopolies ; and in this, having partially succeeded, his government left a claim for gratitude which is remaining still.[1]

In resorting to just measures occasionally, however, when they were not found to interfere with his ulterior schemes, Wentworth had taught himself no lesson of refraining from what was unjust. Money was to be had somehow—if justly, well—if not, it was to be had no

---

[1] For the various measures, and the elaborate reasoning with which the lord deputy supported them, see Strafford Papers, vol. i. pp. 67. 90. 106. 202. 308. 393. 307, 400. 521 192. 351. 366. 386. 405. 174. 340. 299. &c. &c. ; and vol. ii. pp. 18. 198. 137. 20. 89. 135. 42. 151. &c. &c.

less. He now, for instance, imposed a licence upon the retail of tobacco, and himself farmed the privilege for an annual rent of 7000*l.*, and, finally, of 12,000*l.* A tax was laid also on brewing, by way of feeler for the introduction of the excise,—an object of mortal hatred with the Irish.

The statutes of wills and uses were introduced, no less beneficial to the crown, and happily more just to the subject. They strengthened the tenure of property, fixed a remedy against fraudulent conveyances, restored widows to their jointures, and heirs to their inheritances. What was vastly more important to Wentworth, they increased the king's fines in the court of wards, by 10,000*l.* a year! A mint, also, was erected in Ireland, in spite of desperate opposition from the officers of the English mint, with the view of remedying the excessive scarcity of coin; workmen were introduced from England, to sink in various parts of the island for saltpetre, which Wentworth fancied might be obtained to commercial purposes; and he made several successful efforts to work the silver mines and marble quarries.[1]

Greater projects, too, than these, occupied the mind

[1] I have already supplied various authorities for these measures, to which I must refer the reader. With one of his packets to the king, Wentworth forwarded "an ingot of silver, of 300 ounces, being the first that ever was got in Ireland;" accompanying it with a proud expression of his hope, that "this kingdom now at length, in these latter ages, may not only fill up the greatness and dominion, but even the coffers and exchequer, of the crown of England. Sure I am, it becomes not this little one that her breasts should ever be dry, nor ought she with a sparing hand to communicate of her strength and wealth there, considering with what mass of treasure and streams of blood she hath been redeemed and preserved by that her elder and more excellent sister. May your majesty's days be as lasting and glorious as the best and purest of metals, and God Almighty prosper and accomplish all your princely thoughts and counsels, be they old or new."—*Strafford Papers*, vol. i. p. 174.

of the lord deputy. Before he set foot in Ireland [1], he had conceived the noble scheme of opening a victualling trade between Ireland and Spain. The distrust with which the patriotic party regarded Spain may have influenced him first, as if in defiance, to rise superior to such "vain apprehensions;"—but be that as it might, his despatches vindicate his plan. They show how admirably the commodities and the wants of the respective kingdoms correspond, and how closely reciprocal are their interests. They even supply a statement, drawn up with enormous pains from the information of various commercial agents, of the commodities which each port in Spain could either receive from Ireland, or give back in return. In one matter especially Wentworth saw the source of enormous advantage,—since the great annual fleets to the colonies, which were so often detained in the Spanish harbours for want of provisions, could clearly be supplied far more conveniently and cheaply from Ireland than from any other country in Europe. Contemporaneously with this measure, the lord deputy had resolved to attempt two other projects. "And surely, sir," he wrote to the king, "if we be able to furnish, and go through with this undertaking,—increase the growth and set up the manufactory of hemp and flax in that your kingdom,—I will hope to leave your subjects there in much happier condition than I found them, without the least prejudice to your subjects here. For this is a ground I take with me, *that to serve your majesty compleatly well in Ireland,—we must not only endeavour to* *enrich* them, *but make sure still to hold them dependant*

---

[1] See Strafford Papers, vol. i. pp. 93, 94. That remarkable despatch was written while waiting at Westminster for the ship that was to convoy him to Dublin.

upon the crown, and not able to subsist without us. Which will be effected, by wholly laying aside the manufacture of wools into cloth or stuff there, and by furnishing them from this kingdom ; and then making your majesty sole merchant of all salts on that side :—for thus shall they not only have their cloathing, the improvement of all their native commodities, (which are principally preserved by salt), and their victual itself from hence (strong ties and enforcements upon their allegiance and obedience to your majesty),—but a means found, I trust, much to advance your majesty's revenue upon salt, and to improve your customs. The wools there grown, and the cloths there worn, thus paying double duties to your crown in both kingdoms; and the salt outward here, both inward and outward there." [1]   In such principles as these, as through the majority of Wentworth's despotic schemes, some good wrestled with the evil. The linen manufacture, for instance, springing out of this monstrous intention, turned out to be a blessing to the island. Having learnt, on his arrival in the country, that no article for export was manufactured there, except a small quantity of coarse woollen yarn, and unwilling, by encouraging this branch, to interfere with the staple of England, he instantly resolved, by introducing the general cultivation of flax, to induce the manufacture of linen. At his own charge and adventure he imported and sowed a quantity of superior flax seed :—the next year, his first crop having outgone his expectation, he expended 1000*l.* on the same venture, erected a vast number of looms, procured workmen from France and Flanders, and at last sent forth a ship to Spain, at his own risk [2], with the

---

[1] Strafford Papers, vol. i. pp. 93, 94.

[2] See his characteristic letter to the duke of Medina, Strafford Papers, vol. ii. pp. 109, 110.

first investment òf linen that had ever been exported from Ireland. Sanguine of hopes so well laid, Wentworth then hazarded a prediction which has since been amply realised! " Very ambitious am I," writes he to sir William Boswell, " to set up a trade of linen-clothing in these parts, which, if God bless, so as it be effected, will, I dare say, be the greatest enriching to this kingdom that ever befel it."[1] The other project he had set up along with this, happily fell to the ground for want of encouragement. In proposing to monopolise the sale of salt, without which the Irish could neither carry on their victualling trade, nor cure their ordinary provisions, and which was at that time either manufactured by patentees or imported from abroad, lord Wentworth reckoned on a considerable increase of revenue, and the reduction of the Irish to a state of complete dependence. The internal manufacture abolished,—it would be next to impossible to smuggle a commodity so bulky and so perishable by sea, and yet, he urged, "again of so absolute necessity, as it cannot possibly stay upon his majesty's hand, but must be had whether they will or no, and may at all times be raised in price so far forth as his majesty shall judge to stand with reason and honour. Witness the Gabelles of salt in France."[2] This once accomplished, Wentworth felt he would have in his own hands the disposal of the food and the clothing of the Irish, and he pressed it with all his vehemence. " Holding them," exclaimed he, " from the manufacture of wool (which, unless otherwise directed, I shall by all means discourage), and then inforcing them to fetch their cloathing from thence, and to take their salt from the

---

[1] Strafford Papers, vol. i. p. 473.
[2] Ibid. vol. i. pp. 192, 193.; and see pp. 182. 333. 346.

king (being that which preserves and gives value to all their native staple commodities), how can they depart from us, without nakedness and beggary? Which in itself is so weighty a consideration as a small profit should not bear it down!" The small profit, however, in consequence of the jealousies of Weston, did bear it down, and the lord deputy was obliged at last to surrender it.

The embarrassments of the Irish treasury had now vanished, no anticipations any longer weakened it, every charge of government was paid to a day,—and, in the fifth year of his power, lord Wentworth announced to the king that the annual revenue would exceed the expenditure by 60,000*l*.

This, then, was being " crowned with the completest success ! " For, according to such political reasoners as M. de Lally Tolendal, the prosperity of the exchequer is the true test of the well-being of the state, and as long as a wretched people can be flattered or terrified into " coining their hearts " in sums, the king is ably served, and the minister is borne out in his exactions. Yet Wentworth deserves better advocates ! and it is perhaps due to his fame as a statesman, to keep in mind that we do not view his system in a perfect state, since the ground, as it were, had only been cleared for the building, when death struck down the builder.

Yorkshire, meanwhile, and Wentworth Woodhouse, had not been forgotten by the lord deputy ! If he had been living simply as a private gentleman in Ireland, instead of being the immediate manager and director of schemes which would have overwhelmed the strength of a dozen ordinary men,—he could not have attended with greater minuteness and apparent ease to his private affairs in England. I cannot resist extracting here some passages from an extraordinary letter to his early tutor, Mr. Greenwood, which occasion has already been taken to refer to. It is one of the most singular proofs that could be found anywhere, of the compatibility of a comprehensive genius with a vigilant attention to the most minute details. From his viceroyalty the lord Wentworth can signify his desire "that my tenants use their grounds and houses, as honest men and good husbands ought to do, according to their several leases; that my woods be preserved, and at due seasons felled and sold to the best profit, spring-woods I mean; that the hedges and fences be preserved; that the ponds, pheasants, partridges, and parks be preserved, and as much profit made of the herbage of Tankersly park as may be without hurt to the deer; that fires be kept in the houses at Woodhouse and Tankersly, and that the housekeepers preserve the rooms sweet, and the stuff without spoil, and principally that the houses be kept dry from taking of rain;"—that "the keeper of Tankersly must have the more immediate care of the woods belonging to Tankersly, especially those within the park, and to see that the pond-heads there be kept up, and the water to have a large and open passage to run away in the time of flood, and the grates so cleansed and firm as they break not, nor yet choak up, in which cases all the fish will be sure to go away with the flood."—And again, that "none of my demains be plowed in any case. I understand in this Richard Marris hath not followed my direction, which indeed, now and then, if a man would never so fain, he would have done. But if upon advice taken with you and Robin Rockley, you find at any time good for the grounds they were broken up, then would I have them plowed for my own use (*for I know right well the profit of those new rift grounds*), taking still care that they be well limed and manured, and so left as fat and full in heart as might be, to which purpose I would have no cost spared, *for I would have the grounds about my houses kept aloft, so as there may be beauty and pleasure communicated even from them to the houses themselves.*" With these desires are conveyed a vast host of minor directions respecting the servants he would have Greenwood reward, promote, confide in, or distrust.   Nor does he forget to —"beseech you to cause my new study there which looks into the hall, to be glazed, strong doors and locks to be set upon it ; and such boxes being made as are at Woodhouse, which Richard Forster will, upon your direction, give notice for, the evidence may be put into those boxes, and set in that study, where they will be more safe and handsomely kept than where they are now. If you could cause like locks to be made for that study, as are at Woodhouse, so that one key might open the locks in both places, it were much the better, and advising a little with Richard Forster, he might so order the matter as to have them so ;"—and to beg that "the red damask bed with stools, canopies, chairs, &c. belonging thereunto, be carefully looked unto." We learn also, from this omniscient despatch, that the death of his steward, Richard Marris,—"troubles me not so much, albeit in truth I loved him very well, as the sadness and indeed fearfulness of the misfortune, thorough which he was lost, most grievous, God knows, for him, and scandalous to all that have relation to him, amongst the rest, I am sure to have my share. *Nor do I think that he was drowned as you write, for then how should one pocket be dry ? But rather that, heavy with drink, he dropped from his horse near the place where his cloak lay, and, so it may be, amazed with the fall, was dragged by the horse, and the girths loosing, left in that wet place, where he was found dead,* and where, doubtless for want of company, and in a cold night and lodging, stormed to death.   But enough of so woful a subject, which I wish might never be mentioned or remembred again, further than to consider in it the just judgments of God, and to deter us from this swinish vice, and all other which may draw down upon ourselves like punishments."   Subjoining this, the course to be pursued with respect to the brother and heir of the deceased is laid down at great length, and in all its possible bearings, coupled with the following characteristic notice :—" I pray you in any case, if it may be, let him be drawn to this by fair and still means ; but if that work not with him, then would I have you let him know, that, until the account be declared betwixt me and his brother, which I am most willing and desirous may be before the next spring fairly examined by auditors indifferently chosen betwixt us, *I will hold the possession both of lands and goods ; that I will assign my debt to the king, and so extend and keep in extent the whole estate, till I be honestly and truly satisfied ;* as also that I will perform that last office in accomplishment of that which I know was his brother's intention, to see all his other creditors justly paid before he meddle with the estate,— but that then at after, I will not be his loss, by the help of God, one farthing.   And I pray you, if the first milder way take not (which if there be either honesty or con- science in the man methinks it should), then to proceed roundly the other way, holding all you have, putting the bonds of Darcy Wentworth and Pieter Man in suit upon the land, and keeping all in the state you have already

so well settled them, till my coming over." The reverend
gentleman had previously been given to understand that,
—" as for all my rents, the course I desire to be held, is
thus. A month after every rent day, I would have a
time appointed when yourself and Robert Rockley may
meet, and all the bailiffs to be appointed to attend you,
—there receive their accounts, giving them strict charge
to gather what shall be behind, and to bring the remainder and finish their account at Thornhill within a
month after. And I beseech you give them no sparing,
for I have suffered very much by it; however, I never
could perceive my tenants were a groat the better:—
besides, when they find they shall be distrained upon,
they will observe their day carefully, so as within a rent
day or two, this course strictly observed, the rents will
come in without any stop." The whole production is,
indeed, impressed with the peculiarities of Wentworth's
subtle and energetic genius; nor was there reason for
Mr. Greenwood to doubt, as he at the close assured, that
the writer "upon a good occasion would not deny his
life to him."

So also, burthened with his mighty schemes, the lord
deputy found time for every office of private service, of
friendship, and of scholarlike amusement. He made his
newsman, Mr. Garrard, forward him copies of Dr. Donne's
poetry[1], which he was amazingly fond of; gathered
antiquities for the king[2]; vanquished Inigo Jones in a
discussion on architecture[3]; reared a young greyhound
among his own children for the little prince of York[4];

---

[1] Strafford Papers, vol. i. p. 338. &c.   [2] Ibid. vol. ii. p. 82.
[3] Ibid. p. 83.
[4] The countess of Dorset had preferred the request, to which
Wentworth instantly answered—" I did, with all gladness, receive
from your ladyship, by this bearer, the first commands it ever

corresponded with old friends in Yorkshire[1]; dis-cussed with Vandyke on various marbles; hunted, hawked[2], and played at the games of primero and mayo. "He played excellently well," says Radcliffe; "and for company sake, in Christmas, and after supper, he would play sometimes; yet he never was much taken with it, nor used it excessively, but as a recreation should be used. His chief recreation was after supper, when, if he had company, which were suitable unto him, that is, honest chearful men, he would retire into an inner room, and set two or three hours, *taking tobacco and telling stories with great pleasantness and freedom:* and this he used constantly, with all familiarity in private, laying then aside all state and that due respect which in publick he would expect."

Never for a single instant, however, were the public affairs suffered to wait his leisure. They threatened now to demand more than ordinary care, for the king had resolutely thwarted the deputy in his desire to continue the parliament. "My reasons," he wrote, "are grounded upon my experience of them here. They are of the nature of cats, they ever grow curst with age, so that if ye will have good of them, put them off handsomely

---

pleased our young master to honour me withal; and before Christmas I will not fail to furnish his highness with the finest greyhound this kingdom affords; till then I shall humbly crave his highness's pardon; *for, to send any before I may have convenient time, under my own eye, to be sure he is of a safe and gentle disposition, and that I may try him here first, how he shall behave himself amongst my own children,* were the greatest indiscretion and boldness in me possible. And albeit, I assure myself your ladyship's care, and other his highness's attendants, would be such, as the dog should do no harm, yet that were no thanks to me."—*Strafford Papers,* vol. i. p. 303.

[1] Strafford Papers, vol. i. p. 116.

[2] "In his later days," Radcliffe observes, "he got little time to see his hawks fly, though he always kept good ones."

when they come to any age, for young ones are ever most tractable. . . . Now that we are well, let us content ourselves therewith."[1]   Charles, at the same time, had urged upon his minister the preferable course of following out their plans (which were far more favoured with himself than even a submissive Irish parliament), of increasing the estates of the crown by a search after defective titles.   Wentworth, upon this, set resolutely to work.   He examined various old records, and discovered that the whole province of Connaught, on the forfeiture of its Irish chieftain, had lapsed, many years ago, to the crown.   It had, indeed, even since that time, again been granted away, but the court lawyers now either found flaws in the conveyances or made them.   It will be recollected that a recognition of the validity of such titles formed one of the obnoxious "graces" which Wentworth had laid to sleep so soundly.

Pledging himself at once to the king, therefore, that he would reduce Connaught to the absolute possession of the crown,—the lord deputy proceeded into the county of Roscommon, summoned a jury composed of "persons of such means as might answer the king a round fine in the Castle-chamber, in case they should prevaricate, and who, in all seeming, even out of that reason, would be more fearful to tread shamefully and impudently aside from the truth, than such as had less, or nothing, to lose,"[2]—told them that his present appeal to them was a mere act of courtesy, and, in return for a series of deep and significant threats, received a ready obedience. The same scenes, with the same results, were acted in

---

[1] Strafford Papers, vol. i. p. 365. Wentworth's previous entreaties for a prorogation will be found at p. 353.

[2] Strafford Papers, vol. i. p. 442. ; a despatch in which the entire proceedings are characteristically given.

Mayo and Sligo, and lord Wentworth went on to Galway.

Here he was prepared for opposition. The people, chiefly Roman catholics, were supported by a formidable body of priests, and had the strenuous countenance and assistance of their hereditary lord, the earl of St. Albans and Clanricarde, a nobleman of esteem at the English court. The spirit of Wentworth rose at the prospect, and he prepared the court, in a memorable despatch, for the measures they were to expect from him :—"If it be followed with just severity," he wrote, "this opposition will prove of great use to the crown, as any one thing that hath happened, since this plantation fell in pro-position. It shall not only, with a considerable addition of revenue, bring security to this county, which of the whole kingdom most requires it, but make all the succeeding plantations pass with the greatest quietness that can be desired. Whereas if this froward humour be negligently or loosely handled, it will not only blemish the honour and comeliness of that which is effected already, but cut off all hope for the future." He sum-moned a jury on the same principle as in the preceding counties. They were obstinate in their refusal to obey him. The sheriff who had selected them was instantly fined 1000*l.*; the jurors themselves were cited into the Castle-chamber, and fined 4000*l.* each ; and the earl of Clanricarde [1] received a heavy reprimand from the court, and was made to suffer severely. Bitter murmurs were heard in Ireland, and men spoke out more strongly in England. But the deputy knew no fear. "This comfort

---

[1] For the representations made by Wentworth against this noble-man, see Strafford Papers, vol. i. pp. 451. 479. 492. ; and vol. ii. pp. 31. 35. 365. 381.

I have to support me against the malice of this race of sturdy beggars, that howbeit they threaten me with a Felton or a Ravillac, yet my master is pleased graciously to accept of my endeavours, and to say publicly at council-board, the crown of England was never so well served on this side, as since my coming to the government." [1]

Exasperated, nevertheless, with these signs of opposition, he now thought to silence them effectually by one terrible warning. His knowledge of the character of the vice-treasurer, the lord Mountnorris, has been already shown, and I have quoted the deeply significant intimation which opened their official connection. Mountnorris had long disregarded this, and had, indeed, omitted no opportunity which his place afforded him, of thwarting in every possible way the schemes of Wentworth. A trifling circumstance now gave the latter an occasion of punishment. Severely afflicted with the gout,—for so frightful were his bodily infirmities, that freedom from one complaint seldom failed to be followed by thraldom to another,—the lord deputy sat one day in the presence-chamber, when one of his attendants—a Mr. Annesley, a distant relation of the lord Mountnorris—accidentally dropped a stool upon his foot. " Enraged with the pain whereof," says Clarendon, " his lordship with a small cane struck Annesley. This being merrily spoken of at dinner at the lord chancellor's table, where the lord Mountnorris was, he said, 'the gentleman had a brother that would not have taken such a blow.'" [2] These words were spoken in the month of April. Eaves-droppers reported

---

[1] Strafford Papers, vol. i. p. 412. ; and see p. 371.

[2] Clarendon, vol. i. p. 174. This statement is borne out by Baillie's letters. Rushworth, on the other hand, gives it as Wentworth's witnesses afterwards swore to it. Collections, vol. iii. p. 187. ; and see Nalson's Collections, vol. i. p. 59.

them to Wentworth, who instantly forwarded a messenger to London to bring back a king's commission for the trial of Mountnorris. It was sent at his request. Not till December, however, was any further step taken, though the interim had been employed in giving security to the lord deputy's purpose.

In December, Mountnorris received a summons to attend a council of war the next morning. Ignorant of the cause of so sudden a movement, he was vainly asking his brother councillors to explain it,—when Wentworth entered, produced the king's commission, charged lord Mountnorris with an attempt to stir up mutiny against himself as general of the army, and ordered the charge to be read. It ran to this effect :—That it having been mentioned at the lord chancellor's table, that Annesley had let a stool fall on the lord deputy's foot, Mountnorris had scornfully and contemptuously said, " Perhaps it was done in revenge of that public affront that my lord deputy did me formerly; but I have a brother who would not have taken such a revenge." In vain the accused fell on his knees, and requested time for consultation; in vain he demanded even a copy of the charge, or permission to retain counsel :—every thing was denied to him; the lord deputy cited two articles of war which rendered him amenable to imprisonment and to death; demanded from the councillors the immediate and summary judgment of a court martial on both the articles; and sternly silenced a proposal which they ventured to submit, of separating the charges. Guilty the accused was to be voted, "of both or of none !" Even lord Moore, one of the councillors— who, with sir R. Loftus, the brother of another councillor, had proved Wentworth's case—was ordered to resume

his seat, and judge the man whom he had accused!
Under the eye of the lord deputy the council then de-
liberated and voted; and their sentence condemned
Mountnorris to imprisonment, deprived him of all his
offices, ignominiously dismissed him from the army,
incapacitated him from ever serving again, and, finally,
left him to be shot, or beheaded, at the pleasure of the
general.   Before the whole court lord Wentworth then
expressed exultation,—" the sentence was just and noble,
and for his part he would not lose his share of the honour
of it!"   He turned afterwards to the unfortunate Mountnorris; told him that now, if he chose, he had only to
order execution; but that he would petition for his life,
and "would sooner lose his hand than Mountnorris
should lose his head."

His purpose was to be more effectually answered, in
truth, by a contemptuous pardon, and this, from the first,
he appears to have designed, trusting to the general
ignominy that would be thrown over Mountnorris, to
crush any after-attempt he might make against his own
power.   The remarks which have been already made on
other personal oppressions, apply here with still greater
force, and to the system which Wentworth had to uphold
should the horror and reproach be carried.   It is certain
that, at the period of this proceeding, lord Clarendon
has justly described the issue to which the positions of
the parties had brought them :—" That either the deputy
of Ireland must destroy my lord Mountnorris while he
continued in his office, or my lord Mountnorris must
destroy the deputy as soon as his commission was determined."[1]   Wentworth was not the man to leave this

[1] The reader may be referred, in case he desires to pursue this
subject further, to the most ample materials of judgment and dis-

issue in the hands of chance,—nor, at the same time, to blind himself to the results of such conduct as the necessity had forced upon him. "But if, because I am necessitated to preserve myself from contempt and scorn, and to keep and retain with me a capacity to serve his majesty with that honour becoming the dignity of that place I here by his majesty's favour exercise, therefore I must be taken to be such a rigid Cato Censorius, as should render me almost inhospitable to humane kind; —yet shall not that persuade me to suffer myself to be trodden upon, by men indeed of that savage and insolent nature they would have me believed to be, or to deny unto myself and my own subsistence so natural a motion as is the defence of a man's self."

The wife of Mountnorris was a kinswoman of the lady Arabella Hollis, whose memory Wentworth cherished with such enthusiasm, and "in the name and by the memory of her" hoping that God would so reward him for it upon "the sweet children of her kinswoman," lady Mountnorris, immediately after the sentence, in a deeply pathetic letter, besought Wentworth to take "his heavy hand from off her dear lord."[1]   Every writer concurs in stating that this letter was coldly and contemptuously disregarded by the lord deputy, but an extract from one of his despatches may at least serve to throw some doubt over such a statement. "I send you," he writes to secretary Cooke, "here inclosed the sentence of the council of war in the case of the lord Mountnorris. . . .

---

crimination as to the character and bearing of the parties.   Strafford Papers, vol. i. pp. 73. 76. 119. 250. 349. 388. 392. 402. *et seq.* 448. 497. *et seq.* 502. 504. 508. *et seq.* 511. *et seq.* 514. 519. ; and to vol. ii. pp. 5. 14. *et seq.* and 145.   The unfortunate want of an index to the Strafford Papers makes these references necessary.

[1] Clarendon's State Papers, vol. i. p. 449.

I foresee full well, how I shall be skirmished upon for it on that side: causeless traducing and calumniating of me is a spirit that hath haunted me through the whole course of my life, and now become so ordinary a food, as the sharpness and bitterness of it in good faith distempers not my taste one jot. Finally, as I formerly signed the sentence together with them, so do I most heartily now join in their letters to you, where we all become humble petitioners to his majesty for his life, which was, God knows, so little looked after by me, that howbeit I hold under favour the sentence most just, yet were it left me in choice, whether he must lose his head, or I my hand, this should redeem that. His lordship was prisoner in this castle some two days, *but upon his physician's certificate, that the badness of his lodging might prejudice his health, I sent him upon good bond restrained only to his own house, where he is like to remain till I receive his majesty's further pleasure concerning him.*" It is most unlikely that such an extraordinary favour as this had been granted on the application of a physician merely, while the lord deputy had an obvious reason for keeping out of sight the influence of the lady.

Some short time after, Mountnorris, on condition of submitting to Wentworth, and acknowledging the justice of his sentence, received his liberty. Prosecutions, however, had been lodged against him meanwhile in the star-chamber, and he felt himself a lowered and well-nigh beggared man. "At my lord Mountnorris his departure hence," writes the deputy, "he seemed wondrously humbled, as much as Chaucer's friar[1], that

---

[1] Chaucer and Dr. Donne appear to have been Wentworth's favourite poets. Chaucer indeed, to the court readers of that day, was as Shakespeare in our own. It is clear too, from the frequent

would not for him any thing should be dead ; so I told him I never wished ill to his estate, nor person, *further than to remove him thence, where he was as well a trouble as an offence unto me ;* that being done (howbeit thorough his own fault with more prejudice to him than I intended) I could wish there were no more debate betwixt us ; and I told him that, if he desired it, I would spare my prosecution against him in the star chamber there." Immediately before this passage occurs, in the same letter, Wentworth had remarked :—" I assure you I have had a churlish winter of this, nor hath the gout been without other attendants that do prognostick no long life for me here below ! Which skills not much. He lives more that virtuously and generously spruds one month,

---

use of peculiar expressions in his despatches, that the lord deputy was not unacquainted, and that intimately, with the great dramatist, though he never, as with Chaucer and Donne, quotes connected passages. It is worth subjoining, as an instance out of many, one of Wentworth's sneers at sir Piers Crosby—that " trifle Crosby," as he elsewhere calls him. " Since his departure I have neither heard from him, nor of him, more than that he vouchsafed with his pretty composed looks to give the Gallway agents countenance and court-ship before the eyes of all the good people that looked upon them, gracing and ushering them to and from all their appearings before the lords ; there is no more to be added in his case but these two verses of old Jeffrey Chaucer—

> ' No where so busy a man as he ther n'as,
> And yet he seemed busier than he was.' "

When the newsmonger Garrard heard of the affair of Mountnorris, he quotes Dr. Donne, as if to communicate some tender sympathy to his lordship in that way :—" When first I heard the news, which was on St. Stephen's day, and how all men talked of it, it disorder'd me, it brake my sleep, I waked at four in the morning, it made me herd the next day less in company ;—not that I believed what was said, but that I had no oracle, no such friend on the sudden to go to, who could give such satisfaction as I desired. Noblest lord, your letter hath done it ; what Dr. Donne writ once is most true, *Sir, more than kisses, letters mingle souls, for thus friends absent speak,* &c."

than some other that may chance to dream out some years, and bury himself alive all the while." The life of the lord deputy had, indeed, in the intensity of sensation it had required for its sustainment, covered a larger span of existence than years can measure, and now the term that remained to it was fated to be dashed with almost unceasing anxieties and troubles, more bitter in proportion to the temperament they wrought on.

His anticipations of the enmity that would be provoked against him by the case of Mountnorris, were more than realised. Laud ventured to intimate to him—"I find that, notwithstanding all your great services in Ireland, which are most graciously accepted by the king, you want not them, which whisper, and perhaps speak louder where they think they may, against your proceedings in Ireland, as being over-full of personal prosecutions against men of quality. . . . . And this is somewhat loudly spoken by some on the queen's side. . . . . I know you have a great deal more resolution in you, than to decline any service due to the king, state, or church, for the barking of discontented persons ; and God forbid but you should : and yet, my lord, if you could find a way to do all these great services and decline these storms, I think it would be excellent well thought on." [1] To this advice succeeded

---

[1] Strafford Papers, vol. i. p. 479. Lord Cottington's account was something different :—"You said right, that Mountnorris his business wou'd make a great noise : for so it hath, amongst ignorant, but especially ill-affected people ; but it hath stuck little among the wiser sort, and begins to be blown away amongst the rest." His lordship, in the same letter, communicates to Wentworth a remarkable sequel to the affair. The lord deputy, in order to procure Mountnorris's offices for his favourites (chiefly young Loftus, the husband of a lady who has been before adverted to), had proposed to distribute 6000*l.* as a sort of purchase of them, to the principal English ministers. (Strafford Papers, vol. i. p. 508.) The sly old courtier Cottington, however, into whose hands the business

other galling announcements. Lord Clanricarde died suddenly, from a broken heart it was said, in consequence of the Galway proceedings; and the death of the sheriff of that county, who had been imprisoned by Wentworth, immediately followed. Both of these deaths were laid at his door. "They might as well," exclaimed the lord deputy, adverting to the first—"they might as well have imputed unto me for a crime, his being threescore and ten years old!" With cooler satire he put off the fate of the sheriff. "They will lay the charge of Darcy the sheriff's death unto me. My arrows are cruel that wound so mortally!—*but I should be more sorry, by much, the king should lose his fine.*" Still this did not subdue the daily increasing murmurs; one exaggeration begot another; and he resolved at last, by a sudden public appearance in England, to confound his accusers, and, even in their very teeth, to throw for new marks of favour.

Permission having been obtained from the king, Wentworth appeared at the English court in May, 1636. He was received with the highest favour, and so delighted the king with his account of the various measures by which he had consolidated the government of Ireland, that he was entreated by his majesty to repeat the details "at a very full council."—"Howbeit I told him, I feared

---

fell, hit on a more notable expedient. "When William Raylton first told me," he writes, "of your lordship's intention touching Mountnorris's place for sir Adam Loftus, and the distribution of monies for the effecting thereof, I fell upon the right way, *which was, to give the money to him that really could do the business, which was the king himself;* and this hath so far prevailed, as by this post your lordship will receive his majesty's letter to that effect; so as there you have your business done without noise." The money happened to be particularly welcome to Charles, who had just been purchasing an estate! See Strafford Papers, vol. i. p. 511.

his majesty might be wearied with the repetition of so long a narrative, being no other than he had formerly heard, and that I desired therefore I might give my account to the lords without his majesty's further expence of time, yet he told me it was worthy to be heard twice, and that he was willing to have it so."[1] No wonder! A more striking description was never spoken. He detailed all the measures he had accomplished for the church, the army, and the revenue, for manufactures and commerce, for the laws and their administration,—and through every vigorous and well-aimed word shone the author of all those measures! Wentworth adverted, towards the close of his relation, to "some particulars wherein I have been very undeservedly and bloodily traduced." He mentioned the slanders that had been circulated, proclaiming him "a severe and austere hard-conditioned man, rather indeed a basha of Buda, than the minister of a pious Christian king." His report of what followed is a direct illustration of much that has been advanced in this memoir. "Howbeit, if I were not much mistaken in myself, it was quite the contrary; *no man could shew wherein I had expressed it in my nature, no friend I had would charge me with it in my private conversation, no creature had found it in the managing of my own private affairs, so as if I stood clear in all these respects, it was to be confessed by any equal mind that it was not any thing within, but the necessity of his majesty's service, which inforced me into a seeming strictness outwardly.* And that was the reason indeed. For where I found a crown, a church, and a people spoiled, 'I could not

---

[1] See Strafford Papers, vol. i. pp. 13—22. The despatch in which Wentworth again, for the third time, details his remarkable narrative, is addressed to Wandesford, who, in the meanwhile, was administering the Irish government.

imagine to redeem them from under the pressure with gracious smiles and gentle looks. It would cost warmer water than so! True it was, that where a dominion was once gotten and settled, it might be stayed and kept where it was by soft and moderate counsels, but where a sovereignty (be it spoken with reverence) was going down the hill, the nature of a man did so easily slide into the paths of an uncontrouled liberty, as it would not be brought back without strength, nor be forced up the hill again but by vigour and force. And true it was indeed, I knew no other rule to govern by, but by reward and punishment :—and I must profess that where I found a person well and intirely set for the service of my master, I should lay my hand under his foot, and add to his respect and power all I might, and that where I found the contrary, I should not handle him in my arms, or soothe him in his untoward humour, but if he came in my reach, so far as honour and justice would warrant me, I must knock him soundly over the knuckles, but no sooner he become a new man, apply himself as he ought to the government, but I also change my temper, and express my self to him, as unto that other, by all the good offices I could do him. If this be sharpness, if this be severity, I desired to be instructed better by his majesty and their lordships, for in truth it did not seem so to me; however, if I were once told, that his majesty liked not to be thus served, I would readily conform myself, follow the bent and current of my own disposition, which is to be quiet, not to have debates and disputes with any. Here his majesty interrupted me and said, that was no severity, wished me to go on in that way, for, if I served him otherwise, I should not serve him as he expected from me."

Wentworth left the court for Wentworth Woodhouse, loaded with the applause of the king and his lords of the council, and followed by the aweful gaze of doubting multitudes.

As he passed through York, he was arrested by enthusiastic friends, and with some difficulty escaped them. "I am gotten hither," he writes to Laud, "at last, to a poor house I have, having been this last week almost feasted to death at York. In truth, for any thing I can find, they were not ill-pleased to see me. Sure I am it much contented me to be amongst my old acquaintance, which I would not leave for any other affection I have, but to that which I both profess and owe to the person of his sacred majesty. Lord! with what quietness in myself could I live here in comparison of that noise and labour I meet with elsewhere; and, I protest, put up more crowns in my purse at the year's end too! But we'll let that pass. For I am not like to enjoy that blessed condition upon earth. And therefore my resolution is set to endure and struggle with it so long as this crazy body will bear it, and finally drop into the silent grave, where both all these (which I now could, as I think, innocently delight myself in) and myself are to be forgotten. And fare them well! I persuade myself *exuto Lepido* I am able to lay them down very quietly."[1]

His rest was extremely short, for he soon re-appeared in York, discharged several of the duties of his presidency, and fell with all his accustomed vigour on the collection of ship-money. That famous tax had recently been levied. The same success waited upon Wentworth's present measures in respect to it, as the capacity and

[1] Strafford Papers, vol. ii. p. 26.

energy which animated all he did almost invariably commanded. In every other county, murmurs, threats, and curses, accompanied the payment,—in Yorkshire, during Wentworth's presence, silence. His letter to the king reads like one of his Irish despatches. "In pursuit of your commands, I have effectually, both in public and private, recommended the justice and necessity of the shipping business, and so clearly shown it to be, not only for the honour of the kingdom in general, but for every man's particular safety, that I am most confident the assessment this next year will be universally and cheerfully answered within this jurisdiction."[1]

The lord deputy, as the time approached for his return to his government, unburthened himself of a suit to the king which he now felt concerned him daily more and more. For the second time he entreated from Charles the honour of an earldom. He begged it in refutation of the malicious insinuations of his enemies, to prove that their calumnies were disbelieved, and to strengthen him in the eyes of the Irish. At the same time he wrote to Laud, telling him plainly the use the enemies of the state were making of the king's withholding from his deputy some public mark of his favour, and urging the danger it threatened to his authority and to the public service. Again Wentworth's suit was rejected. Since Charles's last answer, his reasons for refusal had increased every way. His reply was peremptory. "Believe it, the marks of my favours that stop malicious tongues are

---

[1] In a subsequent letter Wentworth wrote :—"I forgot in my last humbly to offer my opinion, that in case your majesty find or apprehend any backwardness in the south, it were good the next year's writs for the shipping assessment were hastened first down into these parts, where they are sure to find no opposition, or unwillingness, which example may rather further than hinder in the right way, which others ought to follow elsewhere.

neither places nor titles, but the little welcome I give to accusers, and the willing ear I give to my servants." The jest with which his majesty's letter closed did not mend the matter.   "I will end with a rule that may serve for a statesman, a courtier, or a lover,—never make a defence or apology before you be accused."   The lord deputy felt this deeply.   "I wish," he wrote to Laud, "thorough the opinion that I stand not full to his majesty's liking in my service in this place, his majesty's affairs may not suffer as well as myself.   But fall that as it may, I am resolved never to stir that stone more, dead to me it is to be for ever.   Indeed I neither think of it, . nor look for it."   His friend George Butler he recommended to look for rewards and punishments in the next world; "for in good faith, George, all below are grown wonderous indifferent."   Nor did Wentworth scruple to exhibit very broadly to the king the still rankling disappointment.   "Out of the truth of my heart," he wrote, "and with that liberty your majesty is pleased to afford me (which shall nevertheless ever retain all the humility, modesty, and secrecy possible), admit me to say, reward well applied advantages the services of kings extreamly much.   It being most certain, that not one man of very many serve their masters for love, but for their own ends and preferments, and that he is in the rank of the best servants, that can be content to serve his master together with himself.   Finally, I am most confident, were your majesty purposed but for a while to use the excellent wisdom God hath given you in the constant, right, and quick applying of rewards and punishments, it were a thing most easy for your servants in a very few years, under your conduct and protection, so to settle all your affairs and dominions, as should render you, not only at home but abroad also, the most powerful and considerable king in Christendom."[1]

With Laud, Wentworth communicated more freely on this subject, and in one of his more desponding letters suddenly consoles himself with Dr. Donne and Vandyke. "I most humbly thank your lordship for your noble care and counsel tending to the preservation of my health, a free bounty it is of your love towards me, where otherwise of myself I am so wondrous little considerable to any body else. The lady Astrea, the poet tells us, is long since gone to heaven, but under favour I can yet find reward and punishment on earth. Indeed sometimes they are like Doctor Donn's 'anagram of a good face,'[2] the ornaments missed, a yellow tooth, a red eye, a white lip or so! and seeing that all beauties take not all affections, one man judging that a deformity, which another considers as a perfection or a grace, this methinks convinceth the certain incertainty of rewards and punishments. Howsoever he is the wisest commonly, the greatest, and happiest man, and shall surely draw the fairest table of his life, that understands with Vandike, how to dispose of these shadows, best, to make up his own comeliness and advantage."[3] Whereupon his grace of Canterbury warns the lord deputy from Vandyke and

---

[1] Strafford Papers, vol. ii. p. 41.

[2] "Marry and love thy Flavia, for she
   Hath all things whereby others beauteous be;
   For though her eyes be small, her mouth is great;
   Though theirs be ivory, yet her teeth be jet;
      &c.   &c.   &c.
   What though her cheeks be yellow, her hair's red;

   *   *   *   *
   Though all her parts be not in th' usual place,
   She hath yet the anagrams of a good face!"   *Second Elegy.*

[3] Strafford Papers, vol. ii. p. 158.

Dr. Donne, into the book of Ecclesiastes.—"Once for all, if you will but read over the short book of Ecclesiastes, while these thoughts are in you, you will see a better disposition of these things, and the vanity of all their shadows, than is to be found in any anagrams of Dr. Donne's, or any designs of Vandyke. So to the lines there drawn I leave you."[1]

Disappointed of that public mark of favour he had claimed so justly, but strengthened by private instructions[2] from the king which left no bound or limit to his power, lord Wentworth returned to Ireland. He resumed his measures precisely at the point in which he had left them, overawed every effort to disturb the breathless tranquillity which his energy had inspired, and, under his vigilant eye, the infant cultivation, manufactures, and commerce of the country, began to increase and prosper. "While the subject enjoyed security, from the entire suppression of internal insurrections and depredations, the royal revenues, arising from produce and consumption, experienced a rapid increase."[3] This "security," however, was never felt to be other than that of absolutism, for Wentworth, hand in hand with his most striking financial improvements, carried on his inquiries into defective titles with a terrible rigour. He placed at the king's disposal the entire district of Ormond, and in his Irish exchequer the sum of 15,000*l.*, wrung from the family of the O'Byrnes in Wicklow, to redeem their

[1] Strafford Papers, vol. ii. p. 169.

[2] See his letter to Wandesford, Strafford Papers, vol. ii. p. 13. *et seq.*

[3] Mr. MacDiarmid, whose summary of Wentworth's financial measures is very able. I have occasionally availed myself of it. See Lives of British Statesmen, vol. ii. pp. 170—181. The despatches of the lord deputy, in the early portion of the second volume of the Strafford Papers, are singularly powerful.

possessions from a similar award. Successful in every
effort he made, he did not care to call into request the
new powers he had been entrusted with.

Not a messenger or a letter arrived from England,
however, without news that dashed his prosperity and his
pride. He saw as much beyond the narrow vision of the
English courtiers as his sagacity outreached theirs, and,
in the hollow madness of their measures, had already
discerned disastrous issues. The ruin they were pre-
cipitating, he bitterly knew would involve himself; yet
he had not even the poor consolation of feeling, that the
only portion of the king's service that had in it any of
the elements of stability, his own government, had a
single hearty defender in that English court. Their
praises obsequiously waited on his presence alone. Laud,
indeed, was still his friend; but Laud's ecclesiastical
administration had by this time well nigh incapacitated
its master for any purpose of good. The popular party
in England, meanwhile, taking advantage of the occasion,
raised a loud and violent voice of clamour against the
lord deputy of Ireland. He flung it back, in the hasty
self bullying of his will, with a contemptuous scorn [1],—

---

[1] "In truth," he wrote to Laud, "I still wish (and take it also to
be a very charitable one) Mr. Hambden and others to his likeness
were well whipt into their right senses; if that the rod be so used as
that it smarts not, I am the more sorry. One good remedy were to
send for your chimney-sweeper of Oxford, who will sing you a song
made of one Bond, it seems a schoolmaster of the free-school of St.
Paul's, London, and withal show how to jerk, to temper the voice,
to guide the hand, to lay on the rod excellently; sure I am he made
me laugh heartily when I was there last; and the chancellor of the
university might with a word fetch up to your lordship at Lambeth,
both the person and the poems (for I must tell you there is the
second, if not the third part of the song), and then bring but Mr.
Hambden and Bond in place, and it may every way prove a three
man's song. But fetch in the nobleman you mention, and then it
may chance to prove a very full concert! *As well as I think of Mr.
Hambden's abilities*, I take his will and peevishness to be full as

but he knew secretly its power, and in his graver despatches warned the court from leaving him unprotected
to its effects :—" With the disesteem of the governor," he
wrote, " the government shall impair, if not in the existence, sure in the beauty of it, which is as considerable,
as that most men are guided and guide themselves by
opinion. So as, if you will have my philosophy in the
point, let no prince employ a servant longer than he is
resolved to have him valued and esteemed by others,
thorough those powers he shall manifest to be entrusted
with him." Still he saw no symptoms of what he desired,
and at last he wrote personally to the king. "Sir," he
said, "I take my natural inclinations to be extreamly
much more tender and gentle, than the smooth looks and
cheeks of your ministers on that side find in their own
bosoms, and yet heighten the cry upon me!" But
Charles had now the queen's influence in many respects
upon him, and the queen was not displeased to hear of
the sinking fortunes of Wentworth. Lord Holland, her
favourite counsellor, was even heard to insinuate that the
lord deputy was subject to occasional touches of madness.
This, among the other reports, came to Wentworth's ear.
He charged it upon Holland, who denied it, confessing
he might have attributed "hypochondriack humours,"
certainly not madness. Wentworth wrote back to the
king :—"As for the 'hypochondriack humour' his lordship mentions, it is a great word and a courtly phrase;
but if I mistake not the English of it, it is to be civilly
and silently maddish : and if so, I can assure his lordship,

---

great, and without diminution to him, judge the other, howbeit not
the father of the country (a title some will not stick to give unto them
both, to put them if it be possible, the faster and farther out of their
wits), the very *sinciput*, the vertical point of the whole faction."—
Strafford Papers, vol. ii. p. 158.

he shall find as little of that in me, as of any other more active heat. But I shall not stir that matter further, only, if it be denied his lordship said I was mad, it were very easy to shew his memory might fail him sometimes. . . . Your majesty may be pleased to excuse this foul writing, being in truth so tormented in the present with the toothach, as troubles my sense more than the mistaken reports of any others shall do." Sad indeed were the bodily infirmities which exasperated these complainings of the lord deputy. The gout, the toothach, the ague, an intermittent pulse, faint sweats and heaviness, and, to crown all, the frightful disorder of the stone, alternately broke his spirits, and warned him "that no long life awaited him here below!"

What still remained to him, he yet resolved to live out bravely. "A frame of wood," he writes to Laud, "I have given order to set up in a park I have in the county of Wickloe. And, gnash the tooth of these gallants never so hard, I will by God's leave go on with it, that so I may have a place to take my recreation for a month or two in a year, were it for no other reason than to displease them, by keeping myself, if so please God, a little longer in health."[1] Among other reports to his prejudice had been that of "building up to the sky."[2] We find him afterwards adverting to this :—"I acknowledge, that were myself only considered in what I build, it were not only to excess, but even to folly, having already houses

---

[1] Strafford Papers, vol. ii. p. 106.

[2] Ibid. p. 107. His expensive repairs of the castle of Dublin had also been reproached to him. But on his first arrival he had certainly alleged a good case of necessity to Cooke :—"This castle is in very great decay. I have been inforced to take down one of the great towers, which was ready to fall, and the rest are so crasy, as we are still in fear part of it might drop down upon our heads." vol. i. p. 131.

moderate for my condition in Yorkshire :—but his majesty
will justify me, that at my last being in England, I
acquainted him with a purpose I had to build him a
house at the Naas, it being uncomely his majesty should
not have one here of his own, capable to lodge him with
moderate conveniency (which in truth as yet he hath not),
in case he might be pleased sometimes hereafter to look
upon this kingdom; and that it was necessary in a
manner, for the dignity of this place, and the health of
his deputy and family, that there should be one removing
house of fresh air, for want whereof, I assure your lordship, I have felt no small inconvenience since my coming
hither; that when it was built, if liked by his majesty, it
should be his, paying me as it cost, if disliked, *a suo
damno*, I was content to keep it and smart for my folly.
His majesty seemed to be pleased with all, whereupon I
proceeded, *and have in a manner finished it, and so contrived it for the rooms of state, and other accommodations
which I have observed in his majesty's houses, as I had
been, indeed, stark mad ever to have cast it so for a private
family.*"[1]

Between these two royal residences Wentworth now
divided a great portion of his time.   His mode of living
equalled in magnificence the houses themselves.   At his
own charge he maintained a retinue of 50 attendants,

---

[1] The remains of this building, which was called Juggarstowne
Castle, are visible still, and, I am informed by gentlemen who have
seen them, sufficiently indicate its extraordinary grandeur and extent.
They cover several acres.   They are close to the road side, about
sixteen Irish miles from Dublin, and provoke, even now, from many
an unreflecting passer by, a curse upon the memory of " Black Tom."
Such is the name by which the Irish peasantry still remember
Strafford.   When M. Boullaye-le-Gouz visited Ireland, he found
this castle in the property and possession of sir George Wentworth,
Strafford's brother, and guarded by forty English soldiers.—*Mr.
Croker's MS.*

besides his troop of 100 horse, which he had originally raised and equipped at an expense of 6000*l.*, and kept up at an enormous yearly cost. This style of living, which he took care to bear out in every other respect, he characteristically vindicated to Cottington as "an expence not of vanity, but of necessity, *judging it not to become me, having the great honour to represent his majesty's sacred person, to set it forth, no not in any one circumstance, in a penurious mean manner, before the eyes of a wild and rude people.*"[1] Nor did he scruple to conceal the fact, that his own private fortune had been assisted, in these vast charges, by certain public profits. "It is very true," he writes to Laud, "I have, under the blessing of Almighty God, and the protection of his majesty, 6000*l.* a year good land, which I brought with me into his service; and I have a share for a short term in these customs, which, whilst his majesty's revenue is there increased more than 20,000*l.* by year, proves nevertheless a greater profit to me than ever I dreamt of." When Laud read this passage to Charles, the king observed, impatiently, "but he doth not tell you how much," and plainly intimated that he grudged the minister his share of profit.[2] Wentworth had few occasions of gratitude to Charles during a life worn out in his service! In respect of these customs, it is not to be doubted that Charles's suspicions were grossly unjust. He would have had more of abstract justice with him in objecting to a different source of his lord deputy's revenue, that of the tobacco monopoly, for, on the latter

[1] Strafford Papers, vol. i. p. 128.

[2] Laud writes:—"I have of late heard some muttering about it in court, but can meet with nothing to fasten on : only it makes me doubt some body hath been nibbling about it."—See Strafford Papers, vol. ii. p. 127.

ground, undoubtedly, Wentworth was open to grave charges, though, even here, the king was the last person from whom with any propriety they could issue.

The lord deputy's private habits have been described. He hawked, he hunted[1], and fished[2], whenever his infirmities gave him respite. He passed some of his time also among books, and, in one portion at least of these studies, had his thoughts upon a stormy political

[1] Wittily he writes to Laud :—" We are in expectance every hour to hear what becomes of us and the lord chancellor—*to say the plain truth, whether we shall have a government or no ; and to the intent that I might be the better in utrumque paratus, at this present I am playing the Robin Hood,* and here in the country of mountains and woods hunting and chacing all the out-lying deer I can light of. .But to confess truly, I met with a very shrewd rebuke the other day : for, standing to get a shoot at a buck, I was so damnably bitten with midges, as my face is all mezled over ever since, itches still as if it were mad.   The marks they set will not go off again, I will awarrant you, this week.   I never felt or saw such in England. Surely they are younger brothers to the muskitoes the Indies brag on so much.   I protest, I could even now well find in my heart to play the shrew soundly, and scratch my face in six or seven places." —*Strafford Papers*, vol. ii. p. 173.   This allusion to the lord chancellor had reference to a judgment recently given against that dignitary by Wentworth himself, in a suit brought against him by sir John Gifford, on behalf of sir Francis Ruishe, for an increase of portion to the lady who had married young Loftus :—" According to the lord chancellor's own clear agreement with sir Francis Ruishe, father to the lady."   These are Wentworth's words.   The chancellor refused to submit to the judgment on the ground that the action ought to have been brought in the ordinary courts of law, and that the tribunal before which it was tried was both illegal and partial.   Wentworth upon this had resorted to his usual severity, and was now waiting its issue with the king.   It may be worth stating, that mistakes have been made with respect to the name of the lady chiefly affected in this case, by Mr. MacDiarmid and other writers, in consequence of sir John Gifford having brought the original action.   She was lady Loftus, not lady Gifford.

[2] For some accounts of his fishing exploits, see Papers, vol. ii. p. 213. &c.   Laud appears to have relished the lord deputy's presents of " dryed fish " amazingly, and to have been anything but fond of his " hung beef out of Yorkshire."   His grace had a shrewd eye to appetite :—" Since you are for both occupations, flesh and fish, I wonder you do not think of powdering or drying some of your Irish venison, and send that over to brag too."

future. " I wish," writes his friend lord Conway to him, "you had had your fit of the gout in England, lest you should attribute something of the disease to the air of that country. I send you the duke of Rohan's book, 'Le parfait Capitaine.' *Do not think the gout is an excuse from fighting, for the count Mansfelt had the gout that day he fought the battle of Fleury.*"[1] In the pleasures of the table he indulged little. " He was exceeding temperate," observes Radcliffe, " in meat, drink, and recreations. He was no whit given to his appetite; though he loved to see good meat at his table, yet he eat very little of it himself: beef or rabbits was his ordinary food, or cold powdered meats, or cheese and apples, and in moderate quantity. He was never drunk in his life, as I have often heard him say; and for so much as I had seen, I had reason to believe him: yet he was not so scrupulous but he would drink healths where he liked his company, and be sociable as any of his society, and yet still within the bounds of temperance. In Ireland, where drinking was grown a disease epidemical, he was more strict publickly, never suffering any health to be drunk at his publick table but the king's, queen's, and

---

[1] Strafford Papers, vol. ii. p. 45. Some of lord Conway's letters referred to matters not quite so decent, and the lord deputy's replies gave him no advantage on that score. See Papers, vol. ii. pp. 144 —146. Conway's acquaintance with his intrigues has already received notice, and the following passage from one of Wentworth's letters to this confidant is not a little significant:—" I desire your judgment of the inclosed, which was written to this your servant the other day, and chancing to open and read it in the presence, I burst out before I got it read, that the standers-by wondered what merry tale it might be that letter told me. But I must conjure you to send it me back, not to trust it forth of your hands, only if you will, I am content you shew it my lord of Northumberland, and my lady of Carlile, lest if it were shewn to others they might judge me *Vane*, or something else, of so princely a favour! For less, the least of her commands are not to be taken,—what then may we term these her earnest desires?"

prince's, on solemn days. Drunkenness in his servants was, in his esteem, one of the greatest faults." Throughout his various admirable letters to his young wards, the Saviles, in whose education he took extreme interest always, the hatred of this vice is still more characteristically shown. He returns to the warning again and again, coupling with drunkenness the equal vice of gaming,—the one a " pursuit not becoming a generous noble heart, which will not brook such starved considerations as the greed of winning,"—the other, one " that shall send you, by unequal staggering paces, to your grave, with confusion of face." [1]

No public duty was neglected meanwhile, for, from his country parks and castles, Wentworth in an hour or two could appear in the Dublin presence-chamber. The king sent him every license he required against the lord chancellor Loftus, and that nobleman, for having disputed the judicial functions of the deputy, " that transcendent power of a chancellor," as Wentworth scornfully called him, was deprived of the seals, and committed to prison till he consented to submit to the award and to acknowledge his error.[2]

But while the king thus secretly authorised these acts of despotism, the English court, no less than the English

---

[1] Strafford Papers, vol. i. p. 169, &c. And see an admirable letter at p. 311. of vol. ii.

[2] This case was brought forward at the impeachment, and was much aggravated by a discovery, which has been before named, in reference to the young lady Loftus. " In the prefering this charge," says Clarendon, "many things of levity, as certain letters of great affection and familiarity from the earl to that lady, which were found in her cabinet after her death, others of passion, were exposed to the public view." (vol. i. p. 175.) Ample details of the entire course of the transaction will be found in referring to the Strafford Papers, vol. ii. p. 67. *et seq.* 82. 160. *et seq.* 172. *et seq.* 179. 196. 205. 227. *et seq.* 259. *et seq.* 298. 341. 369. 375. 389.

nation, were known to be objecting to their author. Impatiently he wrote to Laud, demanding at least the charge, something on which to ground an issue—" The humour which offends me," he exclaims, "is not so much anger as scorn, and desire to wrest out from amongst them my charge ; for, *as they say, if I might come to fight for my life, it would never trouble me, indeed I should then weigh them all very light,* and be safe under the goodness, wisdom, and justice of my master. Again, howbeit I am resolved of the truth of all this, yet to accuse myself is very uncomely. I love not to put on my armour before there be cause, in regard I never do so, but I find myself the wearier and sorer for it the next morning."

He could get no satisfactory answer to this, for in truth the English court by this time had enough upon its hands. The king meditated a war with Spain, for the recovery of the palatinate, to which he was the rather urged by the queen, since France had already engaged. Fortunately, before taking this step, he was induced to advise with the lord deputy of Ireland. This was the first time Wentworth had ever been consulted on the general affairs of the kingdom, and he instantly forwarded a paper of opposing reasons to the king, so strongly and so ably stated, that the war project was given up.[1] The queen's indifferent feeling to him, it may well be supposed, was not removed by such policy.[2]

---

[1] The document will be found in the Strafford Papers, vol. ii. p. 60 —64. It is one of the ablest of Wentworth's arguments for his scheme of absolute power. He takes occasion to say in it :—" The opinion delivered by the judges, declaring the lawfulness of the assignment for the shipping, is the greatest service that profession hath done the crown in my time."

[2] It ought to be stated, to Wentworth's honour, that, though he much desired to have stood well with her majesty, he declined to purchase her favour by acts inconsistent with his own public schemes.

The peace, however, which lord Wentworth so earnestly recommended, was now more fatally broken. The whole Scottish nation rose against Charles, in consequence of Laud's religious innovations. Wentworth was not at first consulted respecting these commotions, but he had thrown out occasional advice in his despatches which was found singularly serviceable.[1] He strove as far as possible, by urging strong defensive measures, to prevent an open rupture. " If," he wrote to Charles, " the war were with a foreign enemy, I should like well to have the first blow ; *but being with your majesty's own natural, howbeit rebellious subjects, it seems to me a tender point to draw blood first ;* for till it come to that, all hope is not lost of reconciliation ; and I would not have them with the least colour impute it to your majesty to have put all to extremity, till their own more than words inforce you to it." [2]

Nor did Wentworth serve Charles at this conjuncture with advice alone, for, by his amazing personal energy, he forced down some opening commotions among the 60,000 Scottish settlers in Ulster, and not only disabled them from joining or assisting their countrymen, but

---

See curious evidences of this in Strafford Papers, vol. ii. pp. 221, 222. 257. 329. 425, 426. &c. When she had solicited an army appointment for some young courtier, he wrote an earnest entreaty to her chamberlain, accompanying his reasons for declining the appointment :—" If I may by you understand her majesty's good pleasure, it will be a mighty quietness unto me, for if once these places of command in the army become suits at court, looked upon as preferments and portions for younger children, the honour of this government, and consequently the prosperity of these affairs, are lost." The king himself appears to have made it a personal request of Wentworth, that he should carry himself " with all duty and respect to her majesty." (vol. ii. p. 256.)

[1] See vol. ii. pp. 191, 192. 235. 280. 324. &c.

[2] Strafford Papers, vol. ii. p. 314.

compelled them to abjure the covenant.[1]   Nor this
alone.   He forwarded from Ireland a detachment of
troops to garrison Carlisle ; he announced that the army
of Ireland was in a state of active recruiting and discipline ; he offered large contributions from himself and
his friends towards the necessary expenses of resistance ;
and by every faith of loyalty, and bond of friendship and
of service, he called on every man in Yorkshire to stir
themselves in the royal cause.   "To be lazy lookers on,"
he wrote to the lord Lorne, "to lean to the king behind
the curtain, or to whisper forth only our allegiance, will
not serve our turn ! much rather ought we to break our
shins in emulation who should go soonest and furthest,
in assurance and in courage, to uphold the prerogatives
and full dominion of the crown,—ever remembering ourselves that nobility is such a grudged and envied piece
of monarchy, that all tumultuary force offered to kings
doth ever in the second place fall upon the peers, being
such motes in the eyes of a giddy multitude, as they
never believe themselves clear sighted into their liberty
indeed, till these be at least levelled to a parity as the
other altogether removed, to give better prospect to their
anarchy."[2]

The sluggish and irresolute councils of England looked
ill beside the movements of the deputy.   The king asked
a service from him, but the instructions came too late.
"If his majesty's mind had been known to me in time,"
he wrote to Vane, the treasurer of the household, "I
could have as easily secured it against all the covenanters
and devils in Scotland, as now walk up and down this
chamber.   But where trusts and instructions come too

---

[1] Strafford Papers, vol. ii. pp. 270. 338. 345.
[2] Ibid. p. 210.

late, there the business is sure to be lost." Openly he now expressed his censure of the royal scheme that had prevailed since the death of Buckingham. "I never was in love with that way of keeping all the affairs of that kingdom of Scotland among those of that nation, but carried indeed as a mystery to all the council of England; a rule but over much kept by our master; which I have told my lord of Portland many and often a time, plainly professing unto him, that I was much afraid that course would at one time or other bring forth ill effects; what those are, we now see and feel at one and the same instant." Finally, when Vane had written in an extremely desponding tone, he rallied him with a noble energy. "It is very true you have reason to think this storm looks very foul and dark towards us, so do also myself, for if the fire should kindle at Raby, I am sure the smoke would give offence to our eye-sight at Woodhouse! but I trust the evening will prove more calm than the morning of this day promises. *Dulcius lumen solis esse solet jam jam cadentis.* All here is quiet, nothing colours yet to the contrary. And if I may have the countenance and trust of my master, I hope, in the execution of such commands as his majesty's wisdom and judgment ordain for me, to contain the Scottish here in their due obedience, or if they should stir (our 8000 arms and twenty pieces of cannon arrived, which I trust now will be very shortly) to give them such a heat in their cloaths, as they never had since their coming forth of Scotland! And yet our standing army here is but 1000 horse and 2000 foot, and not fewer of *them* I will warrant you than 150,000, so you see our work is not very easy. The best of it is, the brawn of a lark is better than the carcass of a kite, and the virtue of one loyal subject more than of 1000 traitors. And is not this pretty well, trow you, to begin with?"[1]

No extremity was urged that found Wentworth unprepared. Windebanke hinted the danger he incurred. "I humbly thank you," he answered, "for your friendly and kind wishes to my safety, but if it be the will of God to bring upon us for our sins that fiery trial,—all the respects of this life laid aside, it shall appear more by my actions than words, that I can never think myself too good to die for my gracious master, or favour my skin in the zealous and just prosecution of his commands. *Statutum est semel.*" Another—whom he fancied not unwilling to thwart him, reckoning upon safety from the consequences in the lord deputy's certain destruction— he thus warned :—"Perchance even to those that shall tell you, before their breath I am but as a feather, I shall be found sadder than lead! For let me tell you, I am so confidently set upon the justice of my master, and upon my own truth, as under them and God I shall pass thorough all the factions of court, and heat of my ill-willers, without so much as sindging the least thread of my coat, nor so alone, but to carry my friends along with me." And, in the midst of the storms his measures were raising on all sides round him, he found time and ease enough to amuse himself in tormenting with grave jests a foolish earl of Antrim, whom the king had sent to "assist" him. The despatches he wrote on the subject of the "Antrim negociations" are positive masterpieces of wit and humour.[2] At the same time he did not

---

[1] This letter is dated—"Fairwood Park [the name of his seat in Wicklow], this 16th of April, 1639. I will change it with you, if you will, for Fair Lane."—*Strafford Papers*, vol. ii. pp. 325—328.

[2] See the Strafford Papers, vol. ii. pp. 187. 204. 211. 289. *et seq.* 300. *et seq.* 321. *et seq.* 325. 331. 334 339. 353. 356. It is not too

hesitate to assure the king, that, but for the safety of Ireland, he would " be most mightily out of countenance, to be found in any other place than at his majesty's side ! "

Charles acknowledged these vast services with frequent letters. Wentworth was now his great hope, and he found, at last, that at all risks he must have him in England. He had formerly declined his offered attendance, he now prayed for it. He wished, he said, to consult him respecting the army, " but I have much more," he sorrowfully added, " and indeed too much to desire your counsel and attendance for some time, which I think not fit to express by letter, more than this,—the Scots' covenant begins to spread too far. Yet, for all this, I will not have you take notice that I have sent for you, but pretend some other occasion of business."

Wentworth instantly prepared himself to obey. A short time only he took, to place his government in the hands of Wandesford, and to arrange some of his domestic concerns. His children were his great care. " God bless the young whelps," he said, " and for the old dog there is less matter."[1] Lady Clare, his mother-in-law, had often requested to have the elder girl with

---

much to say, that, in reading these papers, the memory is called to the Swifts of past days, and the Fonblanques of our own. The poor lord's pretensions are most ludicrously set forth, and in a vein of exquisite pleasantry, but little consistent with the popular notion of Strafford's unbending sternness.

[1] See various letters in the course of his correspondence, in which the most tender enthusiasm is expressed for them and for their dead mother. (vol. i. p. 236. ; vol. ii. pp. 122, 123. 146. 379, 380.) Nor was his affection less warmly expressed to the child of his living wife. In several affectionate letters to the latter he never fails to send his blessing to "the baby," or to "little Tom." Shortly before this visit to England, however, the latter died,—and shortly after it, a girl was born.

her, and Wentworth had as often vainly tried to let her leave his side. His passion was to see them all near him in a group together, as they may yet be seen in the undying colours of Vandyke, from whose canvass, also, as though it had been painted yesterday, the sternly expressive countenance of their father still gazes at posterity. The present was a time, however, when the sad alternative of a separation from himself promised him alleviation even, and he resolved to send both sisters to their grandmother. The letter he despatched on the occasion to the Lady Clare remains, and it is too touching and beautiful to be omitted here. A man so burthened with the world's accusations as Strafford, should be denied none of the advantage which such a document can render to his memory. It is unnecessary to direct attention to its singularly characteristic conclusion :—

" My lord of Clare having writ unto me, your ladyship desired to have my daughter Anne with you for a time in England, to recover her health, I have at last been able to yield so much from my own comfort, as to send both her and her sister to wait your grave, wise, and tender instructions. They are both, I praise God, in good health, and bring with them hence from me no other advice, but entirely and cheerfully to obey and do all you shall be pleased to command them, so far forth as their years and understanding may administer unto them.

" I was unwilling to part them, in regard those that must be a stay one to another, when by course of nature I am gone before them. I would not have them grow strangers whilst I am living. Besides, the younger gladly imitates the elder, in disposition so like her blessed mother, that it pleases me very much to see her steps followed and observed by the other.

" Madam, I must confess, it was not without difficulty before I could perswade myself thus to be deprived the looking upon them, who with their brother are the pledges of all the comfort, the greatest at least, of my old age, if it shall please God I attain thereunto. But I have been brought up in afflictions of this kind, so as I still fear to have that taken first that is dearest unto me,—and have in this been content willingly to overcome my own affections in order to their good, acknowledging your ladyship capable of doing them more good in their breeding than I am. Otherways, in truth, I should never have parted with them, as I profess it a grief unto me, not to be as well able as any to serve the memory of that noble lady, in these little harmless infants.

" Well, to God's blessing and your ladyship's goodness I commit them ! where-ever they are my prayers shall attend them, and have of sorrow in my heart till I see them again I must, which I trust will not be long neither. That they shall be acceptable to you, I know it right well, and I believe them so graciously minded to render themselves so the more, the more you see of their attention to do as you shall be pleased to direct them, which will be of much contentment unto me. For whatever your ladyship's opinion may be of me, I desire, and have given it them in charge (so far as their tender years are capable of), to honour and observe your ladyship above all the women in the world, as well knowing that in so doing they shall fulfil that duty, whereby of all others they could have delighted their mother the most; —and I do infinitely wish they may want nothing in their breeding my power or cost might procure them, or their condition of life hereafter may require, for, madam, if I die to-morrow, I will by God's help leave them ten thousand pounds apiece, which I trust, by God's blessing, shall bestow them to the comfort of themselves and friends, nor at all considerably prejudice their brother, whose estate shall never be much burthened by a second venter, I assure you.

"I thought fit to send with them one that teacheth them to write; he is a quiet soft man, but honest, and not given to any disorder; him I have appointed to account for the money to be laid forth, wherein he hath no other direction but to pay and lay forth as your ladyship shall appoint, and still as he wants, to go to Woodhouse, where my cousin Rockley will supply him. And I must humbly beseech you to give order to their servants, and otherwise to the taylors at London, for their apparel, which I wholly submit to your ladyship's better judgment, and be it what it may be, I shall think it all happily bestowed, so as it be to your contentment and theirs, for cost I reckon not of, and any thing I have is theirs so long as I live, which is only worth thanks, for theirs and their brothers all I have must be whether I will or no, and therefore I desire to let them have to acknowledge me for before.

"Nan, they tell me, danceth prettily, which I wish (if with convenience it might be) were not lost,—more to give her a comely grace in the carriage of her body, than that I wish they should much delight or practise it when they are women. Arabella is a small practitioner that way also, and they are both very apt to learn that or any thing they are taught.

"Nan, I think, speaks French prettily, which yet I

might have been better able to judge had her mother lived. The other also speaks, but her maid being of Guernsey, the accent is not good. But your ladyship is in this excellent, as that, as indeed all things else which may befit them, they may, and I hope will, learn better with your ladyship than they can with their poor father, ignorant in what belongs women, and otherways, God knows, distracted, and so awanting unto them in all, saving in loving them, and therein, in truth, I shall never be less than the dearest parent in the world!

" Their brother is just now sitting at my elbow, in good health, God be praised ; and I am in the best sort accommodating this place for him, which, in the kind, I take to be the noblest one of them in the king's dominions, and where a grass time may be passed with most pleasure of that kind. I will build him a good house, and by God's help, leave, I think, near three thousand pounds a year, and wood on the ground, as much, I dare say, if near London, as would yield fifty thousand pounds, besides a house within twelve miles of Dublin, the best in Ireland, and land to it which, I hope, will be two thousand pounds a year,—all which he shall have to the rest, had I twenty brothers of his to sitt beside me. This I write not to your ladyship in vanity, or to have it spoken of, but privately, to let your lady-ship see I do not forget the children of my dearest wife, nor altogether bestow my time fruitlessly for them. It is true I am in debt, but there will be, besides, sufficient to discharge all I owe, by God's grace, whether I live or die. And next to these children, there are not any other persons I wish more happiness than to the house of their grandfather, and shall be always most ready to serve them, what opinion soever be had of me, for no others usage can absolve me of what I owe not only to the memory, but to the last legacy, that noble creature left with me, when God took her to himself.   I am afraid to turn over the leaf, lest your ladyship might think I could never come to a conclusion ; and shall, therefore," &c.

He had arranged everything for his departure, when one of his paroxysms of illness seized him.   He wrestled with it desperately, and set sail.   On landing at Chester he wrote to lady Wentworth a sad description of the effects of the journey upon his gout, and the " flux," which afflicted him.   He rallied, however, and appeared in London in November, 1639.   In a memorable passage, the historian May has described the general conversation and conjecture which had prepared for his approach. Some, he says, remembering his early exertions in the cause of the people, fondly imagined that he had hitherto been subservient to the court, only to ingratiate himself thoroughly with the king, and that he would now employ his ascendancy to wean his majesty from arbitrary counsels.   Others, who knew his character more profoundly, had different thoughts, and secretly cherished their own most active energies.

Wentworth, Laud, and Hamilton, instantly formed a secret council—a "cabinet council," as they were then enviously named by the other courtiers—a "junto," as the people reproachfully called them.   The nature of the measures to be taken against the Scots was variously and earnestly discussed, and Wentworth, considering the extremity of affairs, declared at once for war.

Supplies to carry it on formed a more difficult question still, but it sank before Wentworth's energy.   He proposed a loan,—subscribed to it at once, by way of example, the enormous sum of 20,000*l.*,—and pledged himself to bring over a large subsidy from Ireland if the king would call a parliament there. Encouraged by this assurance, it was resolved to call a parliament in England also. Laud, Juxon, Hamilton, Wentworth, Cottington, Vane, and Windebanke, were all present in council when this resolution was taken. The king then put the question to them whether, upon the restiveness of parliament, they would assist him "by extraordinary ways." They assented, passed a vote to that effect, writs for parliaments in both countries were issued, and Wentworth prepared himself to quit England.

Charles, unsolicited, now invested him with the dignity of earldom. His own very existence seemed dependent on Wentworth's faith, and there was sufficient weakness in the character of the king to render it possible for him to suppose that, even at such a time, the inducement of reward might be necessary as a precaution. The lord deputy was created earl of Strafford and baron of Raby, adorned with the garter, and invested with the title of lord-lieutenant, or lieutenant-general, of Ireland—a title which had not been given since the days of Essex. "God willing," wrote Strafford to his wife immediately after, "you will soon see the lieutenant of Ireland, but never like to have a deputy of Ireland to your husband any more."[1]

On his way to Ireland, the earl was overtaken, at Beaumaris, by a severe attack of gout, yet, still able to move, he hurried on board, notwithstanding the contrary

---

[1] Letter in the Thoresby Museum, Biog. Brit. vol. vii. p. 4182. Some days before he had written to her characteristic news of his children. "The two wenches," he said, "are in perfect health, and now at this instant in this house, lodged with me, and rather desirous to be so than with their grandmother. I am not yet fully resolved what to do with them." They were afterwards sent back to lady Clare, till the lady Strafford arrived in London.

winds, lest he should be thrown down utterly. He wrote at the same time to secretary Cooke, in the highest spirits, to assure him and his master that they need not fear for his weakness. "For," exclaims the lord-lieutenant, "I will make strange shift, and put myself to all the pain I shall be able to endure, before I be any where awanting to my master or his affairs in this conjuncture, and, therefore, sound or lame, you shall have me with you before the beginning of the parliament. I should not fail, though SIR JOHN ELIOT were living! In the mean space, for love of Christ, call upon and hasten the business now in hand, especially the raising of the horse and all together, the rather, for that this work now before us, should it miscarry, we all are like to be very miserable,—but, carried through advisedly and gallantly, shall by God's blessing set us in safety and peace for our lives at after, nay, in probability, the generations that are to succeed us. *Fi a faute de courage, je n'en aye que trop!* What might I be with my legs, that am so brave without the use of them? Well, halt, blind, or lame, I will be found true to the person of my gracious master, to the service of his crown and my friends." Strange that, at such a moment, lord Strafford should have recalled the memory of the virtuous and indomitable Eliot! He was soon doomed to know on whose shoulders the mantle of Buckingham's great opponent had fallen.

In March, 1640, Strafford again arrived in Ireland. The members of the parliament that had just been summoned, crowded round him with lavish devotion, gave him four subsidies, which was all that he had desired, and declared that that was nothing in respect to their zeal, for that "his majesty should have the fee simple of their estates for his great occasions." In a formal declaration, moreover, they embodied all this, declared that their present warm loyalty rose from a deep sense of the inestimable benefits the lord-lieutenant had conferred upon their country, and that all these benefits had been effected " without the least hurt or grievance to any well-disposed subject."[1] The authors of this declaration were the first to turn upon Strafford in his distress. Valuing their praise for its worth in the way of example, the earl forwarded it to England, and requested it to be published to the empire.

He had now been a fortnight in Ireland. Within that time, with a diligence unparalleled and almost incredible, he had effected these results with the parliament, and levied a body of 8000 men as a reinforcement to the royal army.[2] He again set sail for England.

I pause here to illustrate the character of this extraordinary person in one respect, which circumstances are soon to make essential. His infirmities of health have frequently been alluded to, but they come now upon the scene more fatally. No one, that has not carefully examined all his despatches, can have any notion of their frightful nature and extent.

The soul of the earl of Strafford was indeed lodged, to use the expression of his favourite Donne, within a "low and fatal room." We have already seen his friend, Radcliffe, informing us, that in 1622 "he had a great fever, and the next spring a double tertian, and after his recovery a relapse into a single tertian, and a while after a burning fever." It is melancholy to follow the progress

---

[1] See Strafford Papers, vol. ii. pp. 396, 397. Rushworth, vol. iii. p. 1051. Nalson, vol. i. p. 280—284.
[2] See Radcliffe's Essay.

of his infirmities as they are casually recorded by himself!—How the trouble of "an humour, which in strict acceptation you might term the gout," soon increases to "an extreme fit, which renders him unfit, not only for business, but for all handsome civility," and is aggravated by "so violent a fit of the stone, as I shall not be able to stir these ten days—it hath brought me very low, and was unto me a torment for three days and three nights above all I ever endured since I was a man!"—How the eyes that are "these twelve days full of dimness," ere long are "scarce able to guide his pen thorough blindness with long writing;"—and this, too, while "an infirmity I have formerly had in great measure, saluteth me, to wit, an intermitting pulse, attended with faint sweats and heaviness of spirits!"

But ever by the side of the body's weakness we find a witness of the spirit's triumph,—a vindication of the mightiness of will! A lengthened despatch to the secretary is begun in "a fit of the gout which, keeping me still in bed, partly with pain and partly with weariness, makes me unfit for much business."—When he intreats a correspondent to "to pardon my scribbling, for since the gout took me I am not able to write but with both my legs along upon a stool, believe me, which is not only wearisome in itself, but a posture very untoward for guiding my pen aright,"—it is with the consolation that "as sir Walter Raleigh said very well, so the heart lie right, it skills not much for all the rest." —And the advice to "forbear his night watches, and now begin to take more care of his health," is met by the assurance that, "had he fivescore senses to lose, he did and ought to judge them all well and happily bestowed in his majesty's service!"

On the occasion of this last return to England, however, even what has been described would serve little to express what he suffered. Then, when every energy was to be taxed to the uttermost, the question of his fiery spirit's supremacy was indeed put to the issue, by a complication of ghastly diseases! In the letter from Dublin, dated Good Friday, 1640, which assures the king that "from this table I shall go on ship board," he is compelled to add that, "besides my gout, I have a very violent and ill-conditioned flux upon me, such as I never had before. It hath held me already these seven days, and brought me so weak, as in good faith nothing that could concern myself should make me go a mile forth of my chamber. *But this is not a season for bemoaning of myself, for I shall cheerfully venture this crazed vessel of mine, and either, by God's help, wait upon your majesty before the parliament begin,—or else deposit this infirm humanity of mine in the dust!*" And "from the table," on "ship board," he went accordingly, and arrived at Chester on the 4th of April, quite broken down by the fatigues of a rough voyage. "I confess," he writes, "that I forced the captain to sea against his will, and have since received my correction for it. A marvellous foul and dangerous night, indeed, we have had of it!" In this state he despatches the following letter to the king :—" May it please your sacred majesty, —With some danger I wrought thorough a storm at sea, yet light on a greater misfortune here in harbour, having now got the gout in both my feet, attended with that ill habit of health I brought from Dublin. I purposed to have been on my way again early this morning, but the physician disadviseth it; and in truth such is my pain and weakness, as I verily believe I were not able to endure it. Nevertheless, I have provided myself of a litter, and will try to-morrow how I am able to bear travel, which if possible I can do, then by the grace of God will I not rest till I have the honour to wait upon your majesty. In the mean time it is most grievous unto me to be thus kept from those duties which I owe your majesty's service on this great and important occasion. In truth, sir, in my whole life I never desired health more than now, if it shall so please God,—not that I can be so vain as to judge myself equally considerable with many other of your servants, but that I might give my own heart the contentment to be near your commands, in case I might be so happy as to be of some small use to my most gracious master in such a conjuncture of time and affairs as this is. God long preserve your majesty."

Next, he dictates a long despatch to the earl of Northumberland, and attempts, at least, to conclude it with his own hand :—" and yet howbeit, I am much resolved and set on all occasions for your service, will my weary hand be able to carry on my pen not one line further, than only in a word to write myself, in all truth and perfection, your lordship's most humbly to be commanded, STRAFFORD."

I quote also from this despatch to Northumberland an extraordinary incident which occurred on this occasion, and which illustrates his unremitting vigilance in matters which he could hardly have been expected to superintend even under far more favourable circumstances. " Upon my landing at Nesson I observed a Scottish ship there riding upon her anchors, of some six or sevenscore ton, and of some eight or ten pieces of ordnance, and here in town I learn that the ship belongs to Irwin, that she was fraught by some merchants here with sacks, and that the master now in town, is this morning to receive some 600*l.* for freight.   Hereupon, considering the day for the general imbargo is so instant, as your lordship knows, I have privately advised the merchants to stay payment of the freight until to-morrow, and will give present direction for the apprehension of the master and his mate, now in town.   I have also spoken to the customers to send down to Nesson to arrest the said ship upon pretence of cozening the king in his customs, for which the master is to be examined, and, however, the ship to be fraught for the king's service for the transportation of these men.   I have likewise given command to captain Bartlett presently to repair thither, to be assistant therein to the officers of the customs, and before his leaving the port to see execution of all this, as also to take forth of her, all her Scottish mariners, her sails and guns, and to bring them on shore, leaving only aboard such English mariners as shall be sufficient to send the ship there, till further directions.   Thus will she lye fair and open for your arrest, and perchance prove your best prize of that kind, and really being manned with English mariners, which may be pressed for that occasion, be of all other the fittest vessel for the transportation of your men and ammunition to Dunbarton.   If I have been over diligent herein, in doing more than (I confess) I have commission for, I humbly crave your lordship's pardon, and hope the rather to obtain it, in regard it is a fault easily mended,—for my honest blue-cap will be hereby so affrighted, as the delivery back unto him of his freight, goods and ship, will sufficiently fulfil his desires and contentment."

A letter written the following day to Windebanke is

most eminently characteristic :—"I thank you," he says, "for your good wishes, that I might be free of the gout ; but a deaf spirit I find it, that will neither hear nor be persuaded to reason. My pain, I thank God, is gone, yet I am not able to walk once about the chamber, such a weakness hath it left behind. Nevertheless my obstinacy is as great as formerly, for it shall have much more to do before it make me leave my station in these uncertain times. *Of all things I love not to put off my cloaths and go to bed in a storm.* The lieutenant," he proceeds, "that made the false muster, cannot be too severely punished. If you purpose to overcome that evil, *you must fall upon the first transgressors like lightning !"*

Beside such zealousness as Strafford's, the devotion of others was like to come tardily off. The letter to Windebanke proceeds :—" The proxies of the Irish nobility I have received and transmitted over. I cannot but observe how cautious still your great friend, my lord of St. Alban's, is, lest he might seem to express his affections towards the king with too much frankness and confidence. Lord ! how willing he is, by doing something, as good as nothing, to let you see how well contented he would be to deserve the crown, if it were in his power, as indeed it is not. But if his good lordship and his fellows were left to my handling, I should quickly teach them better duties, and put them out of liking with these perverse froward humours. But the best is, by the good help of his friends, he need not apprehend the short horns of such a curst cow as myself,—yet this I will say for him, all your kindness shall not better his affections to the service of the crown, or render him thankful to yourselves longer than his turn is in serving. Remember, sir, that I told you of it. The lord Roch is a person in a lesser volume, of the very self-same edition. Poor soul, you see what he would be at, if he knew how. But seriously let me ask you a question, What would these and such like gentlemen do, were they absolute in themselves, when they are thus forward at that very instant of time, when their whole estates are justly and fairly in the king's mercy? In a word, 'till I see punishments and rewards well and roundly applied, I fear very much the frowardness of this generation will not be reduced to moderation and right reason, but that it shall extreamly much difficult his majesty's ministers, nay, and himself too, in the pursuit of his just and royal designs."

Mr. Brodie has accused Strafford's despatches of heaviness, and certainly every word in them has its weight. This extraordinary letter concludes thus:—
" It troubles me very much to understand by these your letters, that the deputy lieutenants of Yorkshire should shew themselves so foolish and so ingrate as to refuse to levy 200 men and send them to Berwick, without a caution of reimbursement of coat and conduct money. As for the precedent they alledge, they well term them to be indeed of former times, for sure I am none of them can remember any such thing of their own knowledge, or have learnt any such thing by their own practice. What they find in some blind book of their fathers kept by his clerk, I know not, but some such poor business is the best proof I believe they can shew for that allegation. Perchance queen Elizabeth now and then did some such thing; but then it ought to be taken as matter of bounty, not of duty, the law being so clear and plain in that point, as you know. Upon my coming to town I will inform myself who have been the chief leaders in this business, and thereupon give my gentlemen something

to remember it by hereafter. But, above all, I cannot sufficiently wonder that my lords at the board should think of any other satisfaction than sending for them up, and laying them by the heels, especially considering what hath been already resolved on there amongst us. What, I beseech you, should become of the levy of your 30,000 men, in case the other counties of the kingdom should return you the like answer? And therefore this insolence of theirs ought, in my poor opinion, to have been suffocated in the birth, and this boldness met with a courage, which should have taught them their part in these cases to have been obedience, and not dispute. Certain I am, that in queen Elizabeth's time (those golden times that appear so glorious in their eyes, and render them dazzled towards any other object), they would not have had such an expostulation better cheap than the fleet. The very plain truth is, and I beseech you that it may humbly on my part be represented to his majesty in discharge of my own duty, that the council-board of late years have gone with so tender a foot in those businesses of lieutenancy, that it hath almost lost that power to the crown ; and yet such a power it is, and so necessary, as I do not know how we should be able either to correct a rebellion at home, or to defend ourselves from an invasion from abroad, without it. All which, nevertheless, I mention with all humility in the world, without the least imputation to any particular person living or dead, and humbly beseech his majesty to cause the reins of this piece of his government to be strongly gathered up again, which have of late hung too long loose upon us his lieutenants and deputy lieutenants within the kingdom."

Notwithstanding his desperate state, Strafford caused

himself to be pushed on to London. A desire of the king that he should not hazard the journey, reached him already engaged in it.[1] He persisted in being transported thither in a litter by easy journeys. In London a greater and final occasion was yet to be afforded him, for the display of an indomitable nature triumphantly baffling disease and decay, and still, with the increasing and imperious urgency of the need, towered ever proudlier the inexhaustible genius of Strafford.

The parliament had met, and the earl immediately took his seat in the house of lords. Their proceedings, and their abrupt dissolution, belong to history. After that fatal state error, an army, to the command of which Northumberland had been appointed, was marched against the Scots. Severe illness, however, held Northumberland to his bed, and the king resolved to appoint Strafford in his place. "The earl of Strafford," observes Clarendon, "was scarce recovered from a great sickness, yet was willing to undertake the charge out of pure indignation to see how few men were forward to serve the king with that vigour of mind they ought to do; but knowing well the malicious designs which were contrived against himself, he would rather serve as lieutenant-general under the earl of Northumberland, than that he

[1] It is worth quoting as almost the only expression of care and sympathy Charles had hitherto given to his minister. "Having seen divers letters, Strafford, to my lord of Canterbury, concerning the state of your health at this time, I thought it necessary by this to command you, not to hazard to travel before ye may do it with the safety of your health, and in this I must require you not to be your own judge, but be content to follow the advice of those that are about you, whose affections and skill ye shall have occasion to trust unto. If I did not know that this care of your health were necessary for us both at this time, I would have deferred my thanks to you for your great service lately done, until I might have seen you. So praying to God for your speedy recovery, I rest your assured friend."

should resign his commission: and so, with and under that qualification, he made all possible haste towards the north before he had strength enough for the journey."[1] The same noble historian, after saying that Strafford could with difficulty, in consequence of illness, sit in his saddle, describes the shock he experienced in receiving intelligence of the disgraceful flight of a portion of the king's troops at Newbourne on the Tyne, and proceeds thus :—" In this posture the earl of Strafford found the army about Durham, bringing with him a body much broken with his late sickness, which was not clearly shaken off, and a mind and temper confessing the dregs of it, which, being marvellously provoked and inflamed with indignation at the late dishonour, rendered him less gracious, that is, less inclined to make himself so, to the officers upon his first entrance into his charge: it may be, in that mass of disorder not quickly discerning to whom kindness and respect was justly due. But those who by this time no doubt were retained for that purpose, took that opportunity to incense the army against him, and so far prevailed in it, that in a short time it was more inflamed against him than against the enemy."[2] In this melancholy state, with a disgraced and mutinous force, Strafford fell back upon York.

From this moment he sank daily. Intrigues of the most disgraceful character, carried on by Holland, Hamilton, and Vane, and assisted every way by the queen, united with his sickness to break him down. Still he was making desperate efforts to strengthen and animate his army, when suddenly he found that a treaty with the Scots had actually commenced, and that his especial enemy, lord Savile, was actively employed to

---

[1] History, vol. i. p. 114.   [2] Vol. i. p. 115.

forward it. Ultimately, these negotiations were placed in the hands of sixteen peers, every one of whom were his personal opponents. And the crowing enemy was behind,—"an enemy," as lord Clarendon observes, "more terrible than all the others, and like to be more fatal, *the whole Scottish nation*, provoked by the declaration he had procured of Ireland, and some high carriage and expressions of his against them in that kingdom."[1] They illustrated this eminent hatred, by peremptorily refusing, in the midst of much profession of attachment to the king and the English nation, to hold any conferences at York, because it was within the jurisdiction of him whom they called that "chief incendiary," their "mortal foe," the lord-lieutenant of Ireland.

In this there was exaggeration. Notwithstanding the assertions of nearly all the histories, that Strafford's continual counsel to Charles was to rely on arms alone, it is quite certain, from the minutes of the council of peers at York[2], that this is erroneous. When he sent the commission to Ormond to bring over his own army of 20,000 men from Ireland, the negotiations had not been resumed, and, on the resumption of them, that

---

[1] The hatred was, indeed, mutual. Strafford more than once, in his despatches, shows that he even disliked, and was disposed to turn into ridicule, their mode of speech. Alluding to a Scotchman, for instance, a Mr. Barre, whom he supposed to have been favoured by the court intriguers against him, he writes from Ireland thus :— "Then on that side he procures, by some very near his majesty, access to the king, there whispering continually something or another to my prejudice ; boasts familiarly, how freely he speaks with his majesty, what he saith concerning me, and *nou'ant pleese your mejesty ea werde mare anent your debuty of Yrland*, with many such like botadoes, stuffed with a mighty deal of untruths and follies amongst." And see Rushworth, vol. iii. p. 1293.

[2] Printed in the Hardwicke State Papers. And see a very able and impartial view of Strafford's conduct and character, in the History continued from Mackintosh.

commission was withdrawn. Now, however, thwarted and exasperated on all sides, he resolved to furnish one more proof (it was destined to be the last!) of the possibility of recovering the royal authority, by a great and vigorous exertion. During the negotiations no actual cessation of arms had been agreed to by the Scots, and he therefore secretly despatched a party of horse, under a favourite officer, to attack them in their quarters. A large body of the enemy were defeated by this manœuvre, all their officers taken prisoners, the army inspirited, and the spirits of Strafford himself restored. Again he spoke confidently of the future, when suddenly the king, prevailed on by others, commanded him to forbear. In the same moment, without any previous warning, he was told that a parliament was summoned.

Strafford saw at once the extent of his danger. He had thrown his last stake and lost it. He prayed of the king to be allowed to retire to his government in Ireland, or to some other place, where he might promote his majesty's service, and not deliver himself into the hands of his enraged enemies. Charles refused. He still reposed on the enormous value of his minister's genius, and considered that no sacrifice too great might be incurred, for the chance of its service to himself in the coming struggle. At the same time he pledged himself by a solemn promise, that, "while there was a king in England, not a hair of Strafford's head should be touched by the parliament!" The earl arrived in London.

"It was about three of the clock in the afternoon," says Clarendon, "when the earl of Strafford (being infirm and not well disposed in health, and so not having stirred out of his house that morning,) hearing that both houses still sate, thought fit to go thither. It was believed

by some (upon what ground was never clear enough)
that he made that haste there to accuse the lord Say,
and some others, of having induced the Scots to invade
the kingdom ; but he was scarce entered into the house
of peers, when the message from the house of commons
was called in, and when Mr. Pym at the bar, and in the
name of all the commons of England, impeached
Thomas, earl of Strafford (with the addition of all his
other titles) of high treason ! "

Upwards of twelve years had elapsed since sir Thomas
Wentworth stood face to face with Pym. Upon the eve
of his elevation to the peerage, they had casually met
at Greenwich, when, after a short conversation on public
affairs, they separated with these memorable words,
addressed by Pym to Wentworth. " You are going to
leave us, but I will never leave you, while your head is
upon your shoulders ! "[1] That prophetic summons to a
more fatal meeting was now at last accomplished!

Strafford had entered the house, we learn from one
who observed him, with his usual impetuous step—
" with speed," says Baillie, " he comes to the house ; he
calls rudely at the door ; James Maxwell, keeper of the
black rod, opens ; his lordship with a proud glooming
countenance, makes towards his place at the board head ;
but at once many bid him void the house ; so he is
forced, in confusion, to go to the door till he was called.
. . He offered to speak, but was commanded to be gone
without a word. In the outer room, James Maxwell
required him, as prisoner, to deliver his sword. When
he had got it, he cries, with a loud voice, for his man to

[1] An admirable commentary on this fierce text is supplied by my
friend Mr. Cattermole, at the commencement of the volume. [In
his vignette on the title-page, of Wentworth walking downstairs
from Pym to his boat.]

carry my lord-lieutenant's sword. This done, he makes through a number of people to his coach, all gazing, no man capping to him, before whom that morning the greatest in England would have stood uncovered."

This was a change indeed! Yet it was a change for which Strafford would seem to have been found not altogether unprepared. In all the proceedings preliminary to his memorable trial, in all the eventful incidents that followed, he was quiet and collected, and showed, in his general bearing, a magnanimous self-subduement. It is a mean as well as a hasty judgment, which would attribute this to any unworthy compromise with his real nature. It is probably a juster and more profound view of it, to say that, into a few of the later weeks of his life, new knowledge had penetrated from the midst of the breaking of his fortunes. It was well and beautifully said by a then living poet,—

> "The soul's dark cottage, battered and decayed,
> Lets in new light through chinks that time has made!"

—and when suddenly upon the sight of Strafford broke the vision of the long unseen assembly of the people, with the old chiefs, and the old ceremonies, only more august and more fatal,—when he saw himself in a single hour, disabled by a set of men not greater in vigour or in intellect than those over whom the weak-minded Buckingham had for years contemptuously triumphed,— the chamber of that assembly forsaken for Westminster Hall,—its once imperious master become a timid auditor, listening unobserved through his screening curtains, and unable to repress by his presence a single threatening glance, or subdue a single fierce voice, amongst the multitude assembled to pronounce judgment on his

R

minister,—that multitude grown from the "faithful commons" into the imperial council of the land, and the sworn upholders of its not yet fallen liberties,—Pym no longer the mouth-piece of a faction that might be trampled on, but recognised as the chosen champion of the people of England, "the delegated voice of God;"—when Strafford had persuaded himself that all this vision was indeed a reality before him, we may feel the sudden and subduing conviction which at once enthralled him to itself! the conviction that he had mistaken the true presentment of that principle of power which he worshipped, and that his genius should have had a different devotion. He had not sunk lower, but the parliament had towered immeasurably higher!

The first thing he did after his arrest, was to write to the lady Strafford. "Sweet hart,—You have heard before this what hath befallen me ·in this place, but be you confident, that if I fortune to be blamed, yet I will not, by God's help, be ashamed. Your carriage upon this misfortune I should advise to be calm, not seeming to be neglective of my trouble, and yet so as there may appear no dejection in you. Continue on the family as formerly, and make much of your children. Tell Will, Nan, and Arabella, I will write to them by the next. In the mean time I shall pray for them to God, that he may bless them, and for their sakes deliver me out of the furious malice of my enemies, which yet I trust, through the goodnesse of God, shall do me no hurt. God have us all in his blessed keeping. Your very loving husbande, STRAFFORDE."

A few days after this, having vainly proffered bail, he was committed to the Tower. Thereupon he wrote again to lady Strafford. "Sweet hart,—I never pityed you so

much as I do now, for in the death of that great person
the deputy, you have lost the principal friend you had
there, whilst we are here riding out the storm, as well as
God and the season shall give us leave. Yet I trust lord
Dillon will supply unto you in part that great loss, till it
please God to bring us together again. As to myself,
albeit all be done against me that art and malice can
devise, with all the rigour possible, yet I am in great
inward quietnesse, and a strong beliefe God will deliver
me out of all these troubles. The more I look into my
case, the more hope I have, and sure, if there be any
honour and justice left, my life will not be in danger,
and for any thing els, time I trust will salve any other
hurt which can be done me. Therefore hold up your
heart, look to the children and your house, let me have
your prayers, and at last, by God's good pleasure, we
shall have our deliverance, when we may as little look
for it as we did for this blow of misfortune, which, I
trust, will make us better to God and man. Your loving
husbande, STRAFFORDE."

The preliminary arrangements having been settled,
and some negotiations proposed by Charles with a view
to his rescue having failed, Strafford's impeachment
began. Never had such "pompous circumstances" and
so "stately a manner" been witnessed at any judicial
proceeding in England. One only, since that day, has
matched it. It was not the trial of an individual, but
the solemn arbitration of an issue between the two great
antagonist principles, liberty and despotism. Westminster
Hall, which had alternately witnessed the triumphs of
both, was the fitting scene. Scaffolds, nearly reaching
to the roof, were erected on either side, eleven stages
high, divided by rails. In the upper ranks of these were

the commissioners of Scotland and the lords of Ireland, who had joined with the commoners of England in their accusations. In the centre sat the peers in their parliament robes, and the lord keeper and the judges, in their scarlet robes, were on the woolsacks. At the upper end, beyond the peers, was a chair raised under a cloth of state for the king, and another for the prince. The throne was unoccupied, for the king was supposed not to be present, since, in his presence, by legal construction, no judicial act could legally be done. Two cabinets or galleries, with trellis work, were on each side of the cloth of state. The king, the queen, and their court, occupied one of these [1]—the foreign nobility then in London the other. The earls of Arundel and Lindsey acted, the one as high-steward, and the other as high-constable, of England. Strafford entered the hall daily, guarded by two hundred trainbands. The king had procured it as a special favour, that the axe should not be carried before him. At the foot of the state-cloth was a scaffold for ladies of quality ; at the lower end was a place with partitions, and an apartment to retire to, for the convenience and consultations of the managers of the trial; opposite to this the witnesses entered; and between was a small desk, at which the accused earl stood or sate, with the lieutenant of the Tower beside him, and at his back four secretaries.

The articles of accusation had gradually, during the long and tedious preliminary proceedings, swelled from nine—which was their original number—to twenty-eight.

---

[1] The king, however, observes Baillie, "brake down the screens with his own hands, so they sat in the eyes of all, but little more regarded than if they had been absent, for the lords sat all covered." Baillie was the principal of the college of Glasgow, and present by order of the Scottish party.

Pym, in an able speech, presented them to the house of lords. Strafford entreated that—seeing these charges filled 200 sheets of paper, and involved the various and ill-remembered incidents of fourteen years of a life of severe action—the space of three months should be permitted for the answer. He was allowed three weeks, and, on the 24th of February, 1641, his answers, in detail, to the charges of the commons were read to the house. The 22d of March was then fixed for the commencement of his trial.

On the first reception of the articles, Strafford, with characteristic purpose, wrote to his wife. "Sweet Harte, —It is long since I writt unto you, for I am here in such a trouble, as gives me little or no respitt. The charge is now come in, *and I am now able, I prayse God, to tell you that I conceive there is nothing capitall ;* and for the reste, I know at the worste his majestie will pardon all, without hurting my fortune ; and then we shall be happy, by God's grace. Therefore comfort yourself, for I trust thes cloudes will away, and that wee shall have faire weather afterwardes. Farewell. Your loving husband, STRAFFORDE." He expressed the same opinion in a letter to sir Adam Loftus.

A short summary of the charges will be sufficient for the present purpose. For it is not necessary, after the ample notice which has been given of Strafford's life and actions, to occupy any considerable space with the proceedings, which only further illustrated them here.[1]

The grand object which the leaders of the commons had in view, was to establish against Strafford AN ATTEMPT

---

[1] Rushworth has devoted a large folio volume, to the occurrences of the impeachment alone.

TO SUBVERT THE FUNDAMENTAL LAWS OF THE COUNTRY.[1]
They had an unquestionable right, with this view, to
blend in the impeachment offences of a different degree;
nor was it ever pretended by them that more than one
or two of the articles amounted to treason. Their course
—to deduce a legal construction of treason from actions
notoriously gone "thorough" with in the service and in
exaltation of the king—was to show that, no matter with
what motive, any actions undertaken which had a tendency
to prove destructive to the state, amounted, in legal
effect, to a traitorous design against the sovereign. The
sovereign, it was argued by these great men, could never
have had a contemplated existence beyond, or independent of, the state. It could never have been the object,
they said, to have defended the king by the statute of
Edward III., and to have left undefended the great body
of the people associated under him. This principle
Strafford had himself recognised in his support of the
petition of right, and it is truly observed by Rushworth,
that " all the laws confirmed and renewed in that petition
of right were said to be the most envenomed arrows that
gave him his mortal wound." The proofs by which it
was proposed to sustain the tremendous accusation, were
to be deduced from a series of his actions infringing the
laws, from words intimating arbitrary designs, and from
certain counsels which directly tended to the entire ruin
of the frame of the constitution.

Over the three great divisions of his public functions
the articles of impeachment were distributed. As pre-

---

[1] They had passed this vote in the house of commons, and against
it not a voice was raised, even by the earl's most ardent supporters.
" That the earl of Strafford had endeavoured to subvert the ancient
and fundamental laws of the realm, and to introduce arbitrary and
tyrannical government."

sident of the council of York, he was charged with having procured powers subversive of all law, with having committed insufferable acts of oppression under colour of his instructions, and with having distinctly announced tyrannical intentions, by declaring that the people should find "the king's little finger heavier than the loins of the law." As governor of Ireland, he was accused of having publicly asserted, "That the Irish was a conquered nation, and that the king might do with them as he pleased." He was charged with acts of oppression towards the earl of Cork, lord Mountnorris, the lord chancellor Loftus, the earl of Kildare, and other persons. He had, it was alleged, issued a general warrant for the seizure of all persons who refused to submit to any legal decree against them, and for their detention till they either submitted, or gave bail to appear before the council table: he had sent soldiers to free quarters on those who would not obey his arbitrary decrees: he had prevented the redress of his injustice, by procuring instructions to prohibit all persons of distinction from quitting Ireland without his express licence: he had appropriated to himself a large share of the customs, the monopoly of tobacco, and the sale of licences for the exportation of certain commodities: he had committed grievous acts of oppression in guarding his monopoly of tobacco: he had, for his own interest, caused the rates on merchandise to be raised, and the merchants to be harassed with new and unlawful oaths: he had obstructed the industry of the country, by introducing new and unknown processes into the manufacture of flax: he had encouraged his army, the instrument of his oppression, by assuring them that his majesty would regard them as a pattern for all his three kingdoms: he had enforced an illegal oath on the Scottish

subjects in Ireland : he had given undue encouragement to papists, and had actually composed the whole of
his new-levied troops of adherents to that religion.   As
chief minister of England, it was laid to his charge that
he had instigated the king to make war on the Scots, and
had himself, as governor of Ireland, commenced hos-
tilities : that, on the question of supplies, he had declared,
" That his majesty should first try the parliament here,
and if that did not supply him according to his occasions,
he might then use his prerogative to levy what he
needed ; and that he should be acquitted both of God
and man, if he took some other courses to supply
himself, though it were against the will of his subjects : "
that, after the dissolution of that parliament, he had said
to his majesty, " That, having tried the affections of his
people, he was loose and absolved from all rules of
government, and was to do every thing that power would
admit ; that his majesty had tried all ways, and was
refused, and should be acquitted both to God and man ;
that he had an army in Ireland, which he might employ to
reduce England to obedience."   He was farther charged
with having counselled the royal declaration which reflected so bitterly on the last parliament ; with the seizure
of the bullion in the Tower ; the proposal of coining
base money ; a new levy of ship-money ; and the loan of
100,000*l.* from the city of London.   He was accused of
having told the refractory citizens that no good would
be done till they were laid up by the heels, and some of
their aldermen hanged for an example.   It was laid to
his charge that he had levied arbitrary exactions on the
people of Yorkshire to maintain his troops : and, finally,
that his counsels had given rise to the rout at Newburn."[1]

[1] Strafford's Trial, pp. 61—75. Nalson, vol. ii. pp. 11—20.

In his answers and opposing evidence Strafford maintained, that "the enlarged instructions for the council of York had not been procured by his solicitations; that the specified instances of oppression in the northern counties were committed after his departure for Ireland; and that the words imputed to him were directly the reverse of those which he had spoken. With regard to Ireland, he vindicated his opinion that it was a conquered country, and that the king's prerogative was much greater there than in England. He contended that all the judgments, charged on him as arbitrary, were delivered by competent courts, in none of which he had above a single voice: that the prevention of persons from quitting the kingdom without licence, as well as placing soldiers at free quarters on the disobedient, were transactions consistent with ancient usages: that the flax manufacture owed all its prosperity to his exertions, and that his prohibition tended to remedy some barbarous and unjust methods of sorting the yarn: that his bargains for the customs and tobacco were profitable to the crown and the country: and that the oath which he had enforced on the Scots was required by the critical circumstances of the times, and fully approved by the government. In regard to his transactions in England, he answered that hostility against Scotland having been resolved on, he had merely counselled an offensive in preference to a defensive war: that his expressions relative to supplies were in strict conformity to the established maxim of the constitution[1]: that, in such emergencies as a foreign invasion, the sovereign was entitled to levy contributions, or adopt any other measure for the public defence: that the words relative to the

---

[1] *Salus populi suprema lex.*

employment of the Irish army were falsely stated, and that he had not ventured to apply to the kingdom of England words uttered in a committee expressly assembled to consider of the reduction of Scotland. He said that his harsh expressions towards the citizens of London were heard by only one interested individual, and not heard by others who stood as near him: that the contributions in Yorkshire were voluntary: and that the proposals for seizing the bullion and coining base money did not proceed from him.[1]

The charges which remained untouched by these answers were abandoned by the commons, as irrelative or incapable of proof, and on the 23d of March, 1641, the chief manager, Mr. Pym, rose in Westminster Hall, and opened the case against him.

The "getting up" of that mighty scene has been described, and a few words may serve to put it, as it were, in action.

Three kingdoms, by their representatives, were present, and for fifteen days, the period of the duration of the trial, "it was daily," says Baillie, "the most glorious assembly the isle could afford." The earl himself appeared before it each day in deep mourning, wearing his George. The stern and simple character of his features accorded with the occasion,—his "countenance manly black," as Whitelock terms it, and his thick dark hair cut short from his ample forehead. A poet who was present exclaimed,

---

[1] Strafford's Trial, pp. 61—75. Nalson, vol. ii. pp. 11—20. I have partly availed myself, in the above, of Mr. MacDiarmid's abstract—pp. 251—259. Some of the charges specified, were added in the course of the trial.

> "On thy brow
> Sate terror mixed with wisdom, and at once
> Saturn and Hermes in thy countenance."

—To this was added the deep interest which can never be withheld from sickness bravely borne. His face was dashed with paleness, and his body stooped with its own infirmities even more than with its master's cares. This was, indeed, so evident, that he was obliged to allude to it himself, and it was not seldom alluded to by others. "They had here," he said, on one occasion, "this rag of mortality before them, worn out with numerous infirmities, which, if they tore into shreds, there was no great loss, only in the spilling of his, they would open a way to the blood of all the nobility in the land." His disorders were the most terrible to bear in themselves, and of that nature, moreover, which can least endure the aggravation of mental anxiety. A severe attack of stone [1], gout in one of his legs to an extent even with him unusual, and other pains, had bent all their afflictions upon him. Yet, though a generous sympathy was demanded on this score, and paid by not a few of his worst opponents, it availed little with the multitudes that were present. Much noise and confusion prevailed at all times through the hall; there was always a great clamour near the doors; and we have it on the authority of Rushworth himself, that at those intervals when Strafford was busied in preparing his answers, the most distracting "hubbubs" broke out, lords walked about and chatted, and commoners were yet more offensively loud.[2] This was unfavourable to the recollection, for

---

[1] See Nalson, vol. ii. p. 100. *et seq.*

[2] Baillie adds, that in these periods "flesh and bread" was ate, and "bottles of beer and wine were going thick from mouth to mouth."

disproof, of incidents long passed, and of conversations forgotten![1]   But conscious that he was not to be allowed in any case permission to retire, as soon as one of his opponent managers had closed his charge, the earl calmly turned his back to his judges, and, with uncomplaining composure, conferred with his secretaries and counsel.

He had, indeed, it is not to be forgotten, strong assurances to sustain him secretly.   He had, first, his own conviction of the legal incompetency of the charges, and to this was added the doubly pledged faith of the king.   In his prison he had received the following letter ;—" STRAFFORD,—The misfortune that is fallen upon you by the strange mistaking and conjuncture of these times, being such that I must lay by the thought of employing you hereafter in my affairs, yet I cannot satisfy myself in honour or conscience, without assuring you (now in the midst of your troubles) that upon the word of a king you shall not suffer in life, honour, or fortune.   This is but justice, and therefore a very mean reward from a master to so faithful and able a servant, as you have showed yourself to be,—yet it is as much as I conceive the present times will permit, though none shall hinder me from being your constant and faithful friend, CHARLES."   But against these aids, were opposed certain significant symptoms of a desperate and fatal purpose on the part of the managers of the impeachment. The bishops, on whom he might reasonably have relied, had, on the motion of Williams, withdrawn from attendance "*in agitatione causæ sanguinis,*" surrendering, the

---

[1] Baillie cannot refrain from saying, while he describes the guilt to have been fully proved, that some of the evidence was only " chamber and table-discourse, flim-flams, and fearie-fairies."

right they had, under what was called "the constitutions of Clarendon," of attending in capital trials up to the stage of judgment. Next,—the person on whose evidence Strafford mainly relied in the proof of his answers, sir George Radcliffe, had, by a master-stroke of Pym's, been incapacitated suddenly by a charge of treason against himself,—not preferred certainly without cause, on the presumption of the guilt of the principal, for he had been Strafford's guilty agent in all things, but preferred with a fatal effect to Strafford himself. Again,—though counsel had been granted him, they were restricted by the lords, on conference with the commons, to the argument of points of law. Lastly,—with an irresistible energy, equalled only by Strafford's own, Pym had forced from the king a release for all the members of his secret council from their oath of secrecy, in order to their examination before the committee of impeachment.

"My lords," said Strafford,—alluding to this, and to certain words of his own which such examination had been alleged to have proved,—"My lords, these words were not wantonly or unnecessarily spoken, or whispered in a corner, but they were spoken in full council, where, by the duty of my oath, I was obliged to speak according to my heart and conscience, in all things concerning the king's service. If I had forborne to speak what I conceived to be for the benefit of the king and the people, I had been perjured towards almighty God. And for delivering my mind openly and freely, shall I be in danger of my life, as a traitor? If that necessity be put upon me, I thank God, by his blessing I have learned not to stand in fear of him who can only kill the body. If the question be, whether I must be traitor to man, or perjured to God, I will be faithful to my creator. And whatsoever shall befall me from popular rage or from my own weakness, I must leave it to that almighty being, and to the justice and honour of my judges. My lords, I conjure you not to make yourselves so unhappy, as to disable yourselves and your children from undertaking the great charge and trust of the commonwealth. You inherit that trust from your fathers, you are born to great thoughts, you are nursed up for the great and weighty employments of the kingdom. But if it be once admitted, that a counsellor, delivering his opinion with others at the council-table, *candidè et castè*, under an oath of secrecy and faithfulness, shall be brought into question, upon some misapprehension or ignorance of law,—if every word, that he speaks from a sincere and noble intention, shall be drawn against him, for the attainting of him, his children and posterity,—I know not (under favor I speak it,) any wise or noble person of fortune, who will, upon such perilous and unsafe terms, adventure to be counsellor to the king! Therefore, I beseech your lordships so to look on me, that my misfortune may not bring an inconvenience upon yourselves. And though my words were not so advised and discreet, or so well weighed, as they ought to be, yet I trust your lordships are too honourable and just, to lay them to my charge as high treason. Opinions may make an heretic, but that they make a traitor, I have never heard till now."

Again, in reference to matters alleged against him on the evidence of familiar conversations, he eloquently protested thus :—" If, my lords, words spoken to friends in familiar discourse, spoken in one's chamber, spoken at one's table, spoken in one's sick bed, spoken perhaps to gain better reason, to give himself more clear light and judgment, by reasoning ;—if these things shall be brought against a man as treason, this, under favour, takes away the comfort of all human society,—by this means we shall be debarred from speaking (the principal joy and comfort of society) with wise and good men, to become wiser, and better our lives. If these things be strained to take away life and honour, and all that is desirable, it will be a silent world! A city will become a hermitage, and sheep will be found amongst a crowd and press of people! and no man shall dare to impart his solitary thoughts or opinions to his friend and neighbour!" Noble and touching as this is, let the reader remember, as he reads it, the case of Mountnorris, and the misquoting and torturing of words, in themselves harmless, by which the lord deputy of Ireland sacrificed that man to his schemes of absolute power. It is mournful to be obliged to add that, it is chiefly the genius of a great actor which calls for admiration in this great scene ; for though he was, as we may well believe, sincere in his sudden present acknowledgment of that power of the commons which he had so often braved, the same plea of sincerity cannot serve him in his bold outfacing of every previous action of his power.

As the trial proceeded, so extraordinary were the resources he manifested, that the managers of the commons failed in much of the effect of their evidence. Even the clergy who were present forgot the imprisonment of the weak and miserable Laud (who now lay in prison, stripped of his power by this formidable parliament, which the very despotism of himself and Strafford had gifted with its potently operative force!) and thought of nothing but the "grand apostate" before them. "By this time," says May, "the people began to be a little divided in opinion. The clergy in general were so much fallen into love and admiration of this earl, that the archbishop of Canterbury was almost quite forgotten by them. The courtiers cried him up, and the ladies were exceedingly on his side. It seemed a very pleasant object to see só many Sempronias, with pen, ink, and paper in their hands, noting the passages, and discoursing upon the grounds, of law and state. They were all of his side, whether moved by pity, proper to their sex, or by ambition of being able to judge of the parts of the prisoner. But so great was the favour and love which they openly expressed to him, that some could not but think of that verse :—

> ' Non formosus erat, sed erat facundus Ulysses
>   Et tamen æquoreas torsit amore deas ! ' "

Even the chairman of the committee who prepared his impeachment, the author of the Memorials, observes, "Certainly never any man acted such a part, on such a theatre, with more wisdome, constancy, and eloquence, with greater reason, judgment, and temper, and with a better grace in all his words and gestures, than this great and excellent person did."

Such, indeed, appeared to be a very prevailing feeling, when on the morning of the 10th of April, before the opening of that day's trial, Pym entered the house of commons and announced a communication respecting the earl of Strafford, of vital importance. The members were ordered to remain in their places, and the doors of the house were locked. Pym and the young sir Harry Vane then rose, and produced a paper containing "a copy of notes taken at a junto of the privy council for

the Scots affairs, about the 5th of May last." These
were notes made by sir Henry Vane the elder, and
Clarendon says, that he placed them in the hands of
Pym out of hatred to Strafford. With much more appearance and likelihood of truth, however, Whitelocke
states that the elder Vane, being absent from London,
and in want of some papers, sent the key of his study
to his son, and that the latter, in executing his father's
orders, found this paper, and was ultimately induced by
Pym to allow its production against Strafford. The
commons received this new evidence with many expressions of zealous thankfulness.

On the 13th of April the notes were read in Westminster Hall by Pym. They were in the shape of a
dialogue and conference, and contained opinions delivered by Laud and Hamilton; but the essential words
were words spoken by Strafford to the king. "You
have an army in Ireland that you may employ to reduce
this kingdom to obedience." Vane the elder was then
called. He denied recollection of the words at first,
till it had been asserted by others of the privy council,
that Strafford had used those words, "or the like," when
the earl's brother-in-law, lord Clare, rose and suggested
that "this kingdom," by grammatical construction, might
mean Scotland. With singular ability Strafford directed
all his resources to the weakening of this evidence, but
it was generally regarded as fatal. He urged his brother-
in-law's objection; the very title of the notes, in proof
of the country referred to, "no danger of a war with
Scotland, if offensive, not defensive;" and protested
against a man's life being left to hang upon a single
word. The evidence was, finally, admitted against him,
and he was called upon to make his general defence

s

in person against the facts, leaving the law to his counsel.

He began by adverting to his painful and adverse position, alone and unsupported, against the whole authority and power of the commons, his health impaired, his memory almost gone, his thoughts unquiet and troubled. He prayed of their lordships to supply his many infirmities, by their better abilities, better judgments, better memories. "You alone," he said, "I acknowledge, with all gladness and humility, as my judges. The king condemns no man; the great operation of his sceptre is mercy; he dispenses justice by his ministers; but, with reverence be it spoken, he is not my judge, nor are the commons my judges, in this case of life and death. To your judgment alone, my lords, I submit myself in all cheerfulness. I have great cause to give thanks to God for this, and celebrated be the wisdom of our ancestors who have so ordained."

With great force and subtle judgment, he then argued against the doctrine of arbitrary and constructive treason, and afterwards proceeded—"My lords, it is hard to be questioned upon a law which cannot be shown. Where hath this fire lain hid so many hundred years, without smoke to discover it, till it thus burst forth to consume me and my children? That punishment should precede promulgation of a law, to be punished by a law subsequent to the fact, is extreme hard! What man can be safe, if this be admitted? My lords, it is hard in another respect,—that there should be no token set, by which we should know this offence, no admonition by which we should avoid it. My lords, be pleased to give that regard to the peerage of England, as never expose yourselves to such moot points—such constructive interpretations of laws : if there must be a trial of wits, let the subject matter be of somewhat else than the lives and honours of peers. It will be wisdom for yourselves, for your posterity, and for the whole kingdom, to cast into the fire these bloody and mysterious volumes of constructive and arbitrary treason, as the primitive Christians did their books of curious arts, and betake yourselves to the plain letter of the law and statute, that telleth us what is and what is not treason, without being more ambitious to be more learned in the art of killing than our forefathers ! It is now 240 years since any man was touched for this alleged crime, to this height, before myself. Let us not awaken these sleeping lions to our destructions, by taking up a few musty records, that have lain by the walls so many ages, forgotten or neglected. May your lordships please not to add this to my other misfortunes,—let not a precedent be derived from me, so disadvantageous as this will be in its consequence to the whole kingdom. Do not, through me, wound the interest of the commonwealth :—and howsoever these gentlemen say, they speak for the commonwealth, yet, in this particular, I indeed speak for it, and show the inconveniences and mischiefs that will fall upon it : for, as it is said in the statute 1 Hen. IV., ' No one will know what to do or say for fear of such penalties.' Do not put, my lords, such difficulties upon ministers of state, that men of wisdom, of honour, and of fortune, may not with cheerfulness and safety be employed for the public. If you weigh and measure them by grains and scruples, the public affairs of the kingdom will lie waste, no man will meddle with them who hath any thing to lose. My lords, I have troubled you longer than I should have done, were it not for the interest of those dear pledges a saint in Heaven hath left me." At this word (says the reporter) he stopped awhile, letting fall some tears to her memory; then he went on:—"What I forfeit myself is nothing; but that indiscretion should extend to my posterity woundeth me to the very soul. You will pardon my infirmity; something I should have added, but am not able; therefore let it pass. Now, my lords, for myself, I have been, by the blessing of Almighty God, taught that the afflictions of this present life are not to be compared to the eternal weight of glory, which shall be revealed hereafter. And so, my lords, even so, with all tranquillity of mind, I freely submit myself to your judgment, and whether that judgment be of life or death, *Te Deum laudamus.*"[1]

---

[1] This is from Whitelocke's Memorials. It is the most beautiful and complete report that has been given. I may subjoin a characteristic note from Baillie's letters. "At the end he made such a pathetic oration, for half an hour, *as ever comedian did on the stage.* The matter and expression was exceeding brave. Doubtless if he had grace and civil goodness he is a most eloquent man. One passage is most spoken of; his breaking off in weeping and silence when he spoke of his first wife. Some took it for a true defect in his memory; others for a notable part of his rhetoric; some that true grief and remorse at that remembrance had stopt his mouth; for they say that his first lady, being with child, and finding one of his mistress's letters, brought it to him, and chiding him therefore, he struck her on the breast, whereof she shortly died."— *Letters,* p. 291. The latter statement is only one of a thousand horrible and disgusting falsehoods which, notwithstanding the abundance of true accusatory matter, were circulated at the time against Strafford, and one or two specimens of which may be found in the fourth volume of lord Somer's Collection of Tracts. His friends, however, it is to be remarked, were not less forward in getting up all sorts of fictitious points of sympathy (in some respects, also, unnecessary, since they had plenty of true resources in that regard around him and his memory; and as an instance I may mention that an extremely pathetic letter of sir Walter Raleigh to his wife (the most pathetic, probably, in the language), written while he expected execution, was printed with Strafford's signature, and with the alteration of words to meet the circumstances of Strafford's death. The writers of the Biog. Brit. do not seem to

Great was the struggle to be made against such noble and affecting eloquence, and Pym proved himself not unequal to it. While we yield due admiration to the unexampled demeanour of Strafford in this conjuncture ;—to that quick perception of his exact position, which, while it revealed to him the whole magnitude of the danger, suggested the most plausible defence, and supplied resolution where, to an ordinary spirit, it would have induced despair,—so that, while sinking down the tremendous gulf into which he had been so suddenly precipitated, he displayed the same coolness in catching at every weed, however feeble, that might retard his descent, as though the peril had long been foreseen and the methods of escape long rehearsed,—while we praise this in him, let us not forget the still more extraordinary bearing of his adversary—the triumph of Pym, as unparalleled as the overthrow of Strafford. In either case the individual rose or fell with the establishment or the withdrawal of a great principle. Pym knew and felt this, and that with him it now rested whether or not the privileges so long contested, the rights so long misunderstood, of the great body of the people, should win at last their assured consummation and acknowledgment. In the speeches of Pym the true point is to be recognised, on which the vindication of Strafford's death turns. The defence of the accused was technical, and founded on rules of evidence, and legal constructions of statutes, which, though clearly defined since, were in that day recognised doubtfully, and frequently exceeded. The defence of the accusers, if they are indeed to be put

---

have been aware of this. But see Somers' Tracts, vol. iv. pp. 249, 250. ; and compare with Biog. Brit. vol. v. p. 3478.

upon their defence before a posterity for whose rights they hazarded all things, rests upon a principle which was implanted in man when he was born, and which no age can deaden or obscure. "My lords," said Pym, "we charge him with nothing but what the 'law' in every man's breast condemns, the light of nature, the light of common reason, the rules of common society."[1] Nor can it be doubted, that occasions must ever be recognised by the philosopher and the statesman, when the community may be re-invested in those rights, which were theirs before a particular law was established. If ever such an occasion had arisen, surely, looking back upon the occurrences of the past, and forward upon the prospects of the future, it had arisen here. It was time that outraged humanity should appeal, as Pym afterwards urged, to "the element of all laws, out of which they are derived, the end of all laws, to which they are designed, and in which they are perfected."[2] The public liberty was in danger, from the life of Strafford, and the question of justice reared itself above the narrow limits of the law. For yet, again Pym urged, the law itself can be no other than that "which puts a difference betwixt good and evil, betwixt just and unjust! It is God alone who subsists by himself, all other things subsist in a mutual dependence and relation!"[3] Nor can it be alleged, even by the legal opponents of this impeachment, that the proofs advanced under the fifteenth article, which had charged Strafford with raising money by his own authority, and quartering troops upon the people of Ireland, did not advance far more nearly to a substantive treason, within the statute of Edward III., than many of

---

[1] Rushworth, vol. viii. pp. 108, 109.   [2] Ibid. p. 661.
[3] Ibid. p. 663.

the recognised precedents that were offered. "Neither will this," Pym contended on that ground with a terrible earnestness, "be a new way of blood. There are marks enough to trace this law to the very original of this kingdom ; and if it hath not been put in execution, as he allegeth, this 240 years, it was not for want of a law, but that all that time had not bred a man, bold enough to commit such crimes as these !"

At this moment, it is said, Strafford had been closely and earnestly watching Pym, when the latter, suddenly turning, met the fixed and wasted features of his early associate. A rush of other feelings crowding into that look, for a moment dispossessed him. "His papers, he looked on," says Baillie, "but they could not help him to a point or two, so he behoved to pass them." But a moment, and Pym's eloquence and dignified command returned. He had thoroughly contemplated his commission, and had resolved on its fulfilment. The occasion was not let slip, the energies wound up to this feat through years of hard endurance were not frozen,— and the cause of the people was gained. In the condemnation of Strafford, they resumed an alienated power, and were re-instated in an ancient freedom.

He was condemned. The judges themselves, on a solemn reference by the house of lords for their opinion, whether some of the articles amounted to treason, answered unanimously that upon all which their lordships had voted to be proved, it was their opinion the earl of Strafford did deserve to undergo the pains and penalties of high treason by law.

Meanwhile, before this opinion was taken, the commons had changed their course, and introduced a bill of attainder. This has been sorely reproached to them, and one or two of the men who had acted with them up to this point now receded. Lord Digby was the principal of these. "Truly, sir," he said, on the discussion of the bill, "I am still the same in my opinions and affections, as unto the earl of Strafford. I confidently believe him to be the most dangerous minister, the most insupportable to free subjects, that can be charactered. I believe his practices in themselves as high, as tyrannical, as any subject ever ventured on ; and the malignity of them hugely aggravated by those rare abilities of his, whereof God had given him the use, but the devil the application. In a word, I believe him to be still that grand apostate to the commonwealth, who must not expect to be pardoned in this world, till he be dispatched to the other. And yet, let me tell you, Mr. Speaker, my hand must not be to that dispatch. I protest, as my conscience stands informed, I had rather it were off!" The authority of Digby in this affair, however, may well be questioned, since it has been proved that he had at this time entered into an intrigue to save the life of the prisoner, and though he spoke against the bill with extreme earnestness, he at the same time no less earnestly offered to swear, that he knew nothing of a certain copy of important notes which had been lost, though they were afterwards found in his handwriting, in the royal cabinet taken at Naseby, and it turned out that having access to them, as a member of the impeachment committee, he had stolen them.[1]

The bill of attainder was passed on the 21st of April. While on its way to the lords, the king went to that house and addressed them. "I am sure," he said, " you all know that I have been present at the hearing of this

[1] See Whitelocke, p. 43.

great case from the one end to the other; and I must tell you, that I cannot in my conscience condemn him of high treason :—it is not fit for me to argue the business; I am sure you will not expect that; a positive doctrine best becomes the mouth of a prince." After beseeching them not to treat the earl with severity, he thus concluded :—"I must confess, for matter of misdemeanors, I am so clear in that, that though I will not chalk out the way, yet let me tell you, that I do think my lord Strafford is not fit hereafter to serve me or the commonwealth in any place of trust, no, not so much as that of a constable. Therefore, I leave it to you, my lords, to find some such way as to bring me out of this great strait, and keep ourselves and the kingdom from such inconveniences. Certainly he that thinks him guilty of high treason in his conscience may condemn him of misdemeanor."

When Strafford heard in his prison of this intended interference, he had earnestly protested against it, and, on learning that the step was actually taken, he gave himself up for lost.[1] He had judged truly. The leaders of the commons took advantage of the occasion it offered. The presbyterian pulpits of the following day, which happened to be Sunday, sent forth into every quarter of London, cries of "justice upon the great delinquent;" and on the succeeding morning, furious multitudes, variously armed, thronged the approaches to the house of lords; placarded as "Straffordians, or betrayers of their country," the names of those commoners who had voted against the attainder; and shouted openly for the blood of Strafford.

Pym, meanwhile, had discovered and crushed a con-

----

[1] Clarendon and Radcliffe.

spiracy for his release, which had originated in the court, and was disclosed by the inviolable fidelity of the governor of the Tower.

No hope remained. The lords, proceeding upon the judicial opinion I have named, passed the bill of attainder, voting upon the articles judicially, and not as if they were enacting a legislative measure.

The earl of Strafford, with a generosity worthy of his intellect, now wrote to the king and released him from his pledged word. "To say, sir," he wrote in the course of this memorable letter, "that there hath not been a strife in me, were to make me less man than, God knoweth, my infirmities make me; and to call a destruction upon myself and my young children (where the intentions of my heart at least have been innocent of this great offence), may be believed, will find no easy consent from flesh and blood." Its concluding passages ran thus:—"So now, to set your majesty's conscience at liberty, I do most humbly beseech your majesty, for prevention of evils which may happen by your refusal to pass this bill, and by this means to remove, praised be God, (I cannot say this accursed, but, I confess), this unfortunate thing, forth of the way towards that blessed agreement, which God, I trust, shall ever establish between you and your subjects. Sir, my consent shall more acquit you herein to God, than all the world can do besides. To a willing man there is no injury done. And as, by God's grace, I forgive all the world with a calmness and meekness of infinite contentment to my dislodging soul, so, sir, to you I can give the life of this world, with all the cheerfulness imaginable, in the just acknowledgment of your exceeding favours, and only beg, that in your goodness you would vouchsafe to cast your gracious regard upon my poor son and his three sisters, less or more, and no otherwise, than as their (in present) unfortunate father may hereafter appear more or less guilty of this death."

The singular note which has been preserved by Burnet, and which relates circumstances taken from the lips of Hollis himself, continues the deep interest of this tragic history :—"The earl of Strafford had married his sister : so, though in the parliament he was one of the hottest men of the party, yet when that matter was before them, he always withdrew. When the bill of attainder was passed, the king sent for him, to know what he could do to save the earl of Strafford. Hollis answered that, if the king pleased, since the execution of the law was in him, he might legally grant him a reprieve, which must be good in law ;—but he would not advise it. That which he proposed was, that lord Strafford should send him a petition for a short respite, to settle his affairs, and to prepare for death, upon which he advised the king to come next day with the petition in his hands, and lay it before the two houses, with a speech which he drew for the king, and Hollis said to him, he would try his interest among his friends to get them to consent to it. He prepared a great many by assuring them that, if they would save lord Strafford, he would become wholly theirs in consequence of his first principles, and that he might do them much more service by being preserved, than he could do if made an example upon such new and doubtful points. In this he had wrought on so many, that he believed if the king's party had struck into it he might have saved him."[1]

While the party thus prepared to second Hollis waited

[1] Own Time, book i.

their time, the king suddenly resorted to a different scheme, and, having with tears in his eyes signed the commission for giving assent to the bill, declaring at the same time, that Strafford's condition was happier than his own, sent the lords a letter, written by his own hand, and, as a further proof of his deep interest, with the young prince of Wales as its messenger. " I did yester-day," ran this letter, " satisfy the justice of the kingdom, by passing the bill of attainder against the earl of Strafford ; but mercy being as inherent and inseparable to a king as justice, I desire at this time, in some measure, to show that likewise, by suffering that unfortu-nate man to fulfil the natural course of his life in a close imprisonment.   Yet so, if ever he make the least offer to escape, or offer directly or indirectly to meddle in any sort of public business, especially with me, either by message or letter, it shall cost him his life without farther process.   This, if it may be done without the discontentment of my people, will be an unspeakable contentment to me.   To which end, as in the first place, I by this letter do earnestly desire your approbation, and, to endear it more, have chose him to carry it, that of all your house is most dear to me.   So I desire, that by a conference you will endeavour to give the house of commons contentment, assuring you that the exercise of mercy is no more pleasing to me, than to see both houses of parliament consent, for my sake, that I should moderate the severity of the law in so important a case. I will not say, that your complying with me in this my intended mercy shall make me more willing, but certainly 't will make me more cheerful, in granting your just grievances.   But if no less than his life can satisfy my people, I must say—*fiat justitia.*   Thus again, recom-

mending the consideration of my intention to you, I rest." The following was added as a postscript :—
"*If he must die, it were charity to reprieve him until Saturday.*"

Hollis's scheme was now thoroughly defeated, and death secured to Strafford. This pitiable letter ended all. It is a sorry office to plant the foot on a worm so crushed and writhing as the wretched king who signed it, for it was one of the few crimes of which he was in the event thoroughly sensible, and friend has for once co-operated with foe in the steady application to it of the branding iron. There is in truth hardly any way of relieving the "damned spot" of its intensity of hue, even by distributing the concentrated infamy over other portions of Charles's character. The reader who has gone through the preceding details of Strafford's life can surely not suggest any. For when we have convinced ourselves that this "unthankful king" never really loved Strafford; that, as much as in him lay, he kept the dead Buckingham in his old privilege of mischief, by adopting his aversions and abiding by his spleenful purposes; that, in his refusals to award those increased honours for which his minister was a petitioner, on the avowed ground of the royal interest, may be discerned the petty triumph of one who dares not dispense with the services thrust upon him, but revenges himself by withholding their well-earned reward;—still does the blackness accumulate to baffle our efforts. The paltry tears he is said to have shed only burn that blackness in. If his after conduct indeed had been different, he might have availed himself of one excuse,—but that the man, who, in a few short months, proved that he could make so resolute a stand somewhere, should have judged this event no occasion for attempting it, is either a crowning infamy or an infinite consolation, according as we may judge wickedness or weakness to have preponderated, in the constitution of Charles I.

Sufficient has been said to vindicate these remarks from any, the remotest, intention of throwing doubt on the perfect justice of that bill of attainder. Bills of attainder had not been uncommon in England; are the same in principle as the ordinary bills of pains and penalties; and the resort to that principle in the present case, arose from no failure of the impeachment, as has been frequently alleged [1], but because, in the course of that impeachment, circumstances arose, which suggested to the great leader of the popular cause the greater safety of fixing this case upon wider and more special grounds. Without stretching to the slightest extent the boundaries of any statute, they thought it better at once to bring Strafford's treason to the condemnation of the sources of all law. In this view it is one of their wisest achievements that has been brought within the most hasty and ill-considered censure—their famous proviso that the attainder should not be acted upon by the judges as a precedent in determining the crime of treason. As to Strafford's death, the remark that the people had no alternative, includes all that it is necessary to urge. The king's assurances of his intention to afford him no further opportunity of crime, could surely weigh nothing with men who had observed how an infinitely more disgusting minister of his will had only seemed to rise the higher in his master's estimation for the accumulated curses of the nation. Nothing but the knife of Felton could sever in that case

---

[1] The judges and peers voted judicially even on the bill, as has been already stated.

the weak head and the wicked instrument, and it is to the honour of the adversaries of Strafford that they were earnest that their cause should vindicate itself completely, and look for no adventitious redress. Strafford had outraged the people—this was not denied. He was defended on the ground of those outrages not amounting to a treason against the king. For my own part, this defence appears to me decisive, looking at it in a technical view, and with our present settlement of evidence and treason. But to concede that point, after the advances they had made, would have been in that day to concede all. It was to be shown that another power had claim to the loyalty and the service of Strafford— and if a claim, then a vengeance to exact for its neglect. And this was done.

Nor should the subject be quitted without the remark, that the main principle contended for by Pym and his associates was, at the last, fully submitted to by Strafford. He allowed the full power of the people's assembly to take cognizance of his deeds and to dispose of his life, while most earnestly engaged in defending the former and preserving the latter. Now the calm and magnanimous patience of Strafford was very compatible with a fixed denial of the authority of his judges, had that appeared contestible in his eyes,—but we find no intimation of such a disposition. He would not have the parliament's punishment precede promulgation of a law;" he pleads that "to be punished by a law subsequent to the fact is extreme hard;" and that "it is hard that there should be no token set by which we should know this offence, no admonition by which we should avoid it;" and he is desirous that "a precedent may not be derived from one so disadvantageous as this;"—but, in the mean time, the cause is gained, the main and essential point is given up! The old boasts of the lord lieutenant's being accountable to the king alone, of the king's will being the one and the only law of his service, are no longer heard. It may be said that a motive of prudence withheld Strafford from indignantly appealing to the king in his lurking place, from the unrecognised array of questioners and self constituted inquisitors, who had taken upon themselves to supersede him,—but when the sentence was passed and its execution at hand, when hope was gone and the end rapidly hastening, we still find Strafford offering nothing against the right.

One momentary emotion, not inconsistent with his letter to the king, escaped him when he was told to prepare for death. He asked if the king had indeed assented to the bill. Secretary Carleton answered in the affirmative, and Strafford, laying his hand on his heart, and raising his eyes to heaven, uttered the memorable words,—" Put not your trust in princes, nor in the sons of men, for in them there is no salvation." Charles's conduct was indeed incredibly monstrous.

Three days more of existence were granted to Strafford, which he employed calmly in the arrangement of his affairs. He wrote a petition to the house of lords to have compassion on his innocent children ; addressed a letter to his wife bidding her affectionately to support her courage ; and accompanied it with a letter of final instruction and advice to his eldest son. This is in all respects deeply touching :—" MY DEAREST WILL," he wrote, " These are the last lines that you are to receive from a father that tenderly loves you. I wish there were a greater leisure to impart my mind unto you, but our merciful God will supply all things by his grace, and guide and protect you in all your ways,—to whose infinite goodness I bequeath you. And therefore be not discouraged, but serve him, and trust in him, and he will preserve and prosper you in all things. Be sure you give all respect to my wife, that hath ever had a great love unto you, and therefore will be well becoming you. Never be awanting in your love and care to your sisters, but let them ever be most dear unto you :—for, this will give others cause to esteem and respect you for it, and is a duty that you owe them in the memory of your excellent mother and myself; therefore your care and affection to them must be the very same that you are to have of your self; and the like regard must you have to your youngest sister ; for indeed you owe it her also, both for her father and mother's sake. Sweet Will, be careful to take the advice of those friends, which are by me desired to advise you for your education." And so the tenderness of the father proceeds through many fond and affectionate charges. With characteristic hope he says—" The king I trust will deal graciously with you, and restore you those honours and that fortune, which a distempered time hath deprived you of, together with the life of your father." Advice is next given to meet the occurrence of such a chance. " Be sure to avoid as much as you can to enquire after those that have been sharp in their judgments towards me, and I charge you never to suffer thought of revenge to enter your heart ; but be careful to be informed, who were my friends in this prosecution, and to them apply yourself to make them your friends also ; and on such you may rely, and bestow much of your conversation amongst them. And God almighty of his infinite goodness bless you and your children's children ; and his same goodness bless your sisters in like manner, perfect you in every good work, and give you right understandings in all things. Amen. Your most loving father, THOMAS WENTWORTH."[1]

At one time, probably, a deeper pang would have been involved to Strafford in this affecting surrender of his cherished title, than in that of existence itself. But this was not the time. Nothing but concern for his family and friends disturbed the composure of his remaining hours. He wrote kind and encouraging letters to "dear George," as he called sir George Radcliffe; shed tears for the death of Wandesford, whom he had entrusted with the care of his government and family, but who broke his heart on hearing of the sad events that had fallen on his patron; and requested of the primate of Ireland (Usher), who attended him, to desire "my lord's Grace of Canterbury," his old friend, the now imprisoned and afflicted Laud, "to lend me his prayers this night and to give me his blessing when I go abroad to-morrow, and to be in his window, that, by my last farewell, I may give him thanks for this, and all other, his former favours." He had previously asked the lieutenant of the Tower if it were possible to have an interview with Laud, adding with playful sarcasm, "You shall hear what passes betwixt us. It is not a time either for him to

---

[1] Strafford Papers, vol. ii. p. 416. The letter bears date the 11th of May, 1641, and has the following postscript:—"You must not fail to behave yourself towards my lady Clare, your grandmother, with all duty and observance; for most tenderly doth she love you, and hath been passing kind unto me. God reward her charity for it. And both in this and all the rest, the same that I counsel you, the same do I direct also to your sisters, that so the same may be observed by you all. And once more do I, from my very soul, beseech our gracious God to bless and govern you in all, to the saving you in the day of his visitation, and join us again in the communion of his blessed saints, where is fulness of joy and bliss for evermore. Amen, Amen." The "youngest sister" was the infant of lady Strafford.

plot heresy, or me to plot treason." The lieutenant in reply suggested a petition to the parliament. "No," was the quiet rejoinder. "I have gotten my despatch from them, and will trouble them no more. I am now petitioning a higher court, where neither partiality can be expected, nor error feared."

Laud, old and feeble, staggered to the window of his cell as Strafford passed on the following morning, and, as he lifted his hands to bestow the blessing his lips were unable to utter, fell back and fainted in the arms of his attendant.

Strafford moved on to the scaffold with undisturbed composure. His body, so soon to be released, had given him a respite of its infirmities for that trying hour. Rushworth, the clerk of the parliament, was one of the spectators, and has minutely described the scene. "When he arrived outside the Tower, the lieutenant desired him to take coach at the gate, lest the enraged mob should tear him in pieces. 'No,' said he, 'Mr. Lieutenant, I dare look death in the face, and the people too; have you a care I do not escape; 't is equal to me how I die, whether by the stroke of the executioner, or by the madness and fury of the people, if that may give them better content.'" Not less than 100,000 persons, who had crowded in from all parts, were visible on Tower-hill, in a long and dark perspective. Strafford, in his walk, took off his hat frequently, and saluted them, and received not a word of insult or reproach. His step and manner are described by Rushworth to have been those of "a general marching at the head of an army, to breathe victory, rather than those of a condemned man, to undergo the sentence of death." At his side, upon the scaffold, stood his brother, sir George Wentworth, the bishop of Armagh, the earl of Cleveland, and others of his friends,—and behind them the indefatigable collector Rushworth, who "being then there on the scaffold with him," as he says, took down the speech which, having asked their patience first, Strafford at some length addressed to the people. He declared the inno-cence of his intentions, whatever might have been the construction of his acts, and said that the prosperity of his country was his fondest wish. But it augured ill, he told them, for the people's happiness, to write the com-mencement of a reformation in letters of blood. " One thing I desire to be heard in," he added, "and do hope that for Christian charity's sake I shall be believed. I was so far from being against parliaments, that I did always think parliaments in England to be the happy constitution of the kingdom and nation, and the best means, under God, to make the king and his people happy." [1]

He then turned to take leave of the friends who had accompanied him to the scaffold. He beheld his brother weeping excessively. "Brother," he said, "what do you see in me to cause these tears? Does any innocent fear betray in me—guilt? or my innocent boldness—atheism? Think that you are now accompanying me the fourth time to my marriage bed. That block must be my pillow, and here I shall rest from all my labours. No thoughts of envy, no dreams of treason, nor jealousies, nor cares, for the king, the state, or myself, shall interrupt this easy sleep. Remember me to my sister, and to my wife; and carry my blessing to my eldest son, and to

---

[1] The paper of minutes from which he had spoken this speech, was afterwards found lying on the scaffold, and was printed by Rushworth, vol. viii. p. 761. See Appendix to this Memoir.

Ann, and Arabella, not forgetting my little infant, that knows neither good nor evil, and cannot speak for itself. God speak for it, and bless it!" While undressing himself, and winding his hair under a cap, he said, looking on the block—" I do as cheerfully put off my doublet at this time as ever I did when I went to bed."

"Then," proceeds Rushworth, closing this memorable scene, " then he called, 'Where is the man that shall do this last office (meaning the executioner)? call him to me.' When he came and asked him forgiveness, he told him he forgave him and all the world. Then kneeling down by the block, he went to prayer again by himself, the bishop of Armagh kneeling on the one side, and the minister on the other ; to the which minister after prayer he turned himself, and spoke some few words softly; having his hands lifted up, the minister closed his hands with his. Then bowing himself to the earth, to lay down his head on the block, he told the executioner that he would first lay down his head to try the fitness of the block, and take it up again, before he laid it down for good and all ; and so he did ; and before he laid it down again he told the executioner that he would give him warning when to strike, by stretching forth his hands ; and then he laid down his neck on the block, stretching out his hands ; the executioner struck off his head at one blow, then took the head up in his hand, and showed it to all the people, and said, 'God save the king!'"

Thus, on Wednesday, the 12th of May, 1641, died Thomas Wentworth, the first earl of Strafford. Within a few weeks of his death, the parliament mitigated the most severe consequences of their punishment to his children ; and, in the succeeding reign, the attainder was reversed, the proceedings obliterated, and his son restored to the earldom.

A great lesson is written in the life of this truly extraordinary person. In the career of Strafford is to be sought the justification of the world's "appeal from tyranny to God." In him Despotism had at length obtained an instrument with mind to comprehend, and resolution to act upon, her principles in their length and breadth,—and enough of her purposes were effected by him, to enable mankind to see "as from a tower the end of all." I cannot discern one false step in Strafford's public conduct, one glimpse of a recognition of an alien principle, one instance of a dereliction of the law of his being, which can come in to dispute the decisive result of the experiment, or explain away its failure. The least vivid fancy will have no difficulty in taking up the interrupted design, and by wholly enfeebling, or materially emboldening, the insignificant nature of Charles, and by according some half dozen years of immunity to the "fretted tenement" of Strafford's "fiery soul,"—contemplate then, for itself, the perfect realisation of the scheme of "making the prince the most absolute lord in Christendom." That done,—let it pursue the same course with respect to Eliot's noble imaginings, or to young Vane's dreamy aspirings, and apply in like manner a fit machinery to the working out the projects which made the dungeon of the one a holy place, and sustained the other in his self-imposed exile.—The result is great and decisive! It establishes, in renewed force, those principles of political conduct which have endured, and must continue to endure, "like truth from age to age."

APPENDIX [I.]

LIFE OF THE EARL OF STRAFFORD.

MY HUMBLE OPINION CONCERNING A PARLIAMENT IN THIS YOUR MAJESTY'S KINGDOM OF IRELAND.

CHARLES R.

Sections 1, 2, 3, 4, 5. *Upon these reasons alledged by you, and the confidence which we have that you have well weighed all the circumstances mentioned by you, or otherwise necessary to the calling of a parliament; and especially relying upon your faith and dexterity in managing so great a work for the good of our service; we are fully persuaded to condescend to the present calling of a parliament; which accordingly we authorise and require you to do, and therein to make use of all the motives you here propound.*

1. Albeit the calling of a parliament in this kingdom is at no time of so much hazard, where nothing is propounded as a law before it first borrow motion from your majesty's immediate allowance under your great seal, as it is in England, where there is a liberty assumed to offer every thing in their own time and order; and this subordination, whereunto they have been led by the wisdom of former times, is ever to be held as a sacred prerogative, not to be departed from, in no piece to be broken or infringed. Yet is the proposition always weighty—very necessary to be considered with great deliberation—whether the present conjuncture of affairs doth now advise a parliament or no? And, after a serious discourse with myself, my reason persuades me for the assembling thereof.

2. For, the contribution from the country towards the army ending in December next, your majesty's revenue falls short twenty thousand pounds sterling by the year of the present charge it is burthened withal, besides the vast debt of fourscore thousand pounds, Irish, upon the crown; which yearly payments, alone, are impossible by any other ordinary way to be in time supplied, but by the subject in parliament; and to pass to the extraordinary, before there be at least an attempt first to effect it with ease, were to love

difficulties too well, rather voluntarily to seek them, than unwillingly to meet them, and might seem as well vanity in the first respect so to affect them, as faintness to bow under them, when they are not to be avoided.

3. The next inclination thereunto ariseth in me, from the condition of this country, grown very much more civil and rich since the access of your royal father of blessed memory, and your majesty to the crown ; that all you have here is issued out again amongst them for their protection and safety, without any considerable reservation, for other the great affairs and expences abroad ; that this great charge is sustained, and this great debt contracted through imployments for a publick good, whereof the benefit hitherto hath been intirely theirs ; that there hath been but one subsidy granted in all this time, nor any other supply but this contribution ; in exchange whereof, your princely bounty returned them graces as beneficial to this subject as their money was to your majesty ; so as their substance having been so increased under the guard of your wisdom and justice, so little issued hence from them, the crown so pressed, only for their good, and so modest a calling upon them now for a supply, which in all wisdom, good nature, and conscience, they are not to deny ; should they not conform themselves to your gracious will, their unthankfulness to God, and the best of kings, becomes inexcusable before all the world, and the regal power more warrantably to be at after extended for redeeming and recovering your majesty's revenues thus lost, and justly to punish so great a forfeit as this must needs be judged to be in them.

4. Next, the frightful apprehension, which at this time makes their hearts beat, lest the quarterly payments towards the army, continued now almost ten years, might in fine turn to an hereditary charge upon their lands, inclines them to give any reasonable thing in present, to secure themselves of that fear for the future ; and therefore, according to the wholesome counsel of the physician,— *Dum dolet accipe.*

5. And lastly, If they should meanly cast from them these mighty obligations, which indeed I cannot fear, your majesty's affairs can never suffer less by their starting aside, when the general peace abroad admits a more united power in your majesty, and less distracted thoughts in your ministers, to chastise such a forgetfulness, to call to their remembrance, and to inforce from them other and better duties than these.

Sect. 6, 7, 8, 9. *We appoint the time of the meeting to be in Trinity term next, for the reasons you here alledge.*

6. In the second place, the time your majesty shall in your wisdom appoint for this meeting imports very much ; which with all submission I should advise, might not be longer put off than Easter or Trinity term at farthest ; and I shall crave leave to offer my reasons.

7. The improvements mentioned in my dispatch to the lord treasurer, from which I no ways recede, would not be foreslowed ; wherein we lose much by deferring this meeting ; a circumstance

very considerable in these streights, wherein, if surprised, might be of much disadvantage, in case the parliament answer not expectation; and to enter upon that work before, would be an argument for them to scant their supply to your majesty.

8. Again, a breach of parliament would prejudice less thus than in winter, having at the worst six months to turn our eyes about, and many helps to be gained in that space; where, in the other case, the contribution ending in December next, we should be put upon an instant of time, to read over our lesson at first sight.

9. Then the calling of a parliament, and determining of the quarterly payments, falling out much upon one, might make them apprehend there was a necessity enforcing a present agreement, if not the good one we would, yet the best we could get, and so embolden them to make and flatter themselves to gain their own conditions, and conditions are not to be admitted with any subjects, less with this people, where your majesty's absolute sovereignty goes much higher than it is taken, perhaps, to do in England.

Sect. 10. *We well approve and require the making of two sessions, as you propose. The first to be held in summer for our own supplies; and the second in winter, for passing such laws and graces only, as shall be allowed by us. But this intimation of two sessions, we think not fit to be imparted to any, till the parliament be set. And further, we will admit no capitulations nor demands of any assurance under our broad seal, nor of sending over deputies or committees to treat here with us, nor of any restraint in our b.ll of subsidies, nor of any condition of not maintaining the army; but in case any of these be insisted upon, and that they will not otherwise proceed or be satisfied*

10. And lastly, There being some of your majesty's graces, which being passed into laws, might be of great prejudice to the crown; and yet it being to be feared they will press for them all, and uncertain what humour the denying any of them might move in their minds, I conceive, under favour, it would be much better to make two sessions of it, one in summer, the other in winter; in the former, to settle your majesty's supply, and in the latter, to enact so many of those graces as in honour and wisdom should be judged equal, when the putting aside of the rest might be of no ill consequence to other your royal purposes.

with our royal promise for the second session, or shall deny or delay the passing of our bills, we require you thereupon to dissolve the parliament; and forthwith to take order to continue the contributions for our army, and withal to proceed to such improvements of our revenue as are already in proposition, or may hereafter be thought upon for the advantage of our crown.

Sect. 11. *Concerning the short law to preserve the uttermost benefit of the compositions upon concealments, and the plantations of Connaght and Ormond, we like it well, if you can obtain it, for*

11. All the objections I am able to suggest unto myself, are two: That it might render fruitless the intended improvement upon the concealments, and prejudice the plantations of Con-

confirmation of what you have done, or shall hereafter do about those businesses. But your promising of such a law, we doubt, may hinder the service, and cause them to be satisfy'd with nothing but a special statute.

Sect. 12, 13, 14, 15. For demands to be made for us, we allow your propositions in these sections, both in the matter and in the form; only the last clause, which giveth hope to maintain the army afterwards without further charge to them at all, we conceive may be drawn to a binding assumption; and besides, it is not necessary; the very proposition being sufficient to that effect.

naght and Ormond. The former may easily be helped by a short law, propounded in my dispatch to my lord treasurer; and *posito*, that there no other law pass the first session; the second is likewise sufficiently secured.

12. Then it is to be foreseen, what your majesty will demand, how induce and pursue the same, for the happy settlement of the regal rights and powers in this more subordinate kingdom.

13. My humble advice is, to declare, at the first opening of the meeting, that your majesty intends and promises two sessions; this former for yourself, that latter, in Michaelmas term next, for them; this to ascertain the payments of your army, and to strike off the debts of your crown; that, for the enacting of all such profitable and wholsome laws, as a moderate and good people may expect from a wise and gracious king.

14. That, this being the order of nature, reason, and civility, your majesty expects it should be entirely observed, and yourself wholly intrusted by them; which they are not only to grant to be fit in the general case of king and subjects, but ought indeed to acknowledge it with thankfulness due to your majesty in particular, when they look back, and call to mind, how for their ease you were content to take the sixscore thousand pounds (which their agents gave to be paid in three) in six years; and not barely so neither, but to double your graces towards them the whilst, which they have enjoyed accordingly, much to their advantage and greatly to the loss of the crown.

15. And that considering the army hath been represented over to your majesty from this council, and in a manner from the body of this whole kingdom, to be of absolute necessity, to give comfort to the quiet minds in their honest labours, to contain the licentious spirits within the modest bounds of sobriety, it consists not with your majesty's wisdom to give unto the world, no, not the appearance of so much improvidence in your own counsels, of so much forgetfulness in a case of their safety, as to leave that pillar of your authority, and their peace, unset for continuance, at least one six months before the wearing forth of their contribution.

Sect. 16, 17, 18. We do not conceive that hereby you purpose easily to relinquish any of our demands, for all which

16. Therefore your majesty was well assured in conformity to the rules of reason and judgment, they would presently

you have laid so fair and solid grounds. And considering the payment of the army is absolutely necessary to be born by the country, they cannot pretend by their three subsidies to make a fitting recognition of respect for our coming to the crown, without that last addition to buy in rents and pensions.

grant three subsidies to be paid in three years, to disengage the crown of fourscore thousand pound debt; and continue their quarterly payments towards the army four years longer; in which time it was hopeful (suitable to your gracious intentions) some other expedient might be found out, to maintain the army without further charge to them

at all; which law past, they shou'd have as much leisure to enact for themselves at after, as they could desire, either now, or in winter. Nay your majesty wou'd be graciously pleased, with the assistance of your council, to advise seriously with them, that nothing might remain, either unthought of, or deny'd, conducing to the publick good of this kingdom: but if they made difficulty to proceed with your majesty in this manner, other counsels must be thought of, and little to be rely'd, or expected for from them.

17. I am not to flatter your majesty so far, as to raise any hope, on that side, that all this shou'd be granted, but by pressing both; and especially the continuance of the quarterly payments to the army, which they dread above any earthly thing. I conceive it probable, that to determine and lay asleep (as they think) the contribution, and in acknowledgment of your majesty's happy access to the crown, they may be drawn to a present gift of three subsidies, payable in three years, which alone wou'd keep the army on foot during that time; and if my calculation hold, almost discharge the debt of the crown besides.

18. For thus I make my estimate: the contribution from the country, is now but twenty thousand pounds sterling by the year; whereas I have good reason to trust, each subsidy will raise thirty thousand pounds sterling; and so there will be ten thousand pounds for three years, over and above the establishment: which thirty thousand pounds sterling, well and profitably issued, will, I trust, with honour to your majesty, and moderate satisfaction of the parties, strike off the whole fourscore thousand pounds Irish, which in present presseth so sore upon this crown.

Sect. 19, 20, 21, 22. *We like well the appointing of such a committee, and we refer the nomination to yourself. We have also given order to some of our council here, with the assistance of our attorney general, to consider of the graces, that nothing pass by law which may prejudice our crown.*

19. And then, sir, after that in Michaelmas term, all beneficial acts for the subject be thought of, as many, no fewer nor no more, enacted, than were fit in honour and wisdom to be granted; if for a conclusion to this parliament, we could gain from them other two subsidies, to buy in rents and pensions, to ten thousand pounds yearly

value; (a thing they are inclinable unto, as is mention'd in my dispatch to the lord treasurer) I judge, there were an happy issue of this meeting; and that it shou'd, through God's blessing, appear to the world in a few years, you had without charge made a more absolute conquest of this nation by your wisdom, than all your royal progenitors have been able to accomplish by their armies, and vast expense of treasure and blood.

20. These being the ends, in my poor opinion, which are to be desired and attained, the best means to dispose and fit all concurring causes thereunto, are not to be forgotten; and therefore as preparatives, I make bold to offer these ensuing particulars:—

21. It seems to be very convenient, a committee be forthwith appointed of some few of us here, to take into consideration all the bills intended when there was a parliament to have been called in the time of my lord Falkland; such as shall be judged beneficial, to make them ready; such as may be of too much prejudice to the crown, to lay them aside; and to draw up others, which may chance to have been then omitted. This work may be by the committees either quickened or foreslowen as the parliament proceeds, either warmer or cooler in your majesty's supplies.

22. Next, that your majesty's acts of grace directed to my lord Falkland the 24th of May, 1628, may be considered by such of your council in England as shall please your majesty to appoint; there being many matters therein contained, which in a law, wou'd not futurely so well sort with the power requisite to be upheld in this kingdom, nor yet with your majesty's present profit; which hath persuaded me to except against such as I hold best to be silently passed over, and to transmit a paper thereof to my lord treasurer.

Sect. 23. *We approve the reformation of these pressures and extortions by examples, and by commissions, by our own authority; but by no means to be done by parliament.*

12. It is to be feared, the meaner sort of subjects here, live under the pressures of the great men; and there is a general complaint, that officers exact much larger fees, than of right they ought to do. To help the former, if it be possible, I will find out two or three to make examples of; and to remedy the latter, grant out a commission for examining, regulating, and setting down tables of fees in all your courts: so as they shall find your majesty's goodness and justice, watching and caring for their protection and ease, both in private and publick respects.

Sect. 24. *We allow of this course.*

24. I shall endeavour, the lower house may be so composed, as that neither the recusants, nor yet the protestants, shall appear considerably more one than the other; holding them as much as may be upon an equal ballance; for they will prove thus easier to govern, than if either party were absolute. Then wou'd I, in private discourse, shew the recusant, that the contribution ending in December next, if your majesty's army were not supply'd some other way before, the twelve

pence a Sunday must of necessity be exacted upon them ; and shew the protestant, that your majesty must not let go the twenty thousand pounds contribution, nor yet discontent the other in matters of religion, till the army were some way else certainly provided for ; and convince them both, that the present quarterly payments are not so burdensome as they pretend them to be ; and that by the graces they have had already more benefit, than their money came to. Thus poising one by the other, which single might perchance prove more unhappy to deal with.

Sect. 25. To make captains and officers burgesses we altogether dislike ; because it is fitter they attend their charges at that time. Make your choice rather by particular knowledge of men's interests, and good affections to our service.

25. I will labour to make as many captains and officers, burgesses, as possibly I can, who, having immediate dependance upon the crown, may almost sway the business betwixt the two parties, which way they please.

Sect. 26. In the higher house, for the prelates we have written our special letter to the primate of Armagh, addressing him therein to be directed by yourself.

26. In the higher house, your majesty will have, I trust, the bishops wholly for you. The titular lords, rather than come over themselves, will put their proxies into such safe hands, as

may be thought of on this side. And in the rest, your majesty hath such interest, what out of duty to the crown, and obnoxiousness in themselves, as I do not apprehend much, any difficulty amongst them.

Sect. 27. For the peers, that their proxies may be well disposed, we wou'd have you send with speed the names of those there, in whom you repose special trust. And in case your list cannot be here in time, we will give order that all the proxies be sent to you with blanks to be assigned there. In general for the better preventing of practices and disorders, you shall suffer no meetings during the setting of the houses, save only in publick, and for the service of the houses by appointment, and for no other ends.

27. To these, or to any thing else directed by your majesty, I will with all possible diligence apply myself so soon as I shall understand your pleasure therein ; most humbly beseeching, you will take it into your gracious memory, how much your majesty's speedy resolution in this great business imports the prosperity of your affairs in this place ; and in that respect, vouchsafe to hasten it as much as conveniently may be.

WENTWORTH.

1634, April 12.

The answers contained in the apostiles are made by his majesty, and by his commandment set down in this manner.

JOHN COKE.

———

A Copy of the Paper containing the Heads of the Lord Strafford's last Speech, written by his own Hand, as it was left upon the Scaffold.

1. I come to pay the last debt we owe to sin.
2. Rise to righteousness.
3. Die willingly.
4. Forgive all.
5. Submit to what is voted justice but my intentions innocent from subverting, &c.
6. Wishing nothing more than great prosperity to king and people.
7. Acquit the king constrained.
8. Beseech to repent.
9. Strange way to write the beginning of reformation, and settlement of a kingdom in blood on themselves.
10. Beseech that demand may rest there.
11. Call not blood on themselves.
12. Die in the faith of the church.
13. Pray for it, and desire their prayers with me.

APPENDIX II.

SELECTED PAPERS AND LETTERS PRINTED SINCE THE PUBLICATION OF BROWNING'S *LIFE OF STRAFFORD*.

I.

15 Sept. 1617.   SIR THOS. WENTWORTH TO THE EARL OF BUCKINGHAM.

(*Fortescue Papers* (p. 23).   Camden Society, 1871, 4º.)

Right Honorable and my very good Lord.   Thes are to give your Lordship humble thankes for your respective letters dated from Warwicke the 5 of this instant September, which I receaved the 13 of the same ; the messinger told me your Lordship expected a speedy answear, in observance whearof I must crave your patience in reading a long letter.

Your Lordship was pleased therin to lett me understande, that wheras his Majestie is informed that Sir John Savill yealded up his place of *Custos Rotulorum* voluntarily unto me, his Majestie will take it well att my hands that I resigne itt up to him againe, with the same willingnes, and will be mindfull of me to give me as good prefermentt upon any other occasion.

My Lord : I am with all duty to receave and with all humble thankfullnes to acknowledge his Majesties great favours hearin : both of his espetiall grace to take the consentt of his humblest subject, wher it might have pleased his Majestie absolutely to commaund, as alsoe for soe princely a promise of other prefermentt : and itt wear indeed the greatest good happ unto me, if I had the means wherby his Majestie would be pleased to take notice how much I esteem myself bownd to his princely goodnes for the same.

When your Lordship is informed that Sir Jhon yealded up his place of *Custos Rotulorum* willingly unto me ; under favour, I haue noe reason so to conceave ; for, first, he had noe interest to yeald, and, further, I imagin he would not haue done the same willingly att all, wherof this his desiring itt againe is a sufficientt argumentt. Butt, howsoever, voluntarily unto me I cannot be perswaded, both in respect he neuer acquainted me with this motion, which would haue been done, had I been soe much behoulden unto him as is pretended, and in regard I had then some reason to misdoubt (which I have since found) he was not soe well affected towards me.

Butt if itt please your Lordship to be satisfied of the truth, you shall find Sir Jhon brought into the Staire-chamber for his passionate cariage upon the benche towards one of his fellow commissioners ; upon a motion in that Court for his contempts committed to the Fleet, and, upon reading of an affidavit, thought unfitt to be continued in the Commission of Peace, to which purpose my late Lord Chancelour gave his direction about the 3. of December shallbe tow years ; which Sir Jhon getting notice of, to give the better coullor to his displacing, writt some 3 dayes after to my Lord desiring his Lordship would be pleased to spaire his service in respect of his years ; wher indeed he was in effect out of the Commission before, by vertu of that direction : and so consequently ther was nothing in him to resigne, aither voluntarily or other wayes. This will partly appear by a coppy of Sir Jhon's letter, and my Lord's answear under the same, which this bearer hath to shew your Lordship.

Presently hearupon itt pleased my Lord Chancelour, I being att that time in the cuntry, freely of himself to conferre that place upon me, and, as his Lordship did fully assure me, without any motion made unto him, directly or indirectly, by any frend of mine whoesoever.

Being thus placed I have ever since, according to that poore talent God hath lentt me, applied myself, with all paines, dilligence, care, and sincerity to his Majesties service, bothe according to the common duty of a subject and the particuler duty of my place, wherin if any man can charge me to the contrary, I wilbe ready to justifie my self.

Allbeitt I doe infinittly desire to doe his Majestie service, I may truly say that I am free from ambition to desire places of imployment wherby ether his Majesties service might not be soe well performed, or my owne ends better effected; yett, my Lord, to be removed without any misdeamenour, I trust, that can be alledged against me, the like I thinke hath not been heard of; but thatt Sir Jhon should supply the roome in my place, the world conceaving generally, and I having felt experiencedly, to be very little frendly towards me, itt might justly be taken as the greatest disgrace that could be done unto me, and being that which his Majestie never offered to Sir Jhon during all the time of his displeasure against him, I might well conceave his Majestie to be (to my greatest greef) highly offended with me, by some indirect means of my adversaries.

Thes reasons give me assurance in my hope that his Majestie out of his accustomed goodnes to all sort of persons willbe pleased to deale graciousely with me, espetially when his Majestie shallbe informed of these reasons, which I humbly desire he may by your Lordship's good means, as alsoe if Sir Jhon be soe desirouse to doe his Majestie service (which is all our duties) he may doe itt as effectually, being Justice of peace, as if he wear the *Custos Rotulorum.*

Howsoever, with all due reverence and observance shall I waite his Majesties best pleasure, and willingly and dutifully submitt myself to the same, yett humbly crave to be excused, if, out of thes reasons, I say plainly as yett I finde no willingnesse in myself to yeald up my place to Sir Jhon Savill.

Thus much am I hold to signifie to your Lordship to give you satisfaction, which I doe very much desire, and withall to move your Lordship very humbly that ther may be noe further proceedings hearin, till I attend your Lordship, which shalbe, God willing, with all convenient speed.

Lastly, my Lord, myself never having nourished a thought that might in any sortt draw your Lordship's hard conceitt towards me, I fully rely upon your Lordship's favour, in a matter of this nature, that soe deeply concerns my creditt in the cuntry whear I live, which makes me now therof the more sensible; and shall give me just occasion still to indevour myself to doe you service, and beseeche God to blesse your Lordship with longe life and all happines.

Your Lordship's humbly to be commaunded,
TH. WENTWORTH.

GAWTHORP,
this 15th of September, 1617.

II.

20 Jan. 1625-6. Wentworth to Lord Conway, asking for the place of Lord President of the North. (State Papers, Domestic, Charles I. xviij, 110.)

My much Honored Lorde.

The duties of the Place I now hold, not admitting my absence out of thes parttes, I shallbe bold to trouble *your* lord*ship* with a few lines, wheras otherwayes I would haue attended you in person. Ther is a stronge and generall beleefe wi*th* vs hear, that my Lord Scroope, purposeth to leaue the Presidentshippe of Yorke ; whearvpon many of my frendes, haue earnestly moued me to vse sum meanes to procure itt, and I haue att Last yealded to take itt a little into consideration, more to complye wi*th* them, then out of any violentt, or inordinate desire thervnto in my self : yet as on the one side, I haue neuer thought of itt, vnlesse itt might be effected, wi*th* the good liking of my Lord Scroope ; soe will I neuer moue further in itt, till I knowe allsoe, how this sute may please, my Lord of Buckingham, seeing indeed such a seale of his graciouse good opinion would comfortt me much, make the place more acceptable ; and that I am fully resolued nott to ascende one steppe in this kinde, excepte I may take alonge wi*th* me by the way a spetiall obligation to my Lord Duke, from whose bowntye and goodnesse I doe nott only acknowledge much allready ; but iustified in the truthe of my owne hartte, doe still repose and rest vnder the shadow and protection of his fauoure. I beseeche *your* Lo*rdshi*p therfore be pleased to take sum good oportunity fully to acquainte his Grace hearwi*th*, and then to voutchsafe (wi*th* your accustomed freedum and noblenesse) to giue me your Counsell and direction, w*hi*ch I am prepaired strictly to obserue, as one allbeitt chearfully imbracing better meanes to doe his Ma*ies*tie humble and faithfull seruice in thes parttes whear I liue ; yet can wi*th* as well a contented minde rest wher I am, if by reason of my many imperfections I shall not be iudged capable of nearer imploymentt and trust. Ther is nothing more to adde for the presentt, saue that I must rest much bounden vnto your Lo*rdshi*p, for the light I shall borrow from your iudgmentt, and affection hearin, and soe borrowe itt too, as may better inable me more effectnally to exspresse my self hearafter.

Your lo*rdshi*ps most humble and affectionate
kinsman to be commaunded,
TH. WENTWORTH.

Wentworth this 20th of January, 1625.

(Addressed) To the Right Hono*r*able my much honored Lorde the Lorde Conway Principall Secreta*r*ye to his Ma*ies*tie.

(Endorsed) 20 January 1625 Si*r* Thomas Wentworth to the Lo*rd* Conway, ffor the place of Lo*rd* President of the North.

(Well preserved seal.)

III.

27 May 1627. Sir Thos. Wentworth to the Commissioners for the forced loan. (State Papers, Domestic, Charles I, lxv, 12, ii.)

May itt please you. I haue to day receaued your letter, dated the tenthe of this instant : whearin I am required to be with you att Yorke, on tuesday next ; the occasion is as I perceave concerning the late loan to his Ma*ies*tie by me as yet vnpaid. I should precisely have obserued your time, if infirme bodyes weare as readye ministers of the minde, as pens, out of which reason I trust, my absence willbe rightly interpreted, and held excused by you. This gentle proceeding of the Lordes of the Counsell (whear they might haue sent for me vp by Pursevant) I humbly acknowledge ; and therfore to apply myself vnto ther commaunds in the dutifullest manner, I shall desire, that, with your good leaues, I may present my own answeare att the borde, which I will hearby by God's helpe vndertake to performe, in as short a space as the moderate care of my healthe will well admitt, and ease you therby of any further trouble or burthen. But if itt soe fall forth, as you shall not thinke good to grant me this request, I will then waite upon you before the end of the weeke, albeitt I be carried in a litter. Thus desiring to vnderstande by the bearer your good pleasure hearin I rest.

Your very affectionate freinde,
T. WENTWORTH.

Thornhill, this 27th of May, 1627.

To my Honorable good and much respected freindes, Sir Henry Savile, Barronet, Sir Tho. Fairfaxe, Sir Wm. Ellis, Knights, and Wm. Mallorye, Esquier, att Yorke.

IV.

Dec. 1628. Thomas Lord Viscount Wentworth's speech when he first sate Lord President of the North. (From the Tanner MSS. in the Bodleian Library ; printed by Professor S. R. Gardiner in *The Academy*, June 5, 1875.)

My Lords and Gentlemen,—Much reading or affected elegance in speech are seldom heard without some mixture of ostentacion or levity ; the modest sense, therefore, of my own weakness, the gravity of the persons, the dignity of the place, move us to become comformable to the rule of the architect, *Minervae propter virtutem sine deliciis aedeficia constitui decet.* Indeed, natural, substantial plainness many times persuades, prevails most with sad judgements ; nay, it seems, at least in the opinion of these times, even best becoming the Goddess of wisdom and eloquence herself. Without any shadow or light of art then, I must sett forth myself before you this day for the most obliged man in the world ; an evident, a manifest truth ; my testimonies are your own great trusts. We frequently communicated in diverse Parliaments ; your chearful affections enlarged not present alone, but in my confinement—in a degree exile—when I was as infeccion to others, you vouchsafed then again to take me into your bosoms. What confidence greater ? Or what affection warmer ? But cast the free bounties of my gracious master into the other scale ? there weigh me, within the space of one year a bird, a wandring bird cast out of the nest, a prisoner, planted here again in my own soil amongst the companions of my youth ; my house honoured, myself entrusted with the rich dispensacion of a soveran goodness, nay, assured of all these before I ask'd, before I thought of any. Can you show me so sudden, so strange variety in a private fortune? Tell me, was there ever such over-measure ? The like credit given to so weak a debtor ? Baulked indeed before I begin, owing more both to king and people than I shall ever be able to repay to either. Yet to the joint individual well being of Soverainty and of subjeccion do I here vow all my cares and diligences through the whole course of this my ministry. I confess I am not ignorant how some distemperd minds have of late very farr endeavoured to divide the consideracions of the two ; as if their ends were distinct, not the same, nay in opposition ; a monstrous, a prodigious birth of a licentious conception ; for so we should become all head or all members. But, God be praised, human wisdom, common experience, Christian religion teach us farr otherwise.

Princes are to be indulgent, nursing fathers to their people ; their modest liberties, their sober rights ought to be precious in their eies, the branches of their government be for shadow for habitacion, the comfort of life, repose, safe and still under the proteccion of their scepters. Subjects, on the other side, ought with solicitous eyes of jealousy to watch over the prerogatives of a Crown ; the authority of a King is the key-stone which closeth up the arch of order and government, which contains each part in due relation to the whole, and which once shaken, infirm'd all the frame falls together into a confused heap of foundation and battlement, of strength and beauty. Furthermore subjects must lay down their lives for the defence of Kings freely, till those offer out of their store freely like our best grounds, *Qui majore ubertate gratiam quietis referre solent.*

Verily, these are those mutual intelligences of love and proteccion descending, and loyalty ascending, which should pass, be the entertainments between a king and his people. Their faithfull servants must look equally on both, weave, twist these two together in all their counsells, study, labour to preserve each without diminishing or enlarging either, and by running in the worn, wonted channells, treading the ancient bounds, cutt off early all disputes from betwixt them. For whatever he be which ravells forth into questions the right of a King and of a people, shall never be able to wrap them up again into the comeliness and order he found them.

So I trust you see that by this great access of honour and place, I am not only a stone—so to use a word of art—set upon my own bed for continuance, for lasting, but *acquisitivè positus* too, gainfully, commodiously seated for the service both of king and people. And I take God to witness my chiefest comfort herein is to consider that the occasions whereby to express my duties to God, my faith to my master, my love to you, will be more frequently put into my hands in this than in a privater condicion, which I beseech God I may do as I ought, as I infinitely desire to travail under and out of these great obligacions with vertue, truth, and thankfullness.

Give me leave, therefore, as one who comming forth of the sweets, the ease of a private life, already feel the weight that presseth upon me, to charge, to adjure you each one, by those tender respects which have hitherto, and shall still move me rather to serve you uprightly than myself profitably, by those dear affeccions which you have ever born me, by the care you ought to have of him that will very gladly spend and be spent for you ; by the private interest of your selves and posterity, not to leave me, shrink from me now when I have most need of you ; but by your counsell, by your paines, to be still assisting, aiding towards the performance of this so excellent, so necessary a duty ; surely it is the strongest engagement any mortal man can put upon me ; this is my greatest ambition, above any earthly thing to serve his Ma*i*estie, and you acceptably and fruitfully. I challenge your best help then, I require it of you ; you will not as friends, you may not as Christians, you cannot as lovers of your countrie deny it me.

So as in full affiance thereof, I will leave my self, and observe some rules which concerne the place ; a distinction by which I shall futurely govern my self ; for in relation to my own person, never President expected so little ; in relation to this place, never any more jealous of the honour of his master, never any that lookd for more.

Unity inwards amongst ourselves ; uniform justice outwards to such as come before us, are I trust the *Boni Genii*, the acquir'd habits of this Council. I shall by the way then only do them reverence, entirely submitt myself to their skill, their equal regiment, and so to pass on to the bleeding evill, which unless it be stanched, closed by a ready, a skilfull hand, will quickly let out the very vitals of this Court, I mean prohibitions ; the necessity whereof cries not alone to us that are judges to attend the cure, but as you have heard, his Ma*i*estie himself requires it of us.

Well, the disease is recoverable ; the remedies I propound are two ; the first to assume nothing to ourselves but what is our own, being ever mindfull that the voice which speaks here is *vox ad licitum ;* we can go no farther than our instruccions lead us, move only within their circle ; once take wandring planets out of that sphere, presently the interposicion of other courts shadow, eclipse the influence, the beams of this. Assure yourselves, the way to loose what we have is to embrace more than belongs to us. You that are of the fee must guide us herein, you are answerable for it, it is expected from your learning and experience, and therefore I am confident you will carefully intend it.

Secondly, we must apply a square courage to our proceedings, not fall away as water spilt upon the ground, from that which is once justly, warrantably done ; nor yet give off upon prohibicions till the suitor hath the fruit of his plaint, for the Commonwealth hath no more interest herein than that justice be done, whether with us or elsewhere it skills not ; the inherent rights of a subject are no waies touched upon here ; these are only disputes betwixt courts, actuated many times out of heat, nay out of wantoness. And thus the seats of justice, which should nourish, establish a perfect harmony betwixt the head, the members, and amongst themselves, degenerate, become instruments of strife, of separacion, whiles these furies, like that enraged Turnus in the Poet, catch what comes first to hand, tear up the very bounderstones set by the sobriety of former times, and hurl them at their fellows in government : and therefore I will declare this point clearly, that albeit none before me reverenced the law and the Professors of it more, having the honour to be descended from a Chief Justice myself, yet if we here take ourselves to be within, they there conceive us to be out of our instruccions, I shall no more acknowledge them to be our judges, than they us to be theirs, but with all due respect to their persons, must in these questions of jurisdiction appeal to his Ma*ies*tie, the soverain judge of us all. Neither do I this barely in relation to my master's command, but to retain in ourselves a capacity, 1st, to serve you, for if we yield up our arms, how shall we exercise our vertue amongst you ? 2ly, in consideration of the good and benefit of these parts, for surely however some may desire a dissolucion of this court, yet I persuade myself so soon as the number, the heat of small suites carried farr remote at great charges were multiplied amongst them, they would confess their ancestours to have been much wiser who peticioned, gave a subsidy for erecting the Provinciall Court, than themselves who are now so much for the taking them away. May the tent of this court then be enlarged, the curtains drawn out, the stakes strengthned, yet no farther than shall be for a covering to the common tranquillity, a shelter to the poor and innocent from the proud and insolent.

To this end must I not only profess my entire filial obedience to the Church, but also covet a sound, a close conjunction with the grave, the Reverend clergy that they to us, we to them, may as twins administer help to each other; that ecclesiastical and civil constitutions, the two sides of every state, may not stand alone by themselves upon their own single walls, subject to cleave, fall in sunder, but joind strongly bound together in the angle—where his Ma*ies*tie under God is the Mistress of the Corner—the whole frame may rise up *unitate ordinata*, both in the spirituals and in the temporals.

To this end and no other must I encourage you, the Deputy Lieftenants, to proceed roundly to see the arms of the County fully furnishd, I say encourage, in regard some quicker sighted than those that liv'd before them conceive the law to be scant in that point ; *Reverentius est credere quam scire* is an old rule I could wish were more practis'd nowadaies as well in matters of State as Religion ; for admitt the law were defective, yet then it will be confessed a necessary service for the State, for the defence of ourselves, wives, and children so as we might manifest more discretion to wink at it than thus narrowly to pry into it. But the truth of the case is farr otherwise, his Maiestie hath power coercive.   Let no prevaricating spirit flatter itself, it must be obedient ; for after I saw the statute of 5 II. 4—not printed, I confess—therein, even upon the Peticion of the Commons themselves in Parlament, authority given the King to appoint Commissioners of array for taking view of arms, charging all degrees of men, raising moneys for maintaining them at their discretions ; nay, yet more to imprison the refusers, to destrain upon their lands for the summs so imposed upon them ; I had not then onely the moderacion of our ancestours in singular recommendacions, who never question'd, repin'd at these necessary provisions for the honour the safety of the kingdom ; but plainly said they were the wise intelligent men, and we of these later times the ignorant, the misconceiving.

Again to the same, and no other end must I awaken you that be Justices of the Peace to become vigilant in the execucion of your charges, who—being still upon the place—should seasonably wipe from the face of this government the very complexions towards disorder and idleness ; I say awaken you, in regard you have alwaies ow'd an account unto this Council of your proceedings, we must call upon you for it, we shall strictly require it at your hands, albeit I am well assured the sense of your own honours and conscience will be quicker persuaders to you herein than any thing that can move from hence.

Next must I come to the practisers before us ; amongst them, Mr. Attorney, you are the eye of the Court, to look abrode upon the pressure of the grievances of the subject, to bring delinquents to justice, that so the oppressed may go free.   There is a band of Escheators, Feodaries, Undersheriffs, Clerks of the Market, Attornies, Registers, Bailiffs, and suchlike, which snatch on the right hand and are hungry, eat on the left and are not satisfied.   It is befitting the integrity, the watches expected from you to be a means their fees be reduced to moderacion and certainty ; severity must effect it ; these nettles gently touch'd, sting, bite ; taken up with a closer hand loose their heat, their venom ; this fartherance you have towards the work that we will thoroughly join with you in the undoing this heavy burthen ; therefore if you slip, grow remiss in your duty you are the more to be blamed. So much to you alone.

In the second place, I must admonish you with the rest, that your pleeding be here heard with just regard to the dignity of this Court. The rules I will give you for the present are not many ; they are these.   First, that you do that for one another which we will do for you all, hear out patiently one side without interupcion, so may you with better order, more advantage, defend your client's cause ; secondly, touch not upon the by, the person, the adverse party, but keep close to the matter ; else you will appear more to study the passion of your client, than the respect you owe us, the civility you owe to yourselves. He that pleads more with foul language than reason *imminucionem patitur* saith the Law. So say I too.

Thirdly, in the progress of suits to a hearing, move nothing against the constant, ordinary rules of the Court ; I shall take it for a great presumpcion in any man that offers it.   4ly. After publicacion, the proof before your eyes, inform truth, else your reward must be such as will little please you ; neither shall it serve for a cloak either of your malice, or negligence to say, "it is in my brief ; " where it is your part in this case to take informacion forth of the books themselves.   Look to it then, I say, and remember what Papinian recites : *Advocatum ordine motum ex falsâ recitacione.*   These rules observ'd you will become worthy of your calling indeed, which certainly is one of the noblest ; for what greater comfort, greater honour, than for a man by those abilities God hath lent him above others to vindicate silly naked truth from the vizard, the blemish, craft and power might put upon her.

Finally, I do here offer myself, an instrument for good in every man's hand, he that thus useth me most hath the most of my heart, even to the meanest man within the whole jurisdiccion ; and then excite all to lay aside to forget private respects, to join hands and hearts, that we may go on chearfully as one man in the service of the publick, for where the thoughts of particulars are sever'd then the common business is in danger to be jointly lost.   These are those waies which travail'd with integrity diligence and perseverance shall undoubtedly lead in a direct line to the honour of his Maiestie, bring wealth and peace to his people ; put upon this Court the garment of praise for the spirit of heaviness ; and shew those wanton gallants that alwaies fly upon the superior powers that are next them, the necessity, the comfort of being govern'd by and under it. Thus may we walk and not fainte ; thus may we run and not be weary.

Methinks I hear now the envious viper *mordens in silentio* whisper there is a great space betwixt promise and performance ; it may be, I confess, the objeccion of wisedom too ; therefore I end all with a suit I have to make, which is that in my particular you will proceed prudently, severely, give no credit to your ears, farther than charity wills, which is to hope the best, but call to witnesse your eyes too ; for I had much rather you should take me from the original life of that faithfulnesse, that diligence, wherewith I shall express myself in your service, than from these weak draughts, these imperfect copies of my words.

V.

24 Sept. 1632.   Viscount Wentworth to the Earl of Carlisle (?) on the case of Sir Richard Foulis, the necessity of keeping up the King's power, and Wentworth's devotion to this. (From the Forster MSS. at South Kensington, printed by Prof. S. R. Gardiner in *The Academy*, June 2, 1877.)

My very good Lord

        As for many your other favours, soe am I infinitely much bownde unto you for the honoure of your lines, soe multiplied and with soe highe a hande as I have with one hold receaved three of them from you, thus distant, and thus little able to serve you, answearable to ther meritt.

I must ever acknowledge with all possible comfortt his Maiestyes goodnesse towardes me in this matter betwixt Sir David Fowlis and me, and humbly thanke your Lordship for the particular and authentike relation I have therof from you ; which well weighing with myself I have been bold to write the inclosed to his Maiestye which will be much graced, if you be pleased to present itt with my humble service to his Maiesty.

Nor should I have troubled your Lordship hearin, but that you are pleased to take sum small notice of the man ; therfore I beseech your Lordship lett me detaine you a while with a short accompte of this businesse, and espetially what hath paste heare sinc the gentlemans cumming from London.

Sir David Fowlis, a person raysed by the favoure and bownty of the Crowne to a faire and plentifull fortune, and one I had upon all occasions given the best respectt unto I could, as promising myself helpe and assistance from him, in his Maiesties service, it seemed to me marvelouse strange to heare how ill and mutinously affected he was to his Maiestyes rights and government, soe as takinge the reportte either to be mistaken, or to be grownded upon sum personall mallice I gave noe greate beleefe or regarde thereunto : untill this late rioute of his brake forth with such violence and virulence, as might not with my dutye be longer silenced. The particulares would growe tediouse, but in the word of truthe, I take them to be as highly criminall, being only civill, as maybe, nor shall I need to say more for the presentt, saving that he was as insolent after he understoode the whole matter was knowen unto me, as maliciouse and malevolent before ; albeit I confesse you have sent him me downe humbled with a witnesse, a thing ordinary indeed with thos meane natures to becum as low under the cudgill as penitentt[1] wheare they pride themselves upon the advantadge grownde.

The manner of his appearing and intertainment heare was this ; the Counsell and myself sett upon the Commission for Recusantts, my secretary cam to me and tells me Sir David Fowlis was without, desirouse to speake with me, which in good faithe at first I could not beleeve, but being confirmed it was soe, I sent to knowe wheather it was anything concerning his Maiestyes service, or only concerning myself ; if the former, I was ready to speake with him ; if the latter I desired to be excused. His answer was, it was both. Soe I caused him to be brought inn, and being called to the borde, wee saluted him, and desired him to sitt downe at the borde, as being one of the Kings Counsell ; he cam up to me wheare I satt and gave me a very low salute, I told him that the borde was the kings, that he was very wellcum and might sitt downe.

Sir William Ellis lettinge him knowe we understood he had sum-

---

[1] *sic. ; quære* impenitent ?

thing to acquaint us concerning the kings service, wished him to relate what he had to say.

Sir Davide then professed he had nothing of that nature to impart unto us, and that he only cam to speake to me in sum things touching our owne privats.

Then I told him I was gladde when I hearde he had any thing to offer for the service of our Maister, as that which he had never seemed to looke after, sinc I had the honoure to serve him in this place, allbeit I had exspected and promised myself as much from him in that nature as from any other : but seeing that it now all terminated in particulares of our owne, the kings bord was noe fitt place for thos discourses ; therfore I desired him to excuse me, the matters betwixt him and me being of such a condition as should not be heard betwixt us privately in a chamber, but must passe the file of his Maiesties Courtts of Justice, and soe risse,[1] went my way and left them.

This I haue been more induced to relate prescisly to your Lord-ship, in regarde the condition of the man is to mistake others as much as himself, and to speake with that confidence as if he himself believed he spake the truthe, and that whatever the report be he shall make, that this is squarly and really the truthe.

My Lord, you best knowe how much the regall power is be-cummed infirm, by the easye way such have founde, who with rough hands have laid hold upon the flowers of itt, and with unequall and swaggering paces have trampled upon the rights of the Crowne, and how necessary examples are, (as well for the subject as the Soveraigne) to retaine licentious spiritts within the sober boundes of humility and feare. And surely if in any other, then in the case of this man, who hath the most wantonly, the most disdainefully demeaned himself towards his Maiestye and his Ministers that is possible, so as if he doe not taste of the rodde, itt will be impossible to have his Maiesties Counsell heare to be obayed, and should I say lesse weare to bestray the trust my maister hath honoured me with. I heare he cries out of oppression ; soe did my Lord Fauconberge too, your Lordship hearde with what reason or truthe ; beleeve me, this man hath more witt, but his cause is soe much worse, as he hath notwithstanding lesse to say for himself ; in this, never the lesse, they are tied by the tales togeither that both of them dared to strike the crowne upon my shoulders without being at all concerned in my owne interest, or having any other partte to play then such as innocense and patience shall suggest unto me. And truly give me leave to asseure your Lordship I have much reason to carrye my eyes along with me whearever I goe, and to exspectt my actions from the highest to the lowest, shall all be cast into the ballance and tried wheather heavye or lighte. Content in the name of God ! Lett them take me up and cast me downe, if I doe not fall square, and (to use a word of artte) paragon, in every pointe of my duty to my maister : nay, if I doe not fully complie with that

---

[1]   *i.e.* rose.

publicke and common protection which good kings afforde their good people, let me perishe, and let no man pitty me. In the meane time none of thes clamours or other apprehensions shall shake me, or cause me to decline my maisters honour and service, therby to please or soothe thes populare frantike humoures, and if I miscarry this way, I shall not, even then, be founde either soe indulgent to myself, or soe narrowly harted towards my maister, as to thinke myself too good to die for him. *El deve bastar.*

I confesse indeed *Sir* Davide shewed himself a wise man in apply-ing to yo*u*r Lo*rdshi*p as a mediator for him with me, being a noble freinde who I am ambitiouse the world should see hath power as greate and absolute as with any other servantt you have ; and myself as little will to denie any thing you shall move me unto, as is possible ; and therefore am I much bownde to your tender respectt that are pleased only to mention a reconsiliation, rather as a relation of what he would have then as an injunction of your owne, for which I humbly thanke you, for in truthe you had then putt me too a greate straite betwixt my will to obay you, and my care of the kings service, and this government, w*hi*ch I exspectt to finde now in the time of my absence much shaken or much confermed, by the hande men shall observe to be held with this gentleman in the prosecution of this cause, w*hi*ch I propose to beginn w*i*th him in that Courtt, itt seames (and w*i*th good reason) he most feares, having three weekes since taken a subpena forth against him. Only this I will protest to yo*u*r Lo*rdshi*p in the werdes of truth, I have been hithertoo knowen to this gentleman only by curtesyes ; that I beare noe mallice to his person, or att all consider my owne interests in this proceeding (w*hi*ch in truth are none att all) but simply the honoure and service of his Ma*ie*sty, and the seasonable correcting an humoure and libertye I finde raigne in these partts, of observing a superiour commande noe farther than they like themselves, and of questioning any profitt of the Crowne, called upon by his Ma*ie*sties ministers, w*hi*ch might inable itt to subsiste of it selfe, without being necessitated to accepte of such conditions, as others might vainly thinke to impose upon itt. Tis true this way is displeasing for the presentt, layes me open to calumnye and hatred, causeth me by sum ill disposed people, to bee, it may be ill reported ; wheare as the contrary would make me passe smothe and still along with-out noyse ; but I have not soe learnt my maister, nor am I soe in-dulgent to my own ease, as to see his affaires suffer shipwracke whilste I myself rest secure in harboure. Noe, lett the tempest be never soe greate, I will much rather putt forth to sea, worke forth the storme, or at least be founde deade with the rudder in my handes. And all that I shall desire is that his Ma*ie*sty and my other freinds should narrowly observe me, and see if ever I question any man in my owne interests, but whear they are only interlaced as accessoryes, his Ma*ie*sties service, and the just aspectte towards the publicke and duty of my place sett before them as principalls.

But alas, my Lo*rd*, I weary you extreamly w*hi*ch you will please to pardon, being entered a discourse upon a subjectte w*hi*ch I attende next the saving of a soule, more than all the world besides, and should I lesse take it to hartte I weare of all others the most unthankfull wretche to soe gratiouse a maister. Craving then your pardon for detaining you thus long, I will redeeme my faulte with as much speed as I may, giving you this unfained testimony and assurance of my being

  Your Lordships most humble and most faithfull servantt,

          WENTWORTH.

Yorke, 24 September, 1632.

VI.

24 Oct. 1632. Lord Wentworth to the Earl of Carlisle. His devotion to the King's cause; his dislike and censure of Sir David Fowlis; his appeal for Payler's incest-fine for a Church's pair of Organs. State Papers, Domestic, Chas. I, ccxxiv, 45.

        Yorke, 24th of October 1632.

My very good Lorde.

  The excesse of your fauoure in sending your footman soe long and wearisum a jurney, I must acknowledge, and contemplate your lordships noblenesse to your absentt seruantts; soe truly and soe thankfully, as to keepe my self in an equall temper, (wheareuer god and his Maiesty shall bestowe me), to receaue your commaunds with all chearfullnesse, and to fullfill them, withall readinesse and care. That his Maiestie rests satesfied in the course I hold in this Gouernementt, in my cheefest Exaltation before men, and my fullest contentmentt in my inmost retirementts. And surely I will neuer omitt continually to serue him his owne way, wheare I once vnderstande it; and wheare that beame leaues me, serue him the most profitable way, the dimmer lights of my owne iudgmentt shall by any meanes be able to leade me vnto. In this truthe I will liue and die; all the diuells of Hell, all ther ministers on earth, shall neuer be able to impeatche, or shake itt.

For Sir dauide Fowlis, the vnfortunate subiectt of partte of my letters of late, when I consider him as a gentleman, that hath receaued sum respects from me, neuer the least iniurye, I pitty him; when I consider him your Lordships kinsman, in that relation I am hartely sorrye for him and for myself too, that, being soe cordially an honourour of yours and all that depende on you, should thus misaduenturousely light vpon a man, that hath of your blood running in his vaines: yet cannot without much comfortt in myself without much iniurye to you, but obserue the vigoure of your respectt towards me, in thus passing him ouer to a course of Justice, which libertye you bestowe vpon me, and which I will neuerthelesse exercise with such modesty and moderation, as shall shew you I am as farre from drinking *a la confusion des personnes*, as the frenche man the last summer. When I reade his letter (which of your goodnesse is communicated with me) I finde that insolentt vanitye of his, which hath brought forth all this trouble, written in capitall letters. He sayth it was to the admiration of all men, I would not heare him. Alas, I did heare him and vsed him with all ciuility, but ther was a wonder, (catholike enoughe indeed) in all men, to see him soe poorely, and meanly humble himself in the same tounc, wheare within a few weekes before he had as insolenttly demeaned himself, I dare confidently say, more insolently, then euer any of his Maiesties Counsell heare, and a deputye Lieutenante had dun to the Presidentt, and Kings Lieutenantt.

But, good man, heare is the ieste, he tells vs, that by taking this businesse into his owne hande, his Maiestye shall make a purchaise of him ; a purchaise with a witnesse, soe clogged with wretched wofull incumbrances as makes it nothing worthe. He will leade and perswade others, he will by his example much better the kings seruice, leaues it to be considered by the beste affected how much his disgrace might hurtt his Maiestyes seruice. Lord, with Esopes flie vpon the axeltree of the wheele, what a dust he makes? whear are thos he can leade or persuade ? take him out of the Commission of the Peace, (the instrument of terroure by which he pulled them on along with him by the noses), he gouerned himself with such exactte pride and distemper amongst them, that in good faith I verely beleeue that ther are not halfe a score, that would either followe or be perswaded by him. as for his example of life, itt was soe vertuouse, or so viciouse, as I beleeue wee might finde hundreths scandalled sooner, then one betterd by it. and surely if he leaue it to be considered by the best affected, ther verdict willbe, his Maiestye shall contribute more to his owne auctority, by making him an example of his iustice, then can possibly be gained by taking him inn againe. But this is an arrogance growen frequent now adayes, which I cannot indure, euery ordinary man must putt himself in ballance with the king, as if it weare a measuring cast, betwixt them, whoe weare like to proue the greater loosers vpon the parting. let me then cast this graine of truthe inn, and it shall turn the Scale. Silly wretches, let vs not deceaue our selues, the kings seruice cannot suffer by the disgrace of him and me and forty more such, the grownde whearvpon gouernment standes will not soe easilye be washed away. soe as the sooner wee vnfoole ourselues of this errore, the sooner wee shall learne to know our selues, and shake of that self pride which hath to our owne esteeme, represented vs much bigger, more considerable, then in deed ther is cause for.

But the world will speake of his sufferings, who hath dun soe much seruice for the Crowne, and that a submission, with a sure promise to amende willbe more honorable. his sufferings are 'not like to be other, then such as shallbe measured forth vnto him by the equall and streighte rule of Iustice, and then who can he faulte but himself? what he hath merited of the Crowne in former times I knowe not, but I am sure it is visible he hath serued himself to a faire fortune by the meanes of the crowne, and that of late sine I cam heather, I haue hearde of many disseruices, but not any one seruice he hath paid backe vnto the Crowne. It is true indeed he hath been content to bagge vp fiue or sixe thousande poundes of the Kings money, kept itt close in his stomacke this twenty yeares, in plaine termes cheated the king of it, and now it seemes, that Spiritt being cuniured forth of his pockett againe, he bound to pay it inn ; hath occasioned all this foule wheather w*h*ich he hath blowen vpon other the innocent Ministers of his Ma*ie*sty in other remote quarters, not daring to breathe the least blaste of it vpon thos taller Cedars, that had soe ouerlooked him as to finde him out when he least dreamt of it. And for his sure promise of amends, trust him that list, for he that hath falsified all thos great obligations, let him self loosse from thos strongest bonds of Loue and thankfullnesse, I shall neuer flatter my self to hold him faste by the sliperye ties of feare and strained professions ; and soe I leaue him, and buy or purchaise him that lists, for my partte he shall neuer cost me farthing, or a line more Laboure.

My lo*rd*, hear was one Payler fined by the hie Commission 1000*li*. for an incest, this fine, vpon a sute of this Churche was by his Ma*ie*sty bestowed vpon them, for buying a paire of Organs, adorning the Altar, and such sacred vses. you may be informed by the inclosed how, and by whom it is indeuoured to be carried an other way. Good my lo*rd*, be soe farre a Patron to this Churche, as if you heare any thing of it, cast in a worde to conferme his Ma*ie*sty in soe gratiouse and a piouse an intention. I will detaine yo*ur* lor*d-sh*ip noe longer then in all truthe to asseure you that I am,

Yo*ur* lor*dsh*ips most faithfull most humble seruantt

WENTWORTH.

(Endorsed) L*et*tre Lo*rd* Wentworth to the Earle of Carlisle, Yorke, 24th Octob*er*, 1632.

VII.

12 April 1639. Viscount Wentworth to Chief Justice Sir John Bramston on his (Lord W.'s) suit against Sir Piers Crosby. (Printed in the Newbery House Magazine, from the original in the possession of Mrs. Bramston.)

My very good Lord,
The cause betwixt S*i*r Piers Crosby others and myselfe, is now at last to fall in Judgment before yo*ur* Lo*rdsh*ips in the Starr Chamber towards the beginning of this next Terme. And then I trust, by God's Grace, to be quitt from one of the most impudent and false Conspiracys that, as I think, was ever hatched against soe great a Minister as the Deputy of Irelande is, how meane soever my person in my private Capacity should be. And sure, when I Consider how wickedly I have been delt with-all, it has been God's Great Goodness : not any Innocency or Providence of my owne that hath delivered me out of their hands. For I confesse it never fell into my thoughts that any man Could have beene soe wicked, as to have sworne that I either hurt or Struck Esmond, being soe notoriously and prodigeously false as, had not y*e* Defendants pleading not guilty, brought the Publishing of y*e* Scandall

to be only in Issue amonst us, I had been able to have fully dis-
proved that Single Knight of the Post suborned against me by (I
daresay) a dozen witnesses of Credit at least, as I have allready in
the books by His Ma*ies*ties Secretary of State, and another, though
my Stewarde, yet an Approved Honest and Faithfull person ; and
verily, my Lord, I on this Good Friday (a Day whereon it pleased
God to bring me forth into this world, and the Eternall Sonn of the
Father died for the Sinnes of this world), Renounce all the Blessings
of this Passion, if ever I did, or had it in my thought, to strike
Esmonde ; And when ye poore wand shall be shewen in Court,
wherwith I must have beaten the man to death, the impudent
untruth will further appeare unto you. But all this is extra-iuditiall,
and therefore I will trouble you noe further, only become an humble
Suitour that your *Lordship* will be at the hearing of the Cause, and
there Afford me the Justice that in Honour & Truth your *Lordship*
will iudge me worthy of. My Lord, I wish your *Lordship* all
increase of Greatnesse and Happynesse, allways remaining

Your *Lordships* very faithfull humble servant,

WENTWORTH.

Fairwood Parke, 12*th of April* 1639.

INDEX.

By Mr. B. SAGAR.

THE END.

RICHARD CLAY & SONS, LIMITED,
LONDON & BUNGAY.